STAYING AHEAD OF CRA

WHAT FINANCIAL INSTITUTIONS MUST KNOW TO WIN AT COMMUNITY INVESTMENT

STAYING AHEAD OF CRA

WHAT FINANCIAL INSTITUTIONS MUST KNOW TO WIN AT COMMUNITY INVESTMENT

Jeffrey Marshall

BUSINESS ONE IRWIN
Homewood, Illinois 60430

332·1753
M 36 &

This publication is designed to provide accurate and
authoritative information in regard to the subject matter
covered. It is sold with the understanding that neither the
author nor the publisher is engaged in rendering legal, accounting,
or other professional service. If legal advice or other expert
assistance is required, the services of a competent
professional person should be sought.

*From a Declaration of Principles jointly adopted by a Committee
of the American Bar Association and a Committee of Publishers.*

Project editor: Waivah Clement
Production manager: Diane Palmer
Jacket designer: Michael Finkelman
Typeface: 11/13 Times Roman
Printer: Book Press, Inc.

Library of Congress Cataloging-in-Publication Data

Marshall, Jeffrey.

    Staying ahead of CRA : what financial institutions must know to
  win at community investment / Jeffrey Marshall.

    p.   cm.

    Includes index.

    ISBN 1-55623-448-1

    1. Bank loans—United States. 2. Community development—United
  States. 3. Discrimination in mortgage loans—United States.
  I. Title.

  HG1642.U5M38 1991

  332.1'753'0973—dc20   91-488

Printed in the United States Of America

1 2 3 4 5 6 7 8 9 0 BP 8 7 6 5 4 3 2 1

To my parents
To Judy, Jed, and John
And in loving memory of my grandfather, Earl P. Stevenson,
a believer in community investment.

PREFACE

The Community Reinvestment Act is a young law that is still evolving. For much of the first decade after it was enacted in October 1977, it got only sporadic attention; to bankers, it was initially viewed as an irritant, another compliance program for an industry already swatting at a swarm of pesky regulations.

But CRA, as the law and the programs that go with it have become known, went through a crucible in the late 1980s that appeared to change it forever. Congressional leaders and community activists fomented the change, molding CRA into a potent force for community reinvestment and turning the press and, to a lesser degree, the regulatory agencies into advocates for their agenda. Some banks and thrifts, accustomed to treating CRA as a trifling compliance issue that could be largely ignored unless protesters singled them out, have been steamrollered by the reforged CRA machine. Others, while convinced that they must reach out more to lower-income communities, have complained that CRA compliance is a "moving target," a maddening welter of regulatory and community pressures whose shape is incessantly changing.

How this situation has developed, and the impact of the changing CRA agenda, will be the subject of much of this book. But a key to understanding the change in CRA enforcement is to comprehend some of the key dynamics shaping social policy in the late 1980s.

THE PENDULUM SWINGS BACK

George Bush tapped into something genuine in 1988 when he talked about a "kinder, gentler America." The drive for riches, the merger explosion, and the federal retreat from social programs amid government's push for privatization—the legacy of the Reagan years—had combined to give corporate America something of a bad hangover by that year. The stock market crash of late 1987 has been popularly viewed as the high-water mark of an age of excess that spurred a collective *frisson* of guilt, or at least a belief among many in government and industry that the pendulum had swung too far from caring and feeling. Poverty, homelessness, and environmental despoliation received short shrift under the Reagan regime. By 1990, they had shot near the top of the national agenda.

But the engine that had once driven the assault on these problems was largely out of steam, exhausted by the federal refusal to refuel it in favor of private efforts. Nowhere was this more problematic than in housing programs. Once the domain of the U.S. Department of Housing and Urban Development (HUD), low-cost housing efforts slowed dramatically when Uncle Sam turned away. Between 1981 and 1990, federal housing subsidy appropriations plummeted more than 80 percent in real dollars, according to the National Low Income Housing Coalition. Other programs have not been able to fill that void. One result is that a third of all Americans are "shelter poor," meaning that they cannot afford basic necessities beyond their housing, said the Economic Policy Institute in a 1990 study.

The ongoing federal deficit, too, exacts a continuing toll on housing support. Federal Housing Administration mortgage insurance programs were trimmed by $3.4 billion over five years under the fiscal 1991 appropriation. This cut, according to one estimate, could eliminate up to 100,000 households from qualifying for FHA mortgages. This continued housing need, coupled with the government withdrawal, has been at the heart of the new Community Reinvestment Act (CRA) pressures. "Three years after CRA passed, HUD was essentially disbanded, and CRA became the driving force behind the alternative financing options...CRA became the only way to get anyone to focus on the economics of the city neighborhoods," consultant James Carras told *Banker & Tradesman*.

Urban community reinvestment did not begin with the CRA law, and housing has not been its only objective. However, housing has been dominant. The National Council for Urban Economic Development studied CRA activity in eight major cities and concluded in 1990 that "CRA is perceived mainly as a tool for housing finance, not as a major tool for economic development projects." A Ford Foundation researcher working on the study said the results "seemed to confirm the widely held view that CRA has had very modest impacts on commercial lending activity."

Yet small-business lending and economic development are making a greater impact, often through bank community development corporations or small business enterprise corporations. This is not a new phenomenon in banking; bank-sponsored economic development in distressed urban areas dates back to the 1960s, when banks in several of the nation's largest cities, disturbed by the mounting blight and abandonment, began modest efforts at reinvestment.

Chemical Bank went into East Harlem, one of New York's worst neighborhoods, in the late 1960s and made loans to community groups. Often it was lending against an assignment of a federal grant going to the group, said Federal Reserve Governor John LaWare, then a Chemical Bank executive. Somewhat later, LaWare said, Chemical went into Bedford-Stuyvesant, a terribly depressed and burned-out area in Brooklyn, and set up the only branch within two miles. People lined up around the block on opening day to put money in, and "it was profitable from the start."

Such outposts have been the exception. Banks have pulled out of many urban neighborhoods in the past couple of decades as the areas imploded into an ugly morass of abandoned buildings, drug galleries, and rubble-pocked decay. Some of these communities now sense an awakening spirit, frequently sparked by church groups or housing organizers who are reaching out for an economic boost that government is not providing. Bankers, however, often see nothing there to which to lend, or loan requests so small as to be clearly unprofitable.

"Community development, by definition, involves lending situations to which banks are normally averse," The Office of the Comptroller of the Currency (OCC) noted in "Community Development Finance: Tools and Techniques for National Banks." The OCC document refers to community reinvestment, however, as "a natural extension of bank functions and charter obligations." Clearly, as banks pump money into neighborhoods, their own mortgages and loans stand a better chance of repayment.

Neighborhoods: The word has earned its emphasis. Community reinvestment is chiefly an urban phenomenon—Chicago activists say their city is the birthplace of CRA programs—and most protests have involved urban areas. Rural bankers are often, de facto, serving all of their neighborhoods no matter what their income levels. But that doesn't mean that rural communities have been without CRA protests or agitation, or that regulators are holding nonurban banks to a lesser CRA standard.

The merger mania that engulfed the country in the mid-1980s carried into banking, and this larger dynamic also helped drive CRA activity. Community groups feared that as local banks were devoured by larger statewide or regional institutions, the new owners' attention and concern for local neighborhoods could never match the old levels. Protests and demands centered on merger applications became commonplace.

COMMUNITY ISSUES TO THE FORE

Where is CRA headed? Chapter 7 will take up this question in detail, but clearly, community reinvestment ties in to a growing interest in shelter and social welfare issues in the 1990s. Four of five high-ranking executives at Fortune 1000 companies predict that the 1990s will foster greater concern for others in the community, according to a survey commissioned in 1990 by Chivas Regal. Education and poverty-related issues scored highest among domestic priorities among those surveyed. Popular culture guru Faith Popcorn has dubbed the 1990s "The Decency Decade," in which Americans are expected to continue turning from the glitz and gloss of the 80s to try to help solve society's most intractable troubles.

"My personal feeling is that in the 90s, at least the first part of the 90s, community involvement is going to be the big issue. And it's not only with banks," Security Pacific executive vice president Irving Margol told a California CRA forum in 1990.

"It will be a very good decade for corporate ethics," proclaimed Good Housekeeping in full-page newspaper ads in January 1990. "Corporate America will make an extraordinary new commitment to social responsibility through...outreach programs for their communities; through a new commitment to the environment, and the social needs of the country. You can see this happening now—it will quickly gather speed and momentum."

Yet the political framework for community action is no better formed than it has been. The climate as 1991 dawned seemed uncertain; warring between traditional conservatives and liberals had broken out in both major political parties. "The new buzzwords are empowerment, responsibility, and accountability," said *Newsweek* as 1990 ended. "Politicians are seeking new approaches to old social ills, and with Reaganomics discredited and liberalism all but dead, both parties are racing to reconfigure their beliefs."

A ROLE FOR FINANCIAL INSTITUTIONS

Community development initiatives could be nourished by this public policy empowerment movement. But smart financial institutions know that they, too, have a role. "Whatever specific programs may be devised by the private and public sectors, a mandate to banks for closer attention to the needs and preferences of the low-income consumer is clear," wrote University of Virginia professor Charlotte H. Scott in *The Journal of Retail Banking*.

The dominant CRA issue will remain housing, in part because the Home Mortgage Disclosure Act data—housing loan data—due to be released in late 1991 will give community activists the most detail ever about comparative home lending patterns. The low-income housing crisis remains "the most critical social issue confronting the nation in the 1990s, said the National Low Income Housing Coalition.

Yet housing is just part of a mix of targets. Robert Forrestal, president of the Federal Reserve Bank of Atlanta, talks of an evolving social compact for banking. Legislation protecting consumers from alleged discriminatory practices (including CRA) "express the public desire that the banking compact evolve alongside other social changes that have been making U.S. business and social structure more equitable," he said in a speech.

Forrestal believes CRA "offers a good vehicle for demonstrating the industry's commitment to broadening its reach to all segments of this country's banking market. . . I see no reason why banks in every community cannot come up with ideas that go beyond merely satisfying the supervisory agencies but also make a positive contribution to their local economies." Forrestal added that "a variety of excellent programs has already shown ways that community reinvestment can meet the needs of low- and middle-income neighborhoods and still prove profitable."

Profitability and opportunity are two words many bankers don't associate with CRA. But effective community reinvestment can make money and give an institution a new market or bigger share, a better image, and a greater hold on its destiny. With proactive programs and sustained commitment, institutions can stay ahead in the CRA game.

This book seeks to provide a sense of the evolving nature of community reinvestment and the CRA enforcement process. To give that, some narrative about the law and the changes it has undergone in the public policy kiln are vital to set the stage. The thoughts of scores of bankers, regulators, and consumer and community group leaders help illuminate the ways in which CRA is affecting financial and social policy and what the future holds. The book is intended to be scrupulously objective, based on soundings and observations from all sides in the ongoing debate.

This is not a how-to book or a compliance manual. It is not a catalog of what institutions are doing in one locale or another. A raft of examples is included, however, to give readers a sense of how some institutions are going about approaching CRA-related programs or issues. The lists of associations, nonprofits, and vendors at the end of the book were developed as a sort of bulletin board on the growing host of resources available to improve delivery and monitoring of community reinvestment.

The book's underlying theme is that institutions can stay ahead in the CRA process by being alert, proactive, and creative. Those attributes are what regulators and community advocates want to see, particularly the latter. And the CRA agenda has largely become their agenda. Smart bankers know that, and they know that answering community credit needs and enhancing other goodwill efforts can produce a positive ruling in the court of public opinion—and, very likely, new customers and new deposits along the way.

Jeffrey Marshall

ACKNOWLEDGMENTS

Any book is a collaborative process. While the words and the ideas are mine, the presentation has been burnished by the project editor on the book, Waivah Clement, and the copy editor working with her. They did some judicious tightening of phrases here and there that makes a difference, and their work was painstaking and of a high standard.

I also owe a big debt of thanks to executive editor Ralph Rieves, who gave me encouragement and advice on completing the manuscript, and to others at Business One who worked with me in shaping the proposal and selling the idea of the book.

A special thanks goes to Jay Rosenstein, senior editor at the Federal Deposit Insurance Corporation. A former colleague of mine at *American Banker*, Jay was an invaluable ally in thinking up concepts for the book, offering contacts, and providing a sounding board for ideas. He and his wife, Shelly, were also generous hosts on a couple of research trips to Washington. Another former *American Banker* colleague, Richard Ringer, helped mightily by conducting some interviews in Chicago and by providing intelligence about what was happening in the Chicago market.

Among the people interviewed in the course of my research, I'd like to single out Janice Smith and Ken Quincy at the FDIC. The time they gave me and the information they shared were greatly appreciated.

I'd also like to thank former *American Banker* editor Fred Bleakley, who graciously agreed to let me work a reduced schedule for the bulk of the time I was researching the book.

And last, my wife, Judy, has my undying gratitude for putting up with some financial hardship and a few absences in the course of the research.

J. M.

CONTENTS

CHAPTER 1

COMMUNITY REINVESTMENT: THE RULES CHANGE

THE PRESSURE BUILDS

Much of the apprehension that banks feel toward Community Reinvestment Act (CRA) enforcement can be traced to early 1988, more than a decade after the act was passed in October 1977. In its first 10 years, the CRA movement was like a dormant volcano, occasionally spitting smoke and ash—mostly in the form of protested applications—but rousing few institutions to take more than ordinary precautions.

Indeed, the law as it was written offered institutions little to go on and little obvious incentive to act, unless they were bent on buying other banks or opening new offices. The Community Reinvestment Act is a broad, some say vaguely worded, law that restates the fact that "financial institutions are required by law and regulatory policy to serve the convenience and needs of their communities as a condition for acquiring new deposit facilities," Senator William Proxmire, the sponsor and former Senate Banking Committee chairman, said in hearings on the law. Proxmire added that the bill "does not provide for credit allocation."

No definition of "credit needs" or "community" appear in the law, and there is no guidance about the law's scope or methods for delivering on those needs. Moreover, CRA was not intended to "provide any new authority to the [regulatory agencies]" or to "inject any significantly new element into the deposit facility application approval process," Proxmire said. (For a close look at the requirements of the CRA law, see Chapter 8.)

The recent politicization of CRA owes much to the erosion of federal housing and community development funding during the 1980s. But discontent had welled up in the 1970s, as activists complained about redlining,

1

exporting of capital from urban neighborhoods, and the scarcity of bank funding to reverse city decay. During that time, the Equal Credit Opportunity Act (1974) and the Home Mortgage Disclosure Act (1975) became law; from that base, the Community Reinvestment Act had a certain inevitability.

Inner-city neighborhoods, in particular, were in sorry shape by the late 1970s. And since the economics of those neighborhoods were troubled, activists knew little voluntary financing was likely. Gradually, community groups came to view CRA as an effective pressure tool, a lever for forcing reluctant institutions to undertake loans or programs they might have little stomach for. The overlay of charity, of nominal support for marginal causes, was strong in the financial industry through much of the 1980s.

As regulators have come increasingly to regard the needs of low- and moderate-income communities as the focal point of CRA compliance—giving activists the backing they need to press their cases—bankers have gotten their backs up over pressure tactics centered around demands for loans and other services. Over the years, some bankers have talked of "extortion" or "blackmail," and a few still are.

Vague and Arbitrary

Despite the early paucity of serious commitment to CRA, few institutions were ever rated harshly by compliance examiners, a situation that has frustrated activists and triggered charges that the regulators were too cozy with the regulated. When the agencies did chastise banks, it was usually more of a wrist-slap than a lashing. The vagueness of the process let most institutions just drift along, uncertain how they were supposed to proceed.

"In most instances, banks were doing a credible job," wrote researchers Joseph C. Dawson and Paul S. Forbes in *Understanding CRA*, a 1990 handbook issued by the Consumer Bankers Association. "But often progressives were put in the same class as reactionaries, there were no rewards for doing a good job, and there were no penalties for poor performance. Enforcement was a function of the protest mechanism as utilized by community groups, and the system seemed vague, arbitrary, and unfair."

Still, CRA was easy on banks, critics charged. By one accounting, only eight of more than 50,000 applications for new facilities during the 1977–88 period were rejected on CRA grounds. Weak ratings were almost as rare. Only 3.2 percent of state member banks examined by the Fed—in the

1980–88 period got less than a satisfactory record, and ratings on the existing 1–5 scale (from best to worst) averaged 1.94 for those banks. National banks examined by the Office of the Comptroller of the Currency made out even better. Between 1985 and the end of 1988, only one bank got a 5 under the old rating system, and only 12 received a 4, according to John H. McDowell, director of the consumer activities division. In all, a whopping 97.4 percent of OCC-examined banks scored either 1 or 2 in that period. The story was much the same at the Federal Deposit Insurance Corporation, where 98 percent of state nonmember banks scored 1 or 2 in 1984–88, and less than one third of 1 percent got a 4 or 5.

The figures at savings institutions were very different. Only 2 percent of those examined between 1983 and 1988 got a 4 or a 5, but a mere 5.4 percent got a 1 or 2, according to Jerauld C. Kluckman, Office of Thrift Supervision (OTS) director of compliance programs. That left the vast majority solidly average.

Until 1984, the average number of protested applications to the Federal Reserve was about five per year. Since 1985, that number has jumped significantly, to average more than 25 a year. The numbers are much smaller at the other agencies, primarily because the Fed oversees holding companies, where most of the merger activity has been taking place. At the OCC, for instance, protests were zero in 1984, three in 1985, eight in 1986, one in 1987, and zero again in 1988.

With numbers like these, little wonder that CRA often was virtually an afterthought, especially at smaller nonurban institutions. "For years it was really kind of a ho-hum thing," said Mark Aldrich, an attorney and principal with the Bankers Consulting Group in Irvine, California. "There's been a tremendous explosion in the complexity of compliance in the last eight or nine years. Back then, it was mostly [concerned with] Regulation B and Truth-in -Lending. CRA was not a big issue."

It is big now, and not just in big cities. Protests have flared in areas as remote as rural Montana. CRA agitation has emerged in widely dispersed pockets; some areas have a concentration of community groups, others have little or none. The Northeast, California, and the Midwest have had the most activity.

By 1990, CRA was one of the hottest topics around. Bankers, regulators, and trade groups identified it as such; trade journals devoted mountains of space to it. "Last year, we wanted to be sure our banks were focused on CRA. This year, that's not a problem," Consumer Bankers Association president Joe Belew told a 1990 CRA conference. "I thinkeveryone would agree that this has become certainly one of the thornier issues [in banking]."

Congress Rides Herd

What happened to turn up the heat? While there is no simple answer, experts point first to the public policy pressures that found a ready ear—and a willingness to act—in Congress. Much has happened in those marble halls in the past couple of years, and not just starting with the Financial Institutions Reform, Recovery and Enforcement Act (FIRREA), passed in August 1989. CRA was revisited in March 1988, during which time Senator Proxmire, the act's creator, expressed disappointment with regulators' record.

"Regulators seem to think that we're all living in Lake Woebegone. Like the children of the fictional village, U.S. lenders are all above average," he complained. "Almost all get high ratings year after year, and almost none is ever held back." Noting the mere handful of rejected applications over a decade, he added, "I wish we had graders like that when I was in school."

Changes in personality and political makeup have moved social responsibility issues to the front burner. That is particularly true in the House, where urban Democrats like Charles Schumer of New York and Joseph Kennedy of Massachusetts have championed consumer-oriented legislation. The ascendence of Representative Henry Gonzalez, a Texas liberal, to the chairmanship of the Banking Committee is continuing to drive action on CRA. Unlike fellow Democrat Fernand St Germain, whom he succeeded as chairman, Gonzalez is more than willing to chide the banking community and personally lobby for tougher CRA-related sanctions.

Gonzalez, regarded by many bankers as an unrequited populist, has repeatedly warned of intensified oversight on CRA. He views community reinvestment as an obligation. "For too long, CRA has remained a low priority on the agenda of banks and the regulators, to the detriment of local communities," he said at an August 1990 hearing. "We intend to see that a new emphasis is placed on CRA." Gonzalez had scheduled a number of hearings on community reinvestment in early 1991, and few expect him to tone down his rhetoric on the subject.

The strength of the undertow on social responsibility has caught some Washington observers by surprise. Steven M. Roberts, a former Federal Reserve staffer and now a principal with KPMG Peat Marwick, said he had not expected so many consumer provisions sought by the House Banking Committee to find their way into the FIRREA bill. That event "may be a message for the future," he said.

Senator Proxmire has retired and his successor and banking committee chairman, Senator Donald Riegle, was fighting for his political life at this writing after being snared in the influence-buying flap involving S&L kingpin Charles Keating. But there is momentum on CRA issues in the Senate; Senator Alan Dixon, who chairs the key consumer subcommittee, has made fair housing one of his pet issues and has promised hearings on CRA.

"So long as this kind of congressional pressure exists, the examining agencies can be expected to continue to signal it is no longer business as usual," wrote attorney Warren Traiger in a 1990 report on CRA compliance.

Publicity

Media coverage of financial institutions at the end of the 1980s was dominated by the S&L crisis, and rightfully so. But stories about discrimination in mortgage lending rekindled some of the embers that had been smoldering from the redlining days of the 1970s. The biggest blare was sounded in Atlanta, where in May 1988 the *Atlanta Journal-Constitution* ran a series, "The Color of Money," that reported that whites obtained up to five times more home mortgage loans than blacks with similar incomes. The local Federal Reserve Bank's review of home lending data in Atlanta "essentially confirmed the lending differences, but shed little light on the underlying causes," the bank said.

The Atlanta stories were picked up by other media around the country, and they left a considerable legacy, one of them being a Pulitzer prize. The other major result was a quick though flawed response in the form of a targeted lending program by Atlanta-area institutions. This effort will be examined in Chapter 5.

The *Detroit Free Press* followed with a series entitled "The Race for Money" in August of that year. There were similar allegations of bias and lax enforcement in stories appearing in Wilmington, Delaware, in November 1988 and in *The Boston Globe* in January 1989. All found that mortgage lending patterns were hurting black neighborhoods, as did a study by the Center for

Law and Social Justice, a New York advocacy group that concluded in December 1989 that lenders were in gross violation of CRA requirements. As damning as the data appeared to be, "none of the studies has considered the applicants' qualifications for credit beyond general assumptions about income based on census tract characteristics," noted Atlanta Fed vice president Ronald N. Zimmerman in a report in May 1990. He said the Justice Department has been investigating in Atlanta to see if the allegations of unlawful lending discrimination have any basis, and the General Accounting Office has been reviewing mortgage lending of nonregulated lenders, plus the secondary markets.

The validity of the mortgage studies was also questioned by two Federal Reserve Bank of San Francisco economists, Jonathan Neuberger and Ronald Schmidt. They argued that "redlining studies generally have failed to demonstrate conclusively the existence of neighborhood lending differentials after controlling for relevant demand and supply factors in housing markets." And another Federal Reserve staffer, Paul S. Calem of the Philadelphia bank, wrote that "studies of the distribution of mortgage loans generally cannot measure accurately a neighborhood's demand for loans."

Mortgage surveys aside, CRA issues have become something of a hot button for journalists aware of the rising sway of social responsibility issues. "I think there are very willing ears in the press," said Clifford N. Rosenthal, executive director of the National Federation of Community Development Credit Unions. He expects to see considerable media attention given to poor CRA ratings or bias allegations, noting that "the stories that came out of Atlanta and Boston weren't planted by the Association of Communities Organized for Reform Now (ACORN)," a prominent community group. Pulitzer prizes, he noted, have a tendency to focus journalists' attention.

He doesn't think this should panic lenders, who "have plenty of resources with which to defend themselves."

Community Groups

By the mid-1980s, activism on community reinvestment was surging. Some of that agitation was a direct result of the explosion in bank merger activity; community groups, often advised by national activist organizations, filed scores of protests charging that the acquiring bank had a weak record of meeting community needs.

Publicly, regulators have been flayed almost as badly as the banking industry. Community group leaders have often blamed regulators for any CRA shortcomings, saying they fell asleep at the switch. "The reason we have had so many community protests is that the regulators weren't doing their job. Local community groups had to do it for them; they became de facto regulators," Allen Fishbein of the Center for Community Change told the CBA's Dawson and Forbes.

"It seems the regulators have not taken these regulations that seriously, since they were not having to go public with them," said Jane Ubelhoer, congressional liaison for ACORN. Moreover, what satisfies examiners may not satisfy community groups, so an emphasis merely on compliance is not enough to stave off protests, said Fishbein.

As the number of protests mounted, activists discovered tools that would support their charges, such as home mortgage statistics. "Community groups clearly have become increasingly aware of Home Mortgage Disclosure Act (HMDA) data and more sophisticated in their use of the data, especially in connection with the protests of applications by banks for mergers and acquisitions," wrote David Vandre, district compliance officer for the Federal Reserve Bank of San Francisco, in its newsletter. He noted that HMDA reports "have played and continue to play a major part in most protests."

Community leaders also showed they would play hardball through the media. In Washington, D.C., former banking superintendent Gerald Irons assailed the city's biggest banks for what he termed their deficient lending in poorer neighborhoods; the banks later issued a public defense of their record. And in California, the Greenlining Coalition publicly invited Japanese banks to expand operations in the state, saying that domestic banks were "incapable or unwilling to serve minority communities."

Hardball has had an effect, as have banks' attempts to improve outreach efforts. Contacts between banks and recognized community leaders have become almost routine. It is not uncommon now for community group leaders to go directly to the top for meetings with chief executives. That's a big change from a decade ago, when CRA protestors were referred to the public relations or community affairs areas, activists say.

In 1990, in Los Angeles, a coalition of local activists that included black workers, tenants' rights advocates, local developers, churches, and fair housing advocates met directly with Security Pacific Corporation CEO Robert Smith. The activists made a presentation that led to the drafting of a formal agreement regarding increased credit and services.

New Regulatory Attitudes

While they are reluctant to say so publicly, the combined pressure of congressional scrutiny and increased community group turmoil are making regulators very uncomfortable—and compelling them to make CRA more rigorous. Some in Congress, particularly, have asked sharp questions about the history of positive ratings handed out to almost all banks and thrifts. "If anyone's been banged around more than the banking industry by the federal legislature, it's probably the regulators," said the Consumer Bankers Association's late general counsel, Craig Ulrich.

It's been obvious to anyone in the compliance end of banking that the regulatory agencies are viewing community reinvestment in a new, harsher light. The regulators have staked out a position that an inadequate CRA record is grounds for delay or outright denial of an application. And that has created a lot of anguish among institutions everywhere.

"I think CRA can become banking's version of the 'death penalty,'" Signet Banking Corporation vice chairman Malcolm S. McDonald told a CBA conference, referring to a college rule that can disqualify athletic teams from competing. "If any single bank in your holding company has an unsatisfactory rating, don't bother to apply for anything," he said. "How would you like your bank to be shut out of the approvals window for 18 months?"

The tougher tone has been instigated, some observers say, by a new focus on CRA by the Comptroller's office, the FDIC, and Office of Thrift Supervision. The Federal Reserve is regarded as the most sophisticated of the agencies on CRA, having handled the most protests and developed the most educational programs—something of a sore point for the others. Moreover, the Fed has had separate compliance examinations with a different staff, apart from safety and soundness, since 1977. That was not true at the other agencies, where the creation of specialists is a much more recent event.

Savings and loan officials, preoccupied with the deepening crisis at their institutions in the 1980s, concede that their attention was often elsewhere. "Sometimes, a satisfactory rating was given without the examiners digging in," Jerauld Kluckman, director of compliance at the OTS, told *Savings Institutions.* "We're on the way to changing that." And since CRA's primary focus has been housing, and thrifts were the nation's traditional mortgage lenders, they were often assumed to be doing just fine.

Thrift trade group officials acknowledge that some savings and loans, particularly smaller ones, came into 1990 never having had a compliance examination. The whole world of CRA had largely passed them by. "Some of our members had never participated in community reinvestment programs. They had no good understanding of what it was all about," said John Hartnett of the California League of Savings Institutions. "Some of them are really struggling."

But Fed officials haven't been crowing about being out front. "It was not comfortable for us to be perceived as the bad guys," said one. He added that CRA enforcement "is not an area where you can ultimately satisfy anyone. The contestants are diametrically opposed philosophically. It's not easy to satisfy anyone. It's hard on people like us. No one's happy with us."

The changes in CRA regulation have also been spurred by a desire to alter the monitoring process. By expanding and improving the CRA examination, the agencies are trying to "shift the focus of the CRA evaluation form the highly charged atmosphere of protested applications to the quieter climate of an ordinary examination," noted consultant JoAnn Barefoot in *ABA Banking Journal.* Community groups also are being encouraged to file protests as early as possible rather than during the applications process.

One unfortunate effect of this new arrangement, Barefoot said, might be to create CRA pressures on institutions that have never experienced a protest. But on the whole, "the shift should be healthy for the industry . . . because it will reduce the potential for high-pressure confrontations with community groups."

State regulators, while traditionally playing second fiddle to Uncle Sam on issues like CRA, are not sitting by; states like Massachusetts and New York have implemented rules very similar to the federal regulations for their state-chartered banks. These state agencies do their own CRA examinations, using much the same standards as their federal counterparts.

New York, in fact, is often viewed as the model for the national CRA disclosure law. The Empire State has been issuing public CRA ratings of state-chartered banks since 1984, using senior bank examiners to gauge bank reinvestment performance. Massachusetts has rewritten its laws to comport with federal CRA regulations. It has the same four-tier system and disclosure provisions, and uses essentially the same assessment factors.

While regulators have sought to assuage some of the industry's fears, the messages carry no hint of retreat. Fed Governor John LaWare told a 1990 CRA conference that "the ball game hasn't changed, but we are in extra innings." Banks are being asked to add new dimensions to the programs, he said, and the burden of proof has shifted onto bankers' shoulders. "We hope to be able to do something" to calm the industry's anxieties, said one Fed official, but "it may take a little more work than simply sensitizing the examiners."

Some regulators are saying that they perceive banks' anxiety to be fueled by fears of something unfamiliar. The lack of clear-cut CRA guidelines has frustrated institutions: The rules have changed, but there is no rulebook. Some efforts, while well intentioned, have not scored with regulators.

"One thing, I think, that drives bankers up the wall is that they try to do something like the Atlanta consortium, and then you've got regulators saying, 'That's not the kind of program I like,'" Robert E. Mannion, a Washington attorney, told *Southern Banker*. He was referring to the Atlanta lending program that followed the release of the Atlanta Constitution findings.

In interviews, regulators say that most institutions need to turn their reinvestment efforts up a notch or two and try to establish a positive CRA record. "If I were a banker, I would never want to have the examiners do that for me," said one community affairs official. He added that some banks just haven't gotten the message. "You still see banks popping up as zero" in analyses of loans made by census tract, he said.

Local Governments

A lesser but growing source of CRA-related tensions is coming from municipal governments, particularly in larger cities. Increasingly, cities are reacting to complaints from poorer neighborhoods and making a linkage between an institution's community investment and the city's deposits.

A number of Midwestern cities—Cleveland, Cincinnati, and St. Louis—have passed ordinances linking city deposits and institutions' CRA ratings. California cities like Los Angeles and Oakland have been looking to tie deposits to CRA ratings. Los Angeles also passed a motion in 1990 asking the Federal Reserve and the House Banking Committee to hold hearings there to address community reinvestment.

Boston Mayor Raymond Flynn has come out strongly in favor of more bank reinvestment. "I would hope that Congress could find ways to encourage these institutions—with their large investment portfolios—to play a stronger role in meeting the credit needs of low-income and minority neighborhoods," he told a congressional panel in 1989. He also asked Congress to expand the disclosure provisions of CRA and HMDA beyond their current requirements.

Under a law that went into effect in early 1990, New York City requires banks seeking city deposits to give 90 days' notice of all branch closings. In addition, an institution needs to get positive state and federal CRA ratings. New York has gone so far as to offer a report card on community service efforts by 28 banks in November 1990. While there was no official linkage to CRA, the message was unambiguous. City agencies are to give the grades a 10 percent weighting when deciding which banks to use for services, part of Mayor David Dinkins' "economic justice" program to bring business to low-income communities. Higher ratings could clearly swing a city agency to higher-scoring bank.

The ratings are based on such criteria as branches in low-income areas, mortgages and business loans made there, bilingual facilities, and basic banking. On those criteria, not surprisingly, the lowest scores went to wholesale banks like Bankers Trust Company and Morgan Guaranty Trust Company, and there is some grumbling in those quarters. The highest rating went to Chemical, with Citibank second and Manufacturers Hanover third.

Cities aren't the only local governments to act on community reinvestment concerns. As of December 1990, some 32 states had enacted or implemented some form of reinvestment policy— state CRA laws, linked deposit programs, or standards required by banks buying in from another state. Vermont has what some call the most demanding state law in the country. It requires a yearly ranking of banks, based on their noncommercial loans, by the banking commissioner, and mandates that these rankings be published statewide. Massachusetts, Minnesota, and New York also have rigorous CRA laws.

Consumer and community groups are agitating for state legislators to work in concert with the federal agencies to enhance community reinvestment—and a growing number of statehouses are taking up reinvestment legislation. "States can clarify guidelines for community lending in harmony with the federal CRA evaluation framework, and should work with federal regulators to do so," wrote Robert Stumberg of the Center for Policy Alternatives in a 1990 report. But the dual banking system precludes states from preempting federal regulators at anything other than state-chartered institutions. Stumberg's report suggested that to avoid regulatory competition, state reinvestment standards be tied to the placement of deposits in banks by state governments.

Local governments are well aware of the changing climate of social activism, which has been documented in studies and surveys of various stripes. Some of those surveys underscore the role banks are expected to play. More than 40 percent of those surveyed in the 1990 American Banker Consumer Survey felt that banks should be required to lend locally, even if such lending is not profitable. And 32 percent, including half of nonwhites, said they would switch institutions if their primary institution did not comply with CRA.

Expect more cities and states to make a firm linkage between community investment performance and their deposits and contracts. Unquestionably, institutions that can point to broad programs and obvious commitment will be ahead in the jockeying for their favors.

Warning Shots Are Heard

An accumulation of assorted pressures from 1988, including the tougher Congressional scrutiny and the publicity from the various mortgage surveys, set the stage for seminal events in 1989 that kicked CRA enforcement into a higher gear. These happenings molded the existing regulatory framework for community reinvestment, and it seems almost unthinkable that anything could turn back the clock to the days when CRA was a humdrum concern.

The first event was the Federal Reserve Board's ruling against a merger application by Continental Bank Corporation, the major Chicago banking company, in March 1989. Continental, trying to broaden its geographic reach, wanted to acquire Grand Canyon Bank of Arizona, a community bank. But the Fed rejected the transaction on CRA grounds, saying Continental had not set up proactive community outreach or advertising and marketing for low-income neighborhoods. The Fed also criticized Continental for failing to develop a formal method for translating findings about community credit needs and for weak senior management involvement in CRA issues.

"Continental was specifically chastised for its inaccurate CRA statements and a misunderstanding of CRA on the part of its staff and management," wrote attorney Warren Traiger in a September 1990 white paper on CRA compliance. Yet some prominent community activists in Chicago came to Continental's defense, and it was widely perceived that the Fed and FDIC were embroiled in a turf war over regulating Continental, with a CRA ruling allowing the Fed to gain a distinct edge. Still, the Continental ruling signaled that regulators would indeed hold the feet of one of the nation's most prestigious banks to the fire over CRA.

A few weeks later, on March 21, 1989, the four federal agencies, through the Federal Financial Institutions Examination Council (FFIEC), released a joint statement on CRA that put some muscle behind the tougher talk circulating about enforcement. Intended to dispel uncertainty and provide concrete suggestions to improve CRA performance, the joint statement spelled out in considerable detail what institutions could do to help assure compliance. It also placed new importance on an expanded annual CRA statement to be issued to the public as a report on the institution's community reinvestment activities.

The FFIEC advised institutions to include in the statement a description of how they assess community credit needs, how they communicate with people in the community regarding those needs, and how the institutions try to meet those needs. The joint statement also stressed the importance of comments coming from the community about a bank's services, and said that regulators, when weighing applications, would be governed more by current performance than by promises of corrective action. The contents of the statement will be examined in detail in the next section.

A third major event of 1989 was the August passage of the Financial Institutions Reform, Recovery, and Enforcement Act. Contained in the law, aimed at bailing out the hobbled savings and loan industry, was an amendment sponsored by Representative Joseph Kennedy of Massachusetts to make public for the first time the CRA ratings of all U.S. financial institutions (New York State had been making public the CRA ratings of state-chartered banks since 1985). These ratings would be issued for examinations conducted after July 1, 1990.

FIRREA also stipulated that all of these new ratings be determined by examiners on a new four-tiered system with verbal rather than numerical designations: outstanding, satisfactory, needs to improve, and substantial noncompliance. In addition to the rating, a written description of the institution's CRA performance would be made publicly available.

In addition, FIRREA stiffened the requirements banks and thrifts must meet under the Home Mortgage Disclosure Act (HMDA). The data collection on mortgage loans demanded by HMDA has a central role in CRA compliance that will only increase; for all intents and purposes, CRA compliance and HMDA compliance are part of the same package.

For one thing, FIRREA expanded the sway of the HMDA rules to include lenders not affiliated with financial institutions or their holding companies. That had mortgage bankers screaming foul, saying they were being forced to make the disclosures even if they were not under a bank or thrift regulator. Also, HUD extended HMDA compliance to all FHA lenders, encompassing those who had been exempt because they had under $10 million in assets.

Collecting HMDA data has been a familiar process for years at banks and thrifts, but the agencies are now requiring a more sophisticated "loan/application register," or LAR, to record data on an application-by-application basis, including loans bought on a wholesale basis. Institutions are being told to submit their LARS, in electronic or magnetic form if possible, by March 1, 1991. Later in this chapter, we will see what impact this will have on documentation requirements.

Fed Governor John LaWare told a 1990 CRA conference that the HMDA data has "lots of hidden, important facets." Not to mention lots of numbers. The regulators will be generating 33 tables of information by manipulating raw data. "This will enable us to put a better case to Congress with respect to what is really happening in mortgage lending. I think it will help change the image of banking having a callous record," LaWare said.

"It's important that a bank knows what the data are, and how they got that way," LaWare added. Institutions need to draft an intelligent response to any HMDA problems and provide a path for correcting them, he said. Moreover, if data is missing for the LARs, consequences could be serious. Blank entries, for instance, would be returned by the regulator; there is a cutoff date at which there would no more be submissions, so failing to meet that deadline would put an institution on a delinquent list, subject to potential civil penalties.

For months following the FIRREA law's passage, worried bankers jawboned and tried to give themselves wiggle room on what loomed as a major public relations threat to the industry. They sought assurances that an appeal process would give banks a chance to improve a rating before it was made public, but the agencies have held firm against these appeals. Bankers criticized the subjectivity of the examination process, and regulators made plans for joint training sessions for examiners from each of the agencies. The object: to create as much uniformity of approach as possible.

One clear sign of the sharper focus on CRA issues was the attention given them in several Federal Reserve decisions on merger applications. Close to two thirds of the orders in 1989 decisions involving Security Pacific and Manufacturers Hanover dealt with CRA issues, as did more than half of the late 1989 order giving Provident Bancorp of Cincinnati approval to buy Northern Kentucky Trustcorp.

As 1989 wound down, the message coming from Washington was unmistakably tougher than a year earlier. The phrase "the rules have changed" became a common refrain, and the anxiety level in the industry went up a few degrees as the public-rating era approached.

THE IMPACT OF NEW DEMANDS

The Protest Route

The CRA protest, the biggest weapon in the arsenal of community activists, grew increasingly effective through the 1980s as local leaders got help from national organizations and used HMDA data and other accepted tools to flex their muscles. Picketing and sit-ins have not disappeared, but more and more, activists are toning down physical confrontation and using phone calls and letters to banks and regulators to get attention.

Community groups have been most active when banks are applying for new branches or to buy other institutions, knowing this is the best time to seek concessions. They have learned that banks and thrifts, anxious to avoid costly delays and publicity, usually will agree to certain requests for improved services in poorer areas—below-market loan programs, housing money, basic banking programs, and more. When activists accept the institution's offer, the protests are withdrawn and regulatory approval is usually soon forthcoming. While bankers don't like to admit having made agreements with community groups, "there are about 250 formal agreements out there, and most of them seem to be working fairly well," said Allen Fishbein of the Center for Community Change late in 1990.

The number of protests has fallen as merger activity among financial institutions has slumped in recent years. But Ken Quincy, chief of the special review section at the FDIC, said the protests are more focused and intensive. Bankers should not take community group adversaries lightly.

Intensive is the word for what greeted California's First Interstate Bancorp in 1987 when it tried to acquire Houston-based Allied Banks. Allied itself had been a target of community leaders—its previous examination had been unsatisfactory—and First Interstate was greeted with protests in nine states on a single day, according to *U.S. Banker.* Ten different groups offered lists of demands. While the protests were eventually overruled, the experience was harrowing, senior vice president Julius Loeser told the magazine. And as a condition to approving the acquisition, the Fed said it would review First Interstate Texas every six months for CRA compliance.

The stakes are bigger at a huge multistate concern like First Interstate—and big banks are more frequent targets for activist thunder. But protests are taking a toll at smaller banks as well. Take the $140 million Hyde Park Bank and Trust Company in Chicago, which wanted to buy the $42 million University Financial Savings and Loan in Chicago in 1989. An activist group submitted a protest to the FDIC shortly after the merger application was filed, and the ensuing legal skirmishing and negotiating raised the bank's legal fees and created not a little distress. "It was very surprising because we always felt our lending record was very good," Hyde Park CRA officer Georgene Pavelec told *U.S. Banker.*

Even small black-owned banks are not immune from protests. Highland Community Bank, another small Chicago institution, faced a hearing a few years ago when it tried to buy a branch of a local thrift. A community group in the neighborhood argued that Highland was not meeting its needs. In response, Highland's president said that the group's use of HMDA data in making its case was more appropriate to a thrift than to his bank.

Here and there a foreign-owned institution, too, has found itself staring down the barrel of a CRA protest. In 1990, the East Harlem Coalition for Fair Banking protested the merger between Banco de Ponce and Banco Popular, both of Puerto Rico but with branches in New York City. The two banks headed off the protest by agreeing to boost new housing loans in East Harlem.

Japanese banks, with their colossal size and strength (though that strength is fading somewhat), have had their share of merger-related protests. In one of the most celebrated cases, California First Bank agreed in 1988 when it acquired Union Bank to meet a list of demands from almost 90 community groups; the demands included extending $84 million in credit over two years, the appointment of several minority members to its board, and a huge increase in the use of minority vendors. Other California banks have been complaining about the deal ever since, saying California First—now known as Union—caved in and gave away too much. Union objected to that characterization. It added that a commitment to additional hiring of minority managers was a show of good faith, not a binding arrangement. "The management of this bank feels very strongly that affirmative action is not something that should be included in the CRA kettle of fish," spokesman Larry Boggs told *American Banker*. "It's a separate matter."

But protests involving Japanese banks haven't given community groups everything they wanted. Groups contesting the acquisition of Taiyo Kobe Bank Ltd. in Japan by Mitsui Bank Ltd., Tokyo, and the related acquisition of Taiyo Kobe Bank and Trust Company, a nonbank trust company in New York, found that the Fed was unresponsive to their arguments. The protesters held that the Fed should force the holding companies to commit significant resources to community development in the United States because of Mitsui's ownership of Mitsui Manufacturers Bank in Los Angeles. But the Fed found that "nonbank companies that are affiliated with or that own depository institutions were not included by Congress within the provisions of CRA."

While most banks in the throes of protests are in populous areas, there are exceptions. First Interstate Bank of Colstrip, Montana, a $12 million-asset institution, was being challenged in 1990 by Native Action, an Indian group, in what was believed to be first CRA protest involving an Indian tribe. That challenge was holding up the merger between First Interstate Bancsystems of Montana, First Interstate's parent—no relation to first Interstate Bancorp of California—and the $275 million Commerce Bancshares in Wyoming.

Native Action claimed that the bank altered its lending territory to exclude the Northern Cheyenne tribe. The Indian group also produced 20 demands, among them that the bank lend $5 million over five years to the reservation and that it waive origination fees on loans, according to *U.S. Banker*. The bank countered that it could not be proactive in a wider territory that included the reservation because there was very little demand and it didn't have the resources to deliver loans on that basis.

And in Iowa, the Iowa Citizens for Community Improvement challenged two of the state's biggest banks, Norwest Corporation and Banks of Iowa Incorporated, in an effort to gain greater credit access for small farmers. The group has modeled itself on the work of urban community

18 Chapter 1

activists elsewhere, compelling the two banks to agree to pony up millions in commitments in exchange for its dropping the protests.

The lesson from these rural protests: CRA-related actions can turn up almost anywhere, and country banks that have not experienced any can't assume they are safe from harm.

Delays and Other Difficulties

The almost-inevitable result of a protest is a delay in any approval and a jump in legal fees. Some observers say there is a 30-day delay built in when community groups protest an application, but a month is a quick jog around the block compared to the marathons some institutions have been caught in. A bank may find that, much like during a protracted lawsuit, it can be cheaper to settle than to keep fighting.

Consider two of the protests mentioned above. The FDIC was still reviewing the Hyde Park Bank situation in December 1990, almost a year after the bank was first approached by activists, according to consultant Laurie Glenn. And the Colstrip, Montana, action was a year old in January 1991.

Some of the country's most acquisitive banks have been caught in the CRA vise. A nine-month CRA protest delayed by five months the mega-merger of Citizens & Southern Corporation and Sovran Financial Corporation to form C&S/Sovran. Most of the scrutiny was directed at C&S, which had been roundly criticized in the Atlanta mortgage series. But the Fed eventually found that C&S had put its CRA house in order, and the deal was approved.

Another southeastern deal delayed by a challenge was the First Union Corporation application to acquire Florida National Banks Incorporated. First Union was challenged by two community groups, one in North Carolina and the other in Florida. When it agreed to commit $9 million for low-income neighborhoods in Charlotte, North Carolina, that segment of the protest was dropped, but the other continued. Then the Federal Reserve said it would delay the deal further pending an OCC examination of the lead bank's CRA record. Eventually, the OCC found that First Union's CRA performance was inadequate in some respects, but the Fed approved the merger in January 1990 because Florida National was about to fail.

Security Pacific Corporation encountered a long delay in 1990 over its application for a 20 percent stake in Mitsui Manufacturers, a Los Angeles business bank that, as noted earlier, was itself part of a CRA-related protest involving its Japanese parent and another merger. The Fed delayed the application, saying it wanted to examine the two banks' CRA records, and Security Pacific subsequently got involved in negotiations with a coalition of community groups about boosting its reinvestment efforts.

Delay is one thing; denial is another. That was driven home at Continental after its Arizona bid was rejected. Or at Leader Federal, a large thrift in Memphis, Tennessee, that had an application for a new branch denied after it had started building it. The thrift attributed the decision to the changing regulatory climate—the denial came in 1989—and its own self-assessment that as a leader in community investment, it would not knuckle under to what it saw as a bid for credit allocation to specific neighborhoods.

But Leader had its knuckles rapped, and "we are much more sensitive to low- and moderate-income households" as a result, executive vice president Brad Champlin told *Savings Institutions.*

State agencies, too, can weigh in with denials. The Massachusetts Board of Bank Incorporation early in 1990 denied BayBanks' application to vote the stock of its subsidiaries in any potential reorganization or consolidation. The decision was based on the "less than satisfactory" CRA rating given to BayBanks' lead bank in the Boston area.

CRA has spurred some institutions to postpone or abandon expansion plans. Harris Trust and Savings Bank in Chicago decided to postpone a deal for Frankfort Bancshares in early 1990, reportedly because of anxiety about both companies' CRA records. And Harris was no stranger to community reinvestment, having pledged $35 million as part of a multibank commitment back in 1984 and adding an additional $50 million pledge later. Harris later refiled the application and completed the acquisition.

Another Chicago institution, Bell Federal Savings and Loan Association, decided in mid-1990 to withdraw its application to buy a small local thrift, Archer Federal, after an acrimonious protest hearing held by the OTS. And Imperial Savings Association in San Diego withdrew its application to buy five branches from an area thrift, saying it had not been challenged but had been pursuing a wholesale strategy that had excluded making mortgages in the community. It said it might refile the application after improving its CRA performance.

Forcing New Programs

Not surprisingly, the new focus on CRA has brought added resources to the area and, with that, new programs. The sudden emergence of a staff dedicated to CRA at major banks—"a dozen here and a dozen there"—left him "flabbergasted," said Bank of America executive vice president Donald Mullane.

Nowhere has this proliferation of staff and programs been more evident than in California. Much of that has clearly been merger related, with the state's biggest banks still on a buying binge in 1989-90. Both Wells Fargo & Company and Security Pacific Corporation were tested by protested applications in 1989, and while both got approval, they began forming programs to smooth the road for future acquisitions.

Wells Fargo in 1989 agreed to examine its advertising and direct marketing strategies for special credit products based on local credit needs. Wells was to "initiate a promotion of its Low Income Finance Terms program, which features reduced monthly payments over longer terms and modified employment qualifications, to include advertisements in community-based publications," the Federal Reserve noted in its order approving the company's acquisition of Central Pacific Corporation and the Torrey Pines Group in February 1990. The Fed added that it would review the bank's "progress under the CRA in future applications."

Security Pacific, following a September 1989 merger approval, said that in response to a San Diego protest it would create a community development center to handle Small Business Administration and community development-related lending. The bank also said it would contribute $250,000 towards creation of a nonprofit community development corporation to serve the San Diego area and provide training to branch managers and loan officers on SBA lending.

That promise of future programs evidently sat well with the Fed. "As indicated in the policy statements, commitments offered by an applicant to strengthen specific aspects of its record are appropriate when its past performance reveals no serious deficiencies," the board noted in its approval order.

Banks in other parts of the country have found themselves required to implement new programs or procedures in order to win approvals. The OCC told Shawmut National Corporation, which was seeking to relocate a Rhode Island branch a few blocks in 1989, that it needed to support its documentation of its geographic analysis with a written evaluation. "Final approval for the branch relocation will not be granted until this office finds that the bank's geographic lending analysis has been completed in a thorough and professional manner," wrote David A. Bomgaars, district administrator.

In a similar order, Mercantile National Bank of Indiana was given conditional approval for a new branch in 1990, contingent on the bank getting a satisfactory CRA rating from the OCC. The regulator cited "deficiencies in several areas" but noted that the bank had committed itself to a CRA action plan that should boost its performance to satisfactory.

Branch Closings

It used to be that closing a branch created some ill will in that community but not much else. Now, doing so in a low-income neighborhood without careful groundwork can be like waving a red flag in front of a bull: A CRA protest is almost guaranteed. In the current CRA climate, an institution that does so must document its rationale carefully and be prepared to ride out a wave of protest.

CRA protests over branch closings have succeeded in compelling banks to make credit commitments. In Syracuse, New York, a community group protested a branch closing by Key Bank, leading to a $5.5 million commitment for commercial and housing loans.

But Manufactures Hanover Trust Company (MHTC), which survived a challenge over its application to acquire New York City branches of Goldome in 1989, effectively made its case to the Fed. "The record shows that MHTC has closed branches after consideration of their lack of profitability, the presence of other MHTC branches nearby, and the availability of other banking alternatives in the community," wrote the CBA's Craig Ulrich in analyzing the Fed's decision. The bank also could point to careful consideration on its part: on two occasions, a closing was postponed or canceled after presentations by local community groups.

Boatmen's National Bank in St. Louis has established a careful process for closings that is detailed in its CRA statement. The bank said it is "devoting special resources to ensure that the branch decision, the rationale for the branch decision, and the bank's desire to remain active in the community is effectively communicated" to the general population as well as community leaders. The bank's CRA officer also is charged with reviewing the procedures set up for such closings.

Wells Fargo's community affairs department evaluates the impact of possible branch closings and ensures such a decision is in keeping with the bank's efforts to meet community credit needs. Wells has a "CRA compliance checklist" that must be completed for any branch to be closed, downsized, relocated, or consolidated.

One branch-closing alternative that has worked in several cities is the transferral or sale of the branch to a community development credit union. This concept will be explored in Chapter 2.

Goal-Setting

One response to the increased pressure and higher profile of CRA has been to establish credit goals for low- and moderate-income areas. Whether implemented by a single bank or by a group of banks, these goals are meant to underline an ongoing, irrefutable commitment to community reinvestment.

Chicago Neighborhood Lending Programs was the pioneer in goal-oriented programs and has been perhaps the foremost CRA-triggered housing effort in the nation. Launched in 1984, long before CRA had sounded an alarm in many areas, it began as a five-year agreement between activists and three major banks—First Chicago Corporation, Harris Trust and Savings, and Northern Trust Company. In the first five years ending in 1989, the NLP made 572 loans for a total of $117.5 million, creating almost 5,000 housing units. The same three banks have committed to an increase of funding to more than $200 million by 1993.

Some of these money-target programs involve specific commitments; others are more open ended. First Tennessee Bank in Memphis in 1989 announced a 10-year, $100 million program for mortgage, home-improvement, and small business loans in targeted areas in the state. Boatmen's National Bank in St. Louis announced a $50 million lending pledge for its Community Reinvestment Program in 1986, but had made more than $140 million in loans by the end of 1989.

Goal-setting made headlines in California in 1989, when Wells Fargo and then Security Pacific announced multiyear, billion-dollar goals for community reinvestment lending. Wells put its goal at $1 billion over seven years, and Security Pacific committed to $4 billion over 10 years, $2.4 billion of that in California. Much of that money will be directed to affordable housing.

"These were preemptive strikes by institutions trying to stay ahead" of CRA restrictions, Warren Traiger, a New York attorney specializing in community development, told *American Banker*. Besides making themselves leaders in the CRA race, the commitments took some ammunition from the hands of activists sniping at the banks' community reinvestment efforts.

The rationale for announcing the public goal was that "we were empowering [community groups] more than we should by not giving out those kinds of goals, because they would basically beat their chests" and dispute the bank's commitment, Security Pacific executive vice president Irving Margol told a Consumer Bankers Association conference in 1990. "They could call a news conference every day and get more publicity than we could," he added. "By making that commitment, we took a little of that empowerment away, and gave it to us, where it belongs."

Wells' Steven Hall told the same conference that the bank needed the goals internally and wanted to give community groups a way of measuring its performance. Actually, Wells expects to exceed its annual goals during the seven years, he said, adding that the bank is under constant pressure to break apart the overall goal to concentrate on individual communities or cities.

Donald Mullane of Bank of America said the bank's only publicly announced goal was to make $50 million a year available for affordable housing. Other than that, he said the bank is keeping its goals internal "because we believe that leadership is what you do and not what you say." While he said one community group would love to see such a goal, "we want to head them off by offering them a cornucopia of products serving low-income consumers."

Some Common Programs Emerge

The shape of a lot of CRA efforts follows closely a list of suggestions offered by the regulatory agencies, but the regulators stress that there are no off-the-shelf approaches, no blueprints for effective CRA performance that can be followed by any size institution in any market. A host of tips and suggestions will be offered in Chapter 8, but there are general programs that successful institutions have undertaken. The agencies spelled these out in a joint statement, which consultant Rick Eckman said could be used "as a checklist to find out what works." These programs include:

1. Implementing policies, including the use of more flexible lending criteria, consistent with safe and sound practices, to provide the types of loans and services described in the institution's CRA statement on a more widespread basis.

2. Increasing efforts to make loans to help meet identified credit needs within the community, such as those for home mortgages, home improve-

ment,and small business. This may include participation in various government-insured lending programs, such as FHA-insured or VA-guaranteed mortgage loans and SBA loans, and participation in other types of lending programs such as high loan-to-value-ratio conventional mortgage loans with private mortgage insurance.

3. Implementing and advertising the availability of services of benefit to low- and moderate-income persons, such as cashing government checks or offering low-cost checking accounts.

4. Creating and implementing advertising and marketing efforts through, for example, newspapers, radio, television, and brochures designed to inform low- and moderate-income groups (in languages other than English, where appropriate) of available loan and deposit services.

5. Expanded officer call programs to include targeted groups, such as small-business owners and real estate agents in low- and moderate-income neighborhoods.

6. Establishing a process involving all levels of management in efforts to contact governmental leaders, economic development practitioners, businesses and business associations, and community organizations to discuss the financial services needed by the community.

7. Developing systems to assist customers or potential customers regarding federal, state, or local assistance programs to small business, housing, or other community needs.

8. Adopting a written corporate policy concerning branch closings that has provisions for adequate notice, analysis of the closing's impact on the local community, and efforts that may be made to minimize any adverse effects.

9. Participating or providing assistance to community development programs or projects supported by the Neighborhood Housing Services, Small Business Administration or Economic Development Administration, or Community Development Block Grants.

10. Establishing a community development corporation.

11. Funding a small business investment corporation or creating a minority business investment corporation.

12. Making lines of credit and other financing available, within prudent lending principles, to nonprofit developers or low-income housing and small-business developments, for low-income multifamily rehabilitation and new construction projects, and/or providing a secondary market for nonprofit developer paper.

13. Underwriting or investing in state and municipal bonds.

14. In the case of members of the Federal Home Loan Bank System, participating actively in the Community Investment Fund program.

A number of these specific programs will be taken up in detail in Chapter 2.

The New Landscape

During the first half of 1990, bankers around the country were nervously awaiting the approach of the public ratings system. Many moved quickly to set up an infrastructure, appointing a CRA officer and actively seeking out community development opportunities. Seminars by trade groups and state and federal agencies drew strong crowds.

Thrifts, some of whom had rarely gone through compliance examinations, were being urged to look in the mirror and get ready. "Institutions should take advantage of the window of opportunity before their first public CRA evaluation to perform a thorough self-assessment of their CRA programs. If necessary, an action plan should be developed to address any weaknesses in the institution's CRA plan," wrote Jonathan Fiechter, senior deputy director at the OTS, in a bulletin in June 1990.

Regulators swung into action. Guidelines first issued in the March 1989 joint statement were amended, and question-and-answer booklets on CRA were disseminated to the industry. In May, the agencies starting bringing together examiners for joint training sessions in sites around the country; in all, some 700 examiners went through the sessions. "It's generally been pretty positive," said a Fed official familiar with the training, "[but] there have been some rough spots." Different levels of examiner experience presented a continuing problem for trainers.

Regulators were bracing for criticism, no matter what the ratings. But if anything, they were expected to come down harder on institutions than ever. "The industry is concerned about whether the criticism leveled at regulators for failing to reject a sufficient number of applications on CRA grounds will result in more such rejections," wrote attorney Warren Traiger in a 1990 report.

Agencies like the FDIC have found themselves in a catch-up mode, trying to improve training for examiners and put more personnel in place. In the fall of 1990, for instance, the FDIC had just three community affairs officers for its eight district offices and was interviewing to fill the other slots. The Fed has had such officers in place for years.

Examiners from state agencies, too, have had to cram at seminars to understand the new regulations. The Federal Reserve Bank of Boston has been cited for good programs that involved a number of New England states. And Massachusetts hired four additional examiners in 1990 to keep up with the load.

Institutions saw themselves being hemmed in. "Banks are very frightened because of the growing sophistication within community-based organizations. They're nervous about being challenged," said consultant Laurie R. Glenn in Chicago. Failure to gain a satisfactory rating would put "serious constraints on our strategic options," said Allen Lastinger, Jr., vice chairman at Barnett Banks. Consultant Michael T. Sullivan said he believes that "the levels affected most are the next tier, and two tiers down" from the biggest institutions, as well as savings and loans.

For community banks and small thrifts unaccustomed to treating CRA as a serious concern, there was fear that they simply could not keep up. Small banks in California have been taken aback by the mammoth CRA efforts underway at the biggest banks in that state. One Consumer Bankers Association official said he heard complaints from some of those small fry to the big banks that "you've given us an awfully tall mountain to climb."

Many smaller banks, particularly, grouse at the recordkeeping required under the new CRA mandates—more detailed records from more areas than ever. "CRA is a tremendous burden on small banks," James Olivieri, compliance officer at Community National Bank in Staten Island, New York, told *U.S. Banker.* Echoed Tom Bischof, compliance officer at Community Banks in Millersburg, Pennsylvania: "We are bogged down with paperwork."

A different kind of pressure is at work in New England, where intense heat on real estate examinations diverted the banks' best people away from other examination areas like CRA. Bankers wondered if CRA examiners would be seasoned enough to recognize their woes. "To a degree, I would say there is some truth to the inexperienced examiners claim," said Boston consultant James Carras.

This concern about the examiners—their experience and possible subjectivity—surfaced frequently. The prospect of publishing the ratings "has heightened the importance of the individual examiners in the process," said Merrikay Hall, a partner with Hughes, Hubbard and Reed in New York, which has a number of major savings banks as clients. An examination at one savings bank with an extensive network in the Bronx was "awful," she said. "They got creamed." The thrift spent a lot of time and money on a detailed response, pointing out the multilingual programs it had developed and education aimed at loan applicants. But the subsequent examination was still only satisfactory, and some of the previous deficiencies were rehashed, she said.

Despite the war stories, some observers say institutions are adapting to the new demands of CRA quite well. "I haven't heard complaints about the existence of CRA," said one New York attorney. "I think most banks I know have not been terribly irritated by it." California attorney and consultant Mark Aldrich said, "I've seen some banks do a really good job with this—some have really taken it to heart and appointed a CRA officer and gotten busy making loans and documenting."

Still, some scrambling is under way. "We're just beginning to see the impact of CRA disclosure," Frederick Wacker, community affairs officer at the Federal Home Loan Bank of Atlanta, said in October 1990. He said he can pinpoint where examiners have been by the thrifts that call up and ask for help. What was acceptable in the past is no longer so, and "that's causing some heartburn for some CEOs out there," he said.

Another frequently voiced concern is that institutions involved in a range of noncredit activities that benefit local communities are not getting sufficient credit for those from regulators. These "soft" community service activities, which will be examined in Chapter 6, include charitable giving and aid to the needy and handicapped. Basic checking and savings programs to low-income persons also fall under this noncredit area, though regulators have clearly included them among desirable activities.

Most major banks have made this community service work a major feature of their expanded CRA statements. They consider it a key function of their participation in the community, and many institutions are scoring public relations points that could help them should examiners quiz community leaders about the institution's image as a corporate citizen.

DOCUMENTATION AND PROMULGATION

Documentation: Bank CRA officers have been hearing it until they are blue in the face. The regulators have practically emblazoned in the sky the notion that they want policies and procedures on CRA written down and disseminated, and they want written records of activities the institution is undertaking. When examiners arrive, they should readily find evidence of a thorough tracking process.

The FFIEC joint statement suggests such following documentation: description of CRA policies; procedures for policy review; description of services directed at CRA needs; and an accounting of resources being allocated to those services.

Documentation and attitude are the chief determinants of successful CRA compliance, said John McDowell, director of consumer activities at the Comptroller's office. Even minutes from directors' meetings can be valuable. "You're doing a lot, and sometimes you don't give yourselves credit for it," he told a CRA conference late in 1989. "Some [banks] are doing good things but have no documents to back them up," echoed Janice Smith, the FDIC's director of community affairs. Four out of five of the FDIC-examined banks are under $100 million in assets and may not have a full-time compliance officer, she said.

Good documentation not only pleases compliance examiners, but helps validate a bank's community involvement. "We have found that many banks do not adequately document their efforts to identify and meet community credit needs. Therefore, the public does not fully recognize the extent of the banks' efforts," wrote Deputy Comptroller Clifton A. Poole, Jr., in a directive to banks in the Southeast. An American Bankers Association task force conceded that banks have not done "a good job of documenting and communicating all the community-service activities which banks do on a daily basis in a variety of ways. Banks do not always get the credit they deserve for being good corporate citizens."

Some bankers concede that this has been a weak area at their institution. "We always had a high level of community involvement, but we were not always willing to record that," said John T. Ewing, president of the Bank of Vermont in Burlington.

Consultants hammer at the importance of documentation. "Because data collection is one of the fundamental building blocks of a good CRA program, it is important that this step not be overlooked or short-changed," says State and Federal Associates of Alexandria, Virginia.

But good documentation has a price. The more automated a bank, the easier it becomes, so the burden falls heaviest on the smallest institutions that are the least computerized. "Most of our banks feel they are meeting the community development needs of their communities, that they serve them well," Linda Garvelink, formerly director of services at the Independent Bankers Association of America, told *Freddie Mac Reports*. "The difficulty in complying will largely rest on documentation requirements . . . In general, it may be easier for community banks to comply with CRA except for the documentation."

"What banks used to be able to tell regulators they were doing, they now have to put in writing, which means more memoranda and paperwork," groused Chip Morrow, president of Marathon National Bank in Los Angeles, in an IBAA newsletter. He estimated that the cost of compliance would increase by $50,000 in 1990 at his $116 million-asset bank.

Geocoding

Proof of meeting needs in lower-income communities has come to rest largely on "geocoding," one of the reigning buzzwords of community reinvestment compliance. Regulators say they prefer—and generally use—"geographic distribution analysis." But by whatever label, it is critical.

Geocoding refers to adding census tract, state, metropolitan statistical area (MSA), county, and block group codes to each customer record. This coding enables examiners to assess an institution's lending record in various neighborhoods, still the fundamental means of judging CRA compliance.

Compilation of Home Mortgage Disclosure Act (HMDA) data by census tract, in the expanded form required by FIRREA, is forcing banks to go this route. Vendors have sprung up to provide institutions with sophisticated software that speeds and simplifies the process. But these programs are not necessary, particularly for small institutions, regulators say. "Geocoding, banks assume, means elaborate electronic apparatus. That's not the case," said Ken Quincy, chief of the special review section at the FDIC. "It could be using something as simple as pins on a map."

This HMDA data has been and will remain a central element in any CRA exam. As altered by FIRREA, financial institution responsibilities are expanded considerably. Lenders have to use a prescribed loan/application register to record data on an application-by-application basis; that process began in 1990 and was to continue through March 1, 1991, when the LARs are due with their supervisory agency in a series of 10 separate tables.

The FFIEC then will take the data and produce disclosure statements that cross-tabulate data for each institution. Statements will be sent to institutions, which must then make them available within 30 days of receipt, and lenders will be required to keep these HMDA reports for five years. The FFIEC does not expect, however, that the data will be mailed before October 1991, and officials at several nonprofits said they have been told privately that the data will not likely be available before 1992.

Given the need to track mortgages and other loans, computerized coding and mapping to enhance compliance is certain to remain a growth industry. "Census tract geocoding is an excellent tool for all the CRA assessment factors," Charles Schenk, senior vice president at National Westminster Bank USA, told the Consumer Bankers Association's Dawson and Forbes. "For instance, you can see where your loans and deposits are, and validate your community delineations." Still, he noted that "you don't have a benchmark, a yardstick to show whether what you are doing is good, bad, or indifferent. CRA assessment is an art, not a science."

And good geocoding clearly can sway regulators. Confronted with allegations that it had made an inadequate number of smaller mortgage and multifamily mortgage loans in Brooklyn, as well as shown inadequate participation in federally insured mortgage loan programs, Manufacturers Hanover Trust Company trotted out extensive records on its volume of loans for homes, small businesses, and credit card approvals in the borough. The Fed concluded that there had been no discriminatory lending patterns or practices.

By the same token, First Union probably suffered in 1989 because of inadequate documentation about its lending record, said the CBA's late general counsel, Craig Ulrich. "I thought First Union probably had an excellent case to make with respect to its CRA performance," he told a CRA forum. "But it just goes to show that a lot of this detail work—this documentation, documentation, documentation—really has some substance to it."

Some fears about geocoding are being heard. Consultant JoAnn Barefoot told an ABA forum in late 1990 that requiring banks to geocode could lead to credit allocation. "Once the regulators have the data, the industry could fall prey to fulfilling lending obligations according to census tract," she said—leaving smaller banks, with historic difficulties in documentation, particularly vulnerable.

Outreach

A vital component of any strong CRA program is community outreach, and regulators are looking for stepped-up efforts from institutions that historically have been weak in this area. In its CRA rating profiles, the FFIEC said that an outstanding institution "employs affirmative outreach efforts to determine community credit needs and addresses them through innovative product development."

The existence of well-developed community outreach programs helped Security Pacific and Manufacturers Hanover pass muster in their 1989 examinations by the Fed. Both could demonstrate ongoing contact by departmental staff, as well as specialized marketing in ethnic newspapers and neighborhood weeklies. Manufacturers Hanover has a community reinvestment office that meets with governments, local business, community organizations, and residents to get input on needs and the development of products to meet those needs.

Many banks have institutionalized outreach efforts that go back quite a few years. Chemical Bank, for instance, has had a "Streetbanker" program that it says is "at the heart of Chemical's community development efforts." Each of these specially trained lenders "becomes immersed in the community, learning firsthand from the 'street' what credit facilities are needed to make a community more viable," the bank said in its CRA statement. "The Streetbanker is a personal point of contact allowing the community to express needs and establish a dialogue with Chemical—an opportunity not often created by large financial institutions."

In Boston, Shawmut and Bank of Boston have had internal affairs programs for years in which staffers don't make loans or do compliance. They serve as the banks' eyes and ears in the community and carry loan requests from nonprofits and government agencies, according to consultant James Carras. In 1990, Bank of Boston began a massive needs assessment throughout its service areas in New England in which branch managers were asked to call monthly on community groups to learn about their needs.

Great Western Bank set up a lending unit in its Crenshaw Boulevard branch in Los Angeles in 1974 to seek out lending opportunities, the thrift said in its CRA statement. It added: "Loan agents working out of the Crenshaw office regularly attend weekly meetings of the Consolidated Realty Board, a group of minority real estate brokers whose activities are concentrated in the inner city areas of Los Angeles." Another big California thrift, First Nationwide Bank, has placed community investment loan officers in six major urban areas. Each works extensively with builders and community groups and is backed by a loan processor.

BancOhio National Bank sends out branch personnel and calling officers to a wide array of people in attempt to cover the bases—existing and prospective customers, representatives from hospitals, municipalities, and economic and community developers; nonprofit providers of low- to moderate-income housing; church pastors, cultural groups, and community-based organizations.

Some institutions have taken a collective approach to outreach, making it not just the domain of a small group of community specialists. Cincinnati's Star Bank set up a Community Outreach Committee early in 1989 to bolster its CRA programs. This included various departments such as marketing, human resources, commercial lending, and compliance.

At some banks, a prominent community development specialist may be the point man for spreading the word about the bank's activities and soliciting interest. At Wells Fargo, Mel Carriere, who oversees the bank's affordable-housing loan programs, travels to conferences involving non-profits to let them know that Wells wants to finance housing projects.

Outreach can mean calling community leaders in. Bank of America has done so as part of what executive vice president Donald Mullane calls a "preemptive" strategy. "Where there were areas where we were remiss or where our performance wasn't as good as it was in other areas, we asked for their assistance," he said. "We asked what their needs were."

Another well-developed form of reaching out is holding "fairs" or "nights" at local agency offices or schools to tell the community what the bank is doing—and to take applications. Star Bank, for instance, held a day-long financial fair with workshops to educate the public on everything including college education financing, buying property, financing a small business, and how to get and keep credit. Trust Company Bank in Atlanta holds a series of "homebuyers' workshops" at schools and churches.

Advertising

One specialized form of outreach is advertising. Regulators are looking for evidence of efforts to use nontraditional advertising vehicles and ideas to improve delivery to lower-income communities. In neighborhoods with heavy ethnic concentrations where English is not the first language, banks should show they have tried to advertise in the language used in those areas.

Harris Trust and Savings in Chicago launched an advertising campaign in minority-owned newspapers late in 1990. The information was in the form of money-management columns offering advice to consumers and small business owners, as well as a hot-line number; the ads are appearing in bilingual Spanish-English community newspapers and in the black-owned *Chicago Daily Defender.*

But Harris took some flak for its decision not to advertise in Spanish. One attorney for a local activist group charged that the campaign fell short of CRA guidelines as a result. A Harris official told *American Banker* that it did intend to advertise in Spanish eventually, but didn't have the necessary Spanish-speaking staff to handle calls related to the program.

First Nationwide Bank advertises periodically in Spanish- and Chinese-language newspapers and provides retail product information and ATM instructions in those languages. The thrift noted in 1990 that efforts were under way to translate that information into Vietnamese as well. The Office of Thrift Supervision mentioned the bilingual ATM instruction in giving First Nationwide an "outstanding" rating under CRA Assessment Factor "L."

Print media—particularly newspapers—have been the choice for most bank advertisers. They reach a wide audience, and the message has more "permanence" than it would have on radio or television. Billboards, radio, and television also have been used to make people aware of community reinvestment efforts. In their CRA statements, Boatmen's National Bank and Trust Company Bank both list the radio and television stations used for their advertisements.

Trust Company Bank also makes special note of its minority advertising. "Since a significant percentage of out community's low- and moderate-income households are in minority groups, we use media specifically targeted at minorities," the bank said. It also has helped sponsor programs such as a "black history week" on a local radio station.

A far more generic form of advertising is aimed not at helping individual institutions but the industry's image. The American Bankers Association ran a series of "good neighbor" advertisements in national publications beginning in 1989 to highlight what banks were doing to boost community development. Under the slogan "Why being a good neighbor is good banking," the ABA spotlighted the efforts of banks such as American Security in Washington, First Interstate in California, National Bank of Detroit, and some small nonurban institutions such as Wilbur National Bank in Oneonta, New York, and Farmers Savings Bank of Keota, Iowa. Accompanied by drawings by well-known illustrator Whitney Darrow, Jr., the ad campaign was aimed at giving the industry more leverage in heading off new regulation.

This image campaign did garner a good deal of attention and positive notices. "Americans will be more likely to listen to and accept the arguments of an industry they know is actively engaged" in community reinvestment, wrote attorney Warren Traiger in *American Banker.* But he added that "this promotion will be most effective if done at the grassroots level— i.e., by individual institutions through their local media."

Publicity

A relatively small number of banks are publicizing their community reinvestment efforts through newsletters, brochures, and reports, most often directed at opinion leaders and shareholders. American Security Bank, whose community development lending program will be examined in Chapter 3, has even made a sophisticated color videotape chronicling some of its experiences and urging banks to be more proactive.

Some of the publicity efforts are admittedly defensive. "There's no question that, after going through two protests, we felt we had to be doing more," Ralph F. Desiderio, senior vice president at Midlantic Corporation's Continental Bank in Philadelphia, told *U.S. Banker.* Among its efforts, the bank is publishing a community investment newsletter that goes out to 1,500 readers.

First Bank System put out a social audit report listing loans and mortgages, as well as basic banking, in terms of numbers and dollars, said Charles E. Riesenberg, head of the bank's community development corporation. If banks don't take the initiative, community groups could produce a study "that probably has methodologies that are going to hang you," he said.

National City Corporation in Cleveland late in 1990 issued a "Community Outreach" brochure detailing "our extensive outreach efforts to make every neighborhood we serve a better place to live and work." Copies were mailed to all employees and shareholders.

The debate surrounding publication of the new four-tier ratings will be taken up in Chapter 7. Officials at some institutions that had not gone through the new rating process, however, said they felt constrained that they could not release the federal ratings they received under the old format.

Bank of Vermont president John T. Ewing said he would "love to" publish the rating his bank received after an examination completed by the FDIC shortly before July 1, 1990. But he did say the state of Vermont gave the bank a "1″ for its efforts. Chemical Bank vice president Kenneth Herz said he, too, could not reveal the bank's pre-public federal rating but the New York State rating has been "outstanding all along."

In general, however, consultants and marketing experts seem divided on how institutions should make use of outstanding ratings. Some said banks should trumpet the ratings and incorporate them into a new marketing campaign; others said institutions should be wary about lording high ratings over rivals or provoking community groups who might disagree with the evaluations. For its part, the FFIEC said it "is not placing any limitation on the institutions' prudent use of this information," but noted that any such advertising must not be misleading and must make it clear that the rating involves only an institution's CRA performance, not its financial condition.

WAR OR UNEASY TRUCE?

Some banks and thrifts, particularly the ones with the best-developed community outreach programs, have reached something of an entente with community groups. Others are still in various forms of hostilities, with charges and countercharges being lobbed by both sides amid clouds of suspicion and distrust.

The root cause of the Community Reinvestment Act was charges of redlining, and the basic conflict that emerged from those charges—of allegations and denials that credit was withheld because of discrimination—continues to flavor the CRA stew. Redlining isn't heard that much these days, but like a chilly wind on a spring day, it serves as a reminder of what went before.

The published studies on mortgage lending have only given activists more ammunition for their position. Bankers may question the methodologies used, but the results have been nothing but bad news for the industry. Karl E. Case, a professor of economics at Wellesley College and a CRA advocate, told *U.S. Banker* that after examining the differences in lending patterns between black and white neighborhoods, "One cannot prove somebody wrong who says that banks discriminate."

Another continuing overlay to CRA is the clash between the corporate culture and that of the grass roots. Many people from poor neighborhoods don't speak the standard business language and feel uncomfortable in formal surroundings with people in suits, noted Allen Fishbein, general counsel for the Center for Community Change. And vice versa: bankers are uncomfortable dealing with groups that they may perceive more as a collection of street people than as respectable adversaries. The two sides need to find a common language, Fishbein said.

Chicago consultant Laurie Glenn recalls the time when she was doing economic partnership work at First National Bank of Chicago. The bank was targeting poorer neighborhoods in Chicago, and a meeting was held about upcoming school council elections. One of the bank vice presidents in attendance told the others that he wanted "a high comfort level" with the bank's participation. There was nodding around the table about that, but not from everyone.

"After the meeting, one of the community leaders walked up and to me and asked, 'What's a high comfort level?'" Glenn said. Although all the bankers understood, the people in the community didn't—and their suspicions and uneasiness grew.

Community development experts say that too often the two sides settle into a kind of trench warfare, unwilling to explore ways to make peace. "There's mutual mistrust, so you really need some kind of clarity about the purpose of any discussions," said California activist leader Gilda Haas.

"There was an initial assumption that there was a monolithic bank position and a monolithic community position," Dr. Calvin Bradford told the National Training and Information Center, a community group organizer, after examining a number of reinvestment programs. "But as we studied the programs, we found that different communities had significantly different priorities. Some simply wanted to house the poor. Others wanted a mix of low- and moderate-income loans . . . . We found that the CRA laws permitted and even encouraged a diversity of opinions, values, and goals."

What Activists Want

"CRA is not about grants. It's about loans, and not about documentation," insists Jean Pogge, president of the Woodstock Institute in Chicago, a nonprofit dedicated to neighborhood investment. "A bank's first obligation is to make loans, to figure out how to do that."

Easier said than done, of course. But particularly for institutions that have historically paid minimal attention to CRA, the temptation is strong for a "quick fix"—contributing to loan pools, making grants to nonprofits, or undertaking other hands-off investments that show compliance but don't require loads of staff or effort.

This quick-fix idea disturbs activists, said Fishbein. It has translated into what he contends has been an emphasis on form over substance, with geocoding, expanded CRA statements, and published surveys intended to show bank efforts. "There's a difference between compliance and performance. We need to look more at the latter," he told a CRA conference in 1990.

Without a doubt, community activists are not satisfied with banking's record. Some are agitating for additional laws to compel banks to do still more for poorer neighborhoods. They have urged that banks with poor compliance records be hit with unspecified sanctions, and that the best banks be rewarded with government deposits. Community groups attending a conference in Washington in the fall of 1990 urged that CRA be broadened still further—that both banks and regulators meet affirmative action goals in employment, according to *American Banker*.

The California Reinvestment Coalition, an activist group, has suggested that all banks set concrete annual dollar targets for CRA lending, as Security Pacific and Wells Fargo have. It maintains that these goals send a signal that an institution has a firm commitment to community reinvestment, as well as provide a benchmark for implementation.

Meanwhile, challenges to mergers and other expansion efforts will continue, though Fishbein expects these will be used more sparingly. But he warned bankers at a CRA conference that the challenge process may come back with a vengeance if community groups conclude that CRA has not significantly altered the distribution of bank monies to various neighborhoods.

There is an ongoing push for commercial lending disclosure, though advocates are not seeking anything as rigorous as the HMDA requirements that apply to mortgages. Jean Pogge thinks this loan disclosure is "absolutely critical." Data already exists by census tract in cities like Chicago and Cleveland, she said. "The regulators are saying you must do small-business lending, but the banks don't have the data themselves," she added. "Many are doing it, but they have no proof." Studies "suggest that commercial lending disclosure could be even more valuable" than existing lending disclosure for community development and job creation, said the Center for Policy Alternatives.

Bankers React

The drumbeat of CRA-related pressure from activists and now regulators has put a lot of bankers on the defensive. Reactions have ranged widely, from protests of being misunderstood to carping about the load that banks and thrifts—and not other fiduciaries—are being expected to carry. "A satisfactory rating, as I understand it, is an exceptional performance," the CBA's late general counsel Craig Ulrich told bankers at a CRA forum. "No other business entity will be doing what you're doing."

"Banks can't do it all, but we are an easy target. We're on the front line and because we are regulated, our business is open to scrutiny," James Mynatt of Trust Company Bank in Atlanta told *Business Atlanta*. "There's a difference between funding and extending credit, and that needs to be understood," said Larry Kurmel, executive director of the California Bankers Association. "There's a difference between need and demand, and that needs to be understood."

Institutions are particularly troubled by what they see as demands for credit allocation. "The act is supposed to ensure that there are no deliberate exclusions. That doesn't translate into guaranteed credit allocation," Timothy Goodsell, chairman of Chicago's Hyde Park Bank and Trust Company, told *American Banker*. Robert Bartkowski, a community relations officer for Goldome, the New York savings bank, told the newspaper that an East Harlem group that challenged Goldome has "very little knowledge of what's available to them." The thrift committed $100 million to an affordable mortgage program, but the protest group never tries to go that route, he said.

Another common complaint is that activists frequently are unable to make a coherent case for increased lending in their area. "They had no idea what banking was about. They just followed a script someone had given them," said one former banker, now a consultant, of a protest he was involved with.

The constant hubbub about CRA "has not necessarily made any converts," says Georgeann Abbanat, deputy commissioner for community reinvestment and outreach in Massachusetts. "There are some old-timers who you're not going to convince." More than a few bankers have turned to humor—some might call it gallows humor—to ease the pressure. Frederick D. Wacker, community affairs officer at the Federal Home Loan Bank of Atlanta, said he has heard CRA referred to as "The Community Riot Act" and the "Community Render-Us-Insolvent Act."

Banks continue to chafe at what they see as the ill-defined shape of the regulations. And, unquestionably, that shape has changed in the past few years. For that, regulators are taking a few shots. One Virginia banker said to this writer, "I hope you include a chapter on how the regulators keep changing their minds." Said Security Pacific's Irving Margol, "One of the big problems [with CRA] is, who's the scorekeeper?" Regulators, institutions, and community groups keep score differently, he said.

"The only truth to CRA is that there is no one answer . . . I would do something different tomorrow if someone could show me something better," First Union compliance officer Phillips R. Gay, Jr., told a CRA conference in fall 1990. He added: "I'm not sure I can define a CRA loan. If someone has a good definition, I'd love to see it."

But complaints don't score points with community groups or, in most cases, with regulators. Some of the country's most forward-thinking institutions have concluded that resistance is futile; increasingly, upbeat messages about community reinvestment are being heard, even if that term isn't always used. "The notion of 'reinvestment' is you put it back in because you're told to. 'Development' is reaching out because it's the right thing to do," said James P. Murphy, executive vice president and director of public policy and external relations at Fleet/Norstar Financial Group. Indeed, the phrase *the right thing to do* has appeared in a number of bank CEOs' communications about CRA.

Other messages use loftier images. "There is an interdependence between First National Bank and the community that is forged through personal interaction and financial partnerships," said Leonard V. Hardin, president of the First National Bank of Louisville. "The bottom line isn't drawn until community involvement is defined."

There is widespread acknowledgment of the growing sophistication of community groups and the effect that has had on their tactics. Consultant Michael T. Sullivan said they are much more skillful about analyzing annual reports and pinpointing areas where they can exert pressure. "They are part of networks today. They lobby, they're known by the regulators," a thrift executive told *Savings Institutions*. "The community groups are putting their reputations on the line . . . They want it to work as much as we do."

Community groups "have shown time and again that they can bring their collective knowledge of local markets and programs to the table and help banks fashion appropriate responses to community needs," said Federal Reserve Governor John LaWare.

Risk and Reward

Clearly, the scope of CRA activities that an institution pursues may hinge largely on perceived risk. In a difficult economic environment, those risks loom larger. But without some risk there can be little reward, at least in terms of approbation from community groups and regulatory agencies.

One form of reward can be a bigger market share for "good" institutions. "Indirectly, bank community development may allow the bank to develop or retain important customer relationships with individuals, businesses, and government entities who view bank support for the community as important to their selection of a financial institution," noted the OCC in its "Community Development Finance: Tools and Techniques for National Banks."

Another reward can be a lessening of hostilities that can allow an institution to function better, without constant distractions from fighting minor skirmishes. That process may be started simply by inviting activists to a dialogue. "I try to help banks realize that they need to be inclusive. If they bring people in, hostilities end," says Laurie Glenn in Chicago.

The ultimate risk for an institution may not be to its profitability as much as its public image. Ratings disclosures create "a considerable opportunity for neighborhood, community, state, and nationwide activist groups to pillory banks that do not score well in the rankings," wrote Andrew C. Goldberg, a vice president in crisis communications at Burson-Marsteller in New York, in a commentary in *American Banker* late in 1990. "This could be more than just a hot media issue for those banks that are embarrassed by their rating. With the public esteem accorded the banking industry at new lows, activist groups may be better able to mobilize state and local lawmakers into penalizing banks that get unsatisfactory reviews."

While this media hullabaloo was still simmering below the surface at this writing, it could well boil over later in 1991. To bolster their chances for strong ratings and community approval, institutions everywhere are looking harder at their organizations and pursuing special strategies that go beyond conventional lending. In the next chapter, we will examine these strategies and lean about some of the myriad ways in which institutions can supplement their everyday CRA programs.

CHAPTER 2

SPECIAL STRATEGIES

Even with the foundations of an effective CRA program in place, many banks have implemented special strategies meant to further boost community reinvestment. Each of the programs examined in this chapter, apart from the section on wholesale and specialty banks, should be considered as a possible niche or adjunct to a retail institution's mainstream CRA efforts.

CRA compliance pressures are prodding many of these programs, although bankers are reluctant to admit it. Most of these special strategies, like new kids in town, have seen their popularity surge after it was discovered just what they could do. And positive signals from the regulators have cemented that popularity.

CDCs ADDRESSING NEEDS

Community development corporations have been around longer than many CRA programs and are well rooted in many cities and towns around the country. Some predate the CRA law, going back as far as the mid-1960s, and others are still in formation. They offer enormous variety: for-profit and not-for-profit, inner-city and rural, single-bank and multibank.

Many "community development corporations" are owned by nonprofits and, at least organizationally, have nothing to do with financial institutions, though many receive support from intermediaries that draw resources from banks and thrifts. Our concentration here is on bank-owned or bank-supported CDCs, specifically approved by regulators. And while *bank* is the operative word, thrifts have been involved as investors in some CDCs. In Hazleton, Pennsylvania, for instance, First Federal Savings and Loan is a partner with three local banks in a CDC pushing downtown revitalization.

Regulators have been unequivocal about their approval. "Established a community development corporation" is on the list of steps taken by "institutions with the most effective programs for meeting their CRA responsibilities," according to the FFIEC's 1989 joint statement on CRA. And in February 1990, the Comptroller's office revised its rules on CDCs to encourage more banks to go that route.

"These corporations can be catalytic," the Federal Reserve said in a pamphlet on CDCs. "They can inspire further economic and community development in both urban and rural neighborhoods." For its part, the FDIC says that "formation of, or investment in, a community development corporation may . . . be a viable way to address certain credit needs in the communities of banks of holding company subsidiary banks." Says John Sower, president of Development Finance Corporation in Washington and an authority on bank CDCs: "Regulators want a focus, and a CDC is a logical tool" for focused community investment.

Still, as Price Waterhouse noted in a newsletter to clients, a bank's investments in a CDC "can improve its Community Reinvestment Act performance, but this program is intended to enhance rather than replace a bank's regular community development lending program."

The OCC ruling allows banks to invest in CDCs that would not be "bankable assets" under ordinary circumstances, provided that the CDC project is "of a predominantly civic, community, or public nature and not merely private and entrepreneurial." Investments can be carried as "other assets" if the bank's investment is no more than 2 percent of its capital and surplus for one individual project, or 5 percent in the aggregate. The OCC approved its first bank-organized CDC in 1978.

Currently, bank CDCs are regulated by the Comptroller's office, the Federal Reserve, or by state banking officials. The division is logical: the Fed regulates those under bank holding companies, the OCC those under national banks, and state regulators the CDCs of state-chartered institutions. Structurally, there is tremendous latitude. As noted, they can be for-profit or not-for-profit. They can be organized as wholly owned subsidiaries of a holding company or a single bank, or jointly funded by a number of financial institutions or corporate investors. Moreover, some are joint ventures or partnerships with private or public investors. And, they can invest in the equity of a venture, a clear departure from normal bank investments. In all, CDCs give banks a degree of flexibility in extending credit that they cannot get from conventional lending programs.

Despite this latitude, regulators aren't giving institutions a carte blanche. The Comptroller's office, for instance, advises national banks to get an OCC opinion letter regarding compliance for its proposed unit. This generally means that the bank must submit an investment plan, a request to review any legal considerations, and copies of pertinent incorporation papers. The Fed requires a specific form, and advises holding companies to discuss its proposed CDC as thoroughly as possible with regulators before setting it up.

Some concerns have been heard about the Fed process, which involves approvals at the regional bank level. That can mean a dozen different ideas about what constitutes low or moderate income, as well as different notions of what a small business is, said consultant James A. Vitarello. "The OCC program may be slow [in comparison], but at least it's consistent," he told a 1990 CDC conference.

Any bank CDC should be "intended to stimulate, not compete with, private-sector investment or development companies," the OCC noted. Since nonprofit intermediaries or economic development agencies are often involved in the kinds of projects that a bank CDC would do, this can be a drawback. John Kolesar, the former president of Ameritrust Development Bank in Cleveland, said the holding company decided not to incorporate a CDC because the city already had a host of neighborhood nonprofit developers.

Institutions need to realize that often only nonprofits are eligible to get grant money from foundations and federal and state agencies. So while management may want the additional income stream a CDC can provide— most holding company CDCs are for-profit ventures—setting one up as a for-profit entity may foreclose a potentially key source of project financing. On the other hand, nonprofit CDCs can reinvest their earnings in new development.

Regulatory contact doesn't end when the CDC is up and running. The Comptroller's office, for example, asks banks to address what public benefits have resulted every two years, and it also scrutinizes the CDCs through the regular examination process.

Structure and Philosophy

As distinct subsidiaries, bank CDCs usually have a management team independent of top officers of its parent and an independent board of directors. These need not be bankers; some CDCs are led by city or county officials or economic development professionals who provide the spark for new project ideas. The smaller the community, the smaller the leadership group can be. Most CDCs also have a "second tier," an investment committee, usually made up of bankers, who review and approve investments.

The flexibility of bank CDCs carries into structure, notes John Sower, who has helped quite a few banks set up their programs. "In the smallest operation, one person might carry most of the administrative load," he said. "In others, there is more structure, with regular board meetings, written investment criteria, and formalized application procedures." The board's role is often vital, he said. Members' wisdom, experience, and ongoing involvement "will best assure the success of the bank CDC and the projects that are funded," he wrote in *Organizing Bank CDCs for Local Economic Development*, a booklet published by the U.S. Department of Commerce's Economic Development Administration.

In some instances, local government has played a significant role in the formation and operation of a CDC, particularly if a public-private partnership created the project. In other cases, the private sector is the driving force and there may be little or no governmental role. But the regulators believe in the partnership idea. "We encourage bank holding companies to work with existing organizations," Sandra Braunstein, a program manager with the Fed's Division of Consumer and Community Affairs, told a CDC forum.

The OCC and the Fed differ somewhat on their approach, Sower noted. While the former requires demonstrated community involvement with the bank CDC—usually in the form of community representation on the board of directors—the Fed has no such requirement, though it may ask the holding company to show it has some mechanism for receiving community input. "Community involvement may take any form the holding company views as effective," the Fed stated in a pamphlet on CDCs.

The OCC also requires that a bank CDC provide for continuity, delegating day-to-day activities to one person, either full-time or part-time, who is accountable to directors. "Bank CDCs have provided for management by designating bank staff to work on a half-time basis, by contracting with existing organizations, by contracting with private developers, by hiring bank CDC executive directors, or by using a combination of these approaches," Sower wrote.

Not surprisingly, community development corporations have encompassed a wide variety of goals. As the OCC noted in a pamphlet, these have included:

- Housing development and rehabilitation.
- Downtown and neighborhood commercial revitalization.
- Industrial development and redevelopment.

- Small business and minority business assistance.
- Training, technical assistance, research, and planning for non-profit development groups.

Through CDCs, the agency added, banks have bought, rehabilitated, built, managed, sold, and promoted real estate; made equity investments in real estate, commercial projects, and small businesses; provided loans and grants and leveraged both public and private funding; provided technical assistance in such areas as small-business management and mortgage lending; and done project feasibility and market studies related to development.

Among their advantages, CDCs allow banks to target projects closely related to strategic goals and to "centralize community development financing expertise in one identifiable unit which can serve as a resource for both the bank and the community," the OCC observed. Moreover, CDCs can help a bank control transaction costs associated with public-private partnerships, create a clear identity for itself as a civic advocate, and assume a leadership role in community projects through real estate, small business, or other equity investments.

This ability to invest directly in real estate is a real plus, argues Charles Riesenberg, vice president of the First Bank System Community Development Corporation in Minneapolis. Banks can initiate development rather than wait for it to come to them, he told a Consumer Bankers Association conference. He added, "You can gain site control, study feasibility, and have the benefits of ownership."

Sower finds that local government officials, while well-versed in public economic development programs, often know little about bank CDCs. "They should know that bank CDCs represent a source of private-sector funding and management resources for local economic and community development at a time when federal resources are declining," he wrote. Yet in obtaining funding, bank CDCs do have distinct disadvantages: they have no access to the funding windows or secondary markets that their parent banks have.

Bank CDCs have become a pet idea of the federal Economic Development Administration, which in 1989 undertook a seven-month program to push their development through national promotion and educational materials, establishment of pilot programs, and technical assistance. A half-dozen projects were launched in that period, said Sower, who was the contractor working with the EDA. He added that the program generated more than 125 calls from other bankers interested in learning more about CDCs.

But experts sound a cautionary note about multibank CDCs, saying these need a lead bank and a senior-level person at that bank to carry the ball. "Where you can't find that person, you are just about doomed because bankers in a room together will kill this [idea] if they don't understand it," consultant James Vitarello told a forum on bank CDCs.

Some Existing CDCs

It's hard to generalize about the 82 bank-owned CDCs in place in late 1990. They come in different shapes and sizes and they are meant for different ends. One good way to sketch the breadth of approach and scope is to examine a dozen or so, segregated by their stated mission, and to make some generalized observations about how they work.

General Redevelopment
While most CDCs have a fairly well-defined niche, others, particularly at some of the nation's biggest banks, are broad-based. And major banks **are** generally setting up their own proprietary operations. "Big banks like to do things for themselves," Sower said.

• Take NCNB Corporation, the big superregional banking concern based in North Carolina. NCNB Community Development Corporation, approved by the OCC in March 1978, had developed projects around the state worth a sale or appraised value of more than $110 million by mid-1990. Initially, it targeted areas plagued by high crime and blight in its hometown of Charlotte for housing loans. From that base in housing development, it moved into economic development, fashioning a master plan with the city for a gateway along a main highway.

"We are primarily developers," Dennis Rash, president of the CDC, told a conference on CDC development. "We do not approach economic development or our revitalization activities from a lender's perspective. Banks have plenty of those. What we look to do is initiate in areas with chronic economic distress." But a former executive at a rival bank contended that much of what NCNB did was merely "gentrification."

• Chase Manhattan Corporation, the nation's second-largest banking concern, committed $200 million to a new for-profit CDC that began in 1989. The money was to be distributed to housing and economic development activities in lower-income neighborhoods over five years. The CDC also is providing technical assistance to other Chase units in other states. It underwrites the loans it makes and books many of them through the bank.

Its president, Mark A. Willis, said the Chase CDC offers loan products through five specialized units: a residential mortgage lending unit that offers permanent mortgages in low- to moderate-income areas throughout the city; a third-party lending division that provides funds to community-based intermediaries; an urban lending unit that offers construction loans for rehabilitating single- to four-family homes; a larger-development projects unit to finance rehabilitation of rental properties, in conjunction with the New York City Vacant Building Program and the New York City Housing Partnership Program; and a community-based development unit providing construction loans for residential and commercial projects involving local nonprofits.

• First Chicago Corporation's Neighborhood Development Corporation is, like NCNB's, an old-timer, in existence since 1979. This for-profit venture has changed its focus since the outset, when it served as a joint venture partner with local Chicago community groups developing and financing mostly multifamily subsidized housing in poorer neighborhoods.

Since 1985, the CDC has focused primarily on providing technical support for the bank's neighborhood lending division, which works with community groups to do both housing development and commercial revitalization. The CDC is also the conduit for First Chicago's participation in a leading housing intermediary, the Chicago Equity Fund.

• Central Kankakee Business Development Corporation (CKBDC) in Kankakee, Illinois, is a venture between City National Bank of Kankakee, the lead bank, and First Trust and Savings Bank. Also a for-profit entity, the CKBDC grew from an existing downtown revitalization project. The CKBDC's purchase of a vacant department store was a linchpin in the downtown revitalization program. Using that store as the site for a proposed anchor store for a new mall, the CDC was able to help the city procure a federal urban development grant, a state grant, and draw developers to the project.

Real Estate Management
CDCs around the country have been set up to handle the gamut of functions associated with developing and managing commercial and residential real estate.

• First Rockford CDC in Rockford, Illinois, for example, is a nonprofit begun in 1979 to promote the revitalization of a particular city neighborhood. It will acquire, renovate, develop, lease, manage, and sell properties. One declining residential area was given a boost by the purchase, rehabilitation, and sale of 15 houses. And in a downtown commercial area, the CDC refurbished and sold five buildings and purchased, managed, and sold a sixth.

• Key Bank CDC in Chester, New York, a nonprofit formed in 1986, also handles the range of real estate transactions—acquisition, leasing, mortgaging, promoting, and selling—for both residential and commercial properties. In addition, it gives loans or grants to community-based projects and provides technical assistance in such areas as planning and financing.

Housing Development

This is probably the most popular use for bank CDCs, though consultant James Carras said he sees bank CDCs moving away from it. Former Ameritrust executive John Kolesar told a CBA conference that CDCs, having a history of becoming developers, "tend to bog you down in maybe one or two projects in a specific neighborhood in a given period of time." But the interest in using CDCs to develop low-income housing remains strong.

• Buckeye-Woodland CDC, a for-profit entity led by National City Bank of Cleveland, was created in 1981 to revitalize housing in a distressed area in the city. Huntington Banks and Society National Bank have also invested in the CDC. The corporation buys, rehabilitates, and sells vacant single-family housing at below-market costs by using public and other private financing. It also buys and fixes up multifamily housing for rental and develops new housing for sale.

• First Fidelity CDC in New Jersey, formed in 1982, has essentially functioned as a mortgage lender for first-time homebuyers. By 1990, the corporation had made $15 million in such loans, plus an additional $2.1 million in interim loans for low- and moderate-income residential developments and $500,000 for new ownership housing in Atlantic City built by the corporation. The CDC, an approved FHA lender and a licensed mortgage banker, is one of 10 New Jersey lenders committing a total of $125 million in construction loans to inner-city housing developers.

• City Lands Corporation is a for-profit subsidiary of Shorebank Corporation of Chicago, parent of South Shore Bank, which will be profiled in the next chapter. A real investment subsidiary of the holding company, it has built more than 1,300 units of low- and moderate-income housing since

1978. While its focus has been on multifamily housing, it completed a $10 million shopping center in 1990 in a poor area on Chicago's south side. "If you're just a lender, you're distanced from the actual production," Thomas Moss, president of City Lands, told *American Banker*. "When you have people from the bank involved in the work, it gives you a better understanding of the credit needs and other issues in the community where you work."
• Keystone CDC, a unit of Keystone Financial Incorporated in Harrisburg, Pennsylvania, uses a team approach to housing development. It joins with community organizations, then draws on the resources of its member banks to handle the lending. And those resources need not be the lion's share. In a project involving five vacant houses to be renovated and sold, Keystone is kicking in $50,000, compared to $64,000 from the City of Harrisburg and a $150,000 grant from the Pennsylvania Department of Community Affairs.

Business Opportunities/Job Creation
This is an increasingly popular direction for CDCs, with a number of them formed in rural areas where jobs have been scarce. Sower said he has been involved in establishing CDCs to fill industrial and commercial space, in rural and urban areas, involving from one to as many as seven banks.

• Montgomery County Blacksburg/Christiansburg Development Corporation in Blacksburg, Virginia, is a nonprofit dedicated to diversifying and broadening the employment base in its southern Virginia county. Its goal is to provide venture capital, develop shell building projects to attract new industry, and finance startups and existing businesses. The CDC has been working with several small technology firms seeking capital for expansion.
• In rural Wisconsin, the First National Bank of Hartford's for-profit CDC is developing a small-business "incubator," the chief cog of which is a 43,000-square-foot light industrial building designed to be home to several start-ups at once. A local nonprofit development corporation owns the industrial park where the incubator is located and is matching the bank's investment.
   "I looked upon it as an investment in our community," Bank president Dennis A. Carroll told *Independent Banker*. "It's an opportunity to create some profits, get some small businesses started, and in two [to] three years get them out to their buildings in the industrial park."
• Indiana Community Business Credit Corporation (ICBCC) is perhaps unique among CDCs in that close to 50 banks have pooled resources to set

up a for-profit corporation to make somewhat speculative loans to promising small companies. In 1990, it was working with a pool of $8.3 million and had $4 million in loan balances and unfunded commitments.

The ICBCC is structured very much like a loan consortium. Member institutions make revolving lines of credit to the corporation in amounts equal to 1.5 percent of their capital and surplus; for each project funded, one member must lend at least 50 percent of the needed amount, with the ICBCC providing the balance. The corporation draws this funding from each member's credit line, based on the prorated share of the total base.

Doing the Unconventional

Community development corporations clearly give banks a chance to take on unconventional projects that would be deemed too risky for their bank parents. Many of these would logically be targeted for poorer areas that regulators are certain to focus on during targeted CRA examinations, or hold out the promise of jobs for people living in those areas.

In Seattle, a CDC organized by Security Pacific Bank Washington expanded its work from housing to economic development by investing $500,000 in an organic foods distributor. The company was already a bank client, Sower noted, but since it was being serviced through conventional working capital means, the company didn't qualify for more bank financing. The same CDC is also supporting a T-shirt company called Body Wear; the company got a loan from the CDC and a line of credit from the parent bank.

The CDC investment allowed the organic foods company to make a major expansion. The bank will get to partake in the fruits of that effort because the deal was structured essentially as an unsecured loan with options to purchase stock in the future. "The bank CDC funding is in the risk/reward 'gap' between conventional bank loans and venture capital," Sower observed.

Speculative commercial and industrial space is another area where CDCs are filling a niche. While the stuff of nightmares for conventional lenders, "spec" buildings fall readily into the equity investment role of CDCs. In Norwalk, Ohio, the Norwalk Community Development Corporation provides equity financing for unleased industrial buildings with the aim of attracting new manufacturing firms to the area, hard hit by job losses. These investments have spurred more than $10 million in investments since 1982 and, in at least one case, persuaded a firm with 175 jobs to stay in the area. And seven banks in Wheeling, West Virginia, formed a for-profit CDC to finance a 12,000-square-foot unleased industrial building to attract a new company to the community. Construction there began in 1990.

The Ohio Valley Industrial & Business Development Corporation, as the CDC in Wheeling is known, was trying to spur private investment and create a modern facility that would lure a nonlocal company, said its executive director, Terry Burkhardt. While the CDC is providing 100 percent financing for the project, the developer is responsible for items such as interest, insurance, and taxes, and has personally signed on a note, Burkhardt told a CDC forum.

POOLING RESOURCES WITH OTHERS

While a number of community development corporations involve collective efforts, far and away the most popular form of group initiatives for community reinvestment have been loan pools and other consortiums. Like mushrooms after a heavy rain, consortiums have been springing up around the country in recent years as financial institutions have learned how effectively they can leverage their own lending through collaborative programs.

Such pooled efforts, most focused on generating more affordable housing, clearly have the regulators' blessing. In a 1989 CRA booklet directed at chief executives and compliance officers, the Federal Deposit Insurance Corporation, for instance, said it would "continue to consider favorably" any "participation by financial institutions in public and private partnerships to promote economic and community development efforts." A later FDIC booklet lists purchases of community development loans as a "nontraditional" but clearly acceptable form of community reinvestment for CRA purposes.

The Federal Reserve Bank of San Francisco has been an active supporter of community reinvestment corporations, and is working with a nonprofit affordable housing advocate, the San Francisco Development Fund, in promoting them in its region. The California Community Reinvestment Corporation, an ambitious consortium involving scores of banks in the state, was put together late in 1988 with help from the Fed bank and the development fund to create more affordable housing in California. The CCRC and a dozen other consortia will be examined in detail in Chapter 5.

One major lure for financial institutions looking into such initiatives is the participation of state and local (and occasionally federal) governments, nonprofits, and foundations. Besides legitimizing private efforts, participation by governments and other public entities provides an important wellspring of additional capital. This money is often known as "credit enhancement" or "synthetic equity," and it can transform the economics of a project from submarginal to viable. It can come in a raft of forms, including loan subsidies, compensating balances, operating or technical support expenses, and more. These public entities can also represent an important conduit to the secondary market for lenders.

This public-private partnership idea can be a terrific boon to institutions. Lenders whose attention is generally turned elsewhere and who have few if any contacts in low-income neighborhoods can do good works without an intensive staff effort—a real bonus in a time of earnings pressures. And a loose collection of community activists and nonprofit consultants and developers can be put together with the capital they need to rebuild eroding neighborhoods and bring new life, perhaps, to a local lending market too long in decline.

Consortiums with established nonprofit community development intermediaries, such as the Local Initiatives Support Corporation or Neighborhood Housing Services (both profiled in Chapter 5), have proven an excellent way of leveraging an institution's contribution. That's because the loan money is supplemented by public and foundation funding, including grant programs, and the expertise the intermediaries have built up means that the money will be effectively used.

Much can be done outside the realm of the established intermediaries. In Des Moines, Iowa, seven banks have committed $9 million toward a public-private partnership to restore housing stock in the metropolitan area. The money is going to the Neighborhood Finance Corporation, a nonprofit mortgage finance agency set up by banking and other business leaders; other private companies have pledged $6 million, and the city and Polk County will provide an additional $2 million each. In Kentucky, two dozen financial institutions have formed a $20 million consortium to help needy families obtain closing costs for first homes. Borrowers in the Equity Partners Investing in the Commonwealth program, assisted by the Kentucky Housing Corporation, can obtain up to 60 percent of the closing costs at below-market rates.

In another Kentucky program with a clear CRA intent, local institutions in the Lexington area have formed a pool that can guarantee the top 10 percent to 20 percent of the risk on low- to moderate-income mortgages.

These programs are evidence of a mounting interest in loan pools and consortiums. And consortiums have an obvious appeal for banks and thrifts keen on community development. A 1989 booklet from the Office of the Comptroller of the Currency, "Community Development Finance: Tools and Techniques for National Banks," noted that "participation in a consortium organization for community development purposes provides a number of key advantages for banks. They help banks to:

- Pool and focus their financial resources on particular community development problems.
- Share and diversify risks associated with community development lending.
- Finance projects or activities in which individual institutions may have little experience or expertise.
- Reduce and manage transaction costs through the use of professional staff experts on a shared-cost basis."

Among the advantages of these arrangements, the Comptroller's office noted, is that widespread participation can help stimulate interest and added resources from the business community and individual investors. Moreover, participating community banks have a chance to help finance important projects whose scope is well beyond their lending limits.

Pools also can spread risk to the point that projects that might send individual institutions fleeing will get financed. "There are a lot of risk-reduction issues to be addressed through consortiums," acknowledged Anne Hoskins of the National Center for Policy Alternatives in Washington. A loan pool in California, for instance, approved a $6 million first mortgage loan late in 1990 to construct a single-room occupancy hotel, generally the kind of property that lenders shy from because of the SROs' image as seedy havens for derelicts and transients with no steady income except public assistance.

Economies of Scale

CRA "is certainly a major concern" of the lenders who take part in loan pools, concedes Kathleen Kenny, deputy director at the San Francisco Development Fund, the nonprofit housing advocate. "That's what first gets their attention. It makes a lot of sense [to go to consortium] because of the economy of scale in a loan pool. Particularly for medium to small institutions, they don't have the staff to do that kind of lending. Singularly, they wouldn't get near it. This gives them some kind of comfort, as well as economy."

A loan pool being formed in 1990 in upstate New York, the Community Lending Corporation, will attempt to link up with state programs to leverage its resources, said James Murphy, executive vice president and director of public policy and external relations at Fleet/Norstar Financial Corporation. "Having found that vehicle, the way to do [pooled lending] is with economies of scale," Murphy said. He added, "Pooling gives you the ability to do things on scale, with focus and lobbying."

The economies of scale are particularly compelling when lenders consider major multifamily housing developments, many of which would be far beyond the scope of an individual institution to finance. "In some of the communities where we're working, multifamily is the best way to house people," said Frederick Wacker of the Atlanta Federal Home Loan Bank. Those efforts include some very low-income people making less than 30 percent of an area's median income. "It's hard to imagine those people as homeowners," he said.

Scale economies also come into play when factoring the additional cost required in obtaining information about little-known areas, according to economists from the Federal Reserve Bank of San Francisco. A consortium "serves the purpose of lowering the per-bank costs of obtaining information about low-income neighborhoods," they wrote in the *FRBSF Weekly Letter*.

How Loan Pools Take Shape

There is no one way to create or join in a loan pool. The diversity of approaches among those up and running is testimony to the ingenuity of the public entities and the lenders who have become involved. But some effort at standardization, at least to the extent that it can speed up the process and give the resulting pool immediate credibility, was apparent by 1990.

The San Francisco Development Fund's efforts to launch affordable housing pools in Florida, Hawaii, Nevada, and other regions are being predicated on the CCRC model in California. Based on the framework set up by the fund, the structures would include:

• A board of directors comprising chiefly representatives from member lenders, plus additional people from the community, local government, and the housing industry. In the CCRC, 75 percent of the board is coming from member banks.

- A loan committee that screens all credits. Appointed by the board, this committee would be made up of member lenders and real estate professionals. Loan approval requires the endorsement of a certain percentage of bank members.
- A loan pool drawn down at loan closing, with each member participating in every loan, according to a formula based on assets. The funds then revolve as loans are sold to the secondary market or repaid.

But the Development Fund offers a laundry list of issues it says lenders must resolve if a pool is to succeed. These include corporate structure, membership, and governance; regulatory concerns, licensing and certification, underwriting criteria, selection of loan products, security for participating lenders, accessing the secondary market, legal and accounting issues, selection of the agent bank, lender liability, initial capitalization, organizational and staffing costs, and the creation of real estate documents and other necessary paperwork.

In cases like CCRC, the impetus for the pool came from the Federal Reserve Bank and a number of major commercial banks. At the Savings Association Mortgage Company (SAMCO) in California, also profiled in Chapter 5, a number of leading thrifts in the state carried the ball. Both of these efforts have attracted scores of financial institutions of all stripes—community banks and multinational giants, wholesale banks, even foreign-owned institutions.

A similar group initiative in New York led to the formation of the Community Preservation Corporation. It, too, will be profiled in Chapter 5, but unlike CCRC or SAMCO in California, it involved both banks and thrifts almost from the outset. Its basic funding comes from credit lines to the corporation, which are drawn down as loans are made; members purchase notes secured by long-term mortgages made by the CPC.

Pools can be started by as few as two banks. American Security Bank and National Cooperative Bank in Washington, D.C., for instance, set up a joint pool for financing acquisition/construction costs and permanent mortgages for housing projects. An outgrowth of the Cooperative Housing Finance Program established by the two banks in 1987, the loan pool includes a half-dozen other area institutions and involvement by the District's Department of Housing and Community Development.

Or one bank might take leadership for a program and then "sell" it to other institutions. In other arrangements, "borrowers seeking financing from the pool will be referred to lenders on a revolving basis, so that each bank takes a turn originating loans," according to the OCC booklet. An example of the leadership model comes from Boston, where the First National Bank of Boston's community investment division provided an executive for nine months to help organize and launch the Boston Housing Partnership. Working for the partnership, which is aimed at rehabilitating multifamily housing, the bank's real estate division processed, originated, and serviced a series of construction loans to nonprofit developers.

While housing has been and will continue to be the focus of the biggest pools, some programs have targeted small-business lending and economic development. Four big Boston-area banks have been taking part in the Neighborhood Commercial Development Bank, which provides loans for rehabilitation of commercial and mixed-used properties in specific neighborhoods. Its overriding aim is to provide financing at lower rates and for longer terms than borrowers would ordinarily find.

In the program, the banks have been originating loans at a top rate of 75 percent of the prevailing prime rate. But these loans are not losers dressed up with public purpose. The institutions get what amounts to a market rate of return by using noninterest-bearing balances made by the city of Boston's Public Facilities Department, according to the OCC's community development financing booklet. The deposits are used as loan subsidies, not as collateral, meaning that the funds revolve for future use as the loans are amortized.

A Supplementary Role

While regulators smile on well-targeted loan consortiums, no institution should assume that participation in a pool can turn a weak CRA record into a good one. Particularly for retail banks with significant deposit-gathering operations, pools should be supplementary adjuncts to a multifaceted community reinvestment program. Too many people "are looking for a no-brainer approach," said a prominent community affairs official at one of the federal agencies. "That's not what [CRA is] about. That won't wash with the examiners." Institutions need to show ample evidence of community outreach and specific programs to address credit needs, not just throw a few million dollars into a low-income housing fund.

"We've said all along that the program is only a supplement to other bank efforts," said Robert Fichter of the Massachusetts Bankers Association, speaking of a major statewide community reinvestment program there. "At the beginning, once we got into it, we said the easiest thing is to do a loan pool. But we refused to do just that," he said. "At best, it can be part of a larger plan. It's too easy. As soon as the heat is off, the loan pool goes down to zero and you go back to what you were doing. I think our plan is more firmly rooted than that."

Speaking of the CLC effort in New York State, Fleet/Norstar's James Murphy said the pool there is "not in lieu of what banks should be doing for CRA purposes or in terms of singular responses to community development."

Just how much positive scoring does an institution get for belonging to a consortium, as opposed to developing its own programs? Clearly less, but there are no firm guidelines, and experts say each agency—indeed, each regional office within an agency—may have its sights set somewhat differently. The Consumer Bankers Association says some banks are concerned (as well they should be) "whether this type of lending is being given the same amount of 'credit' that would be given if the loans had been made directly by the institution and had all been made in the institution's delineated community."

This hometown concern has created some confusion and angst, particularly on the part of community banks participating in statewide pools. They wonder how much credit they can get if the pool loans aren't made in their towns. While this remains troubling, some observers say the worry seems to be dissipating as the popularity of the consortium idea grows. "I think there is room within CRA to do something that's not necessarily within the outlook of your bank," says Mark Aldrich, a principal with the Bankers Compliance Group in Irvine, California, which advises community banks on their CRA responsibilities.

Other Potential Problems

Pools do have some other drawbacks, real or imagined. In an area with intense retail bank competition, for instance, a consortium arrangement might create unrealistic expectations because banks are too busy fighting for market share, say some experts. After all, the effectiveness of such a group approach relies on teamwork and the willingness to sacrifice individual glory.

There is also less control on the part of any individual institution participating in a community reinvestment loan. While pools often give each potential lender a chance to share in all the information about a credit, in reality, some banks will rely more on what others are doing than performing their own analysis of the loan.

Julia Seward, community reinvestment officer at Signet Bank/Virginia, said community groups may be disturbed because they think the presence of a consortium puts a layer between them and an individual institution. Beyond that, some community activists decry pools as formulaic, rigid approaches to segmented slices of an institution's market. They may see loan pooling as a cop-out, a join-the-parade approach for an institution unwilling to make a greater effort to understand their needs.

"I like loan pools as part of a strategy that makes sense, rather than as a way for banks to dump their CRA obligations," said Tom Fox, director of the Normal Heights Community Association in San Diego. In a pool for small business, "everyone gets thrown in, but [pool members] limit the amount of credit rather than expand it—it's a limited pool of people they're going after."

One community activist dismisses affordable housing pools, calling them "a form of redlining or credit discrimination. The risk [the institutions take on] is negligible." Fox argues that too often, pools are benefiting private developers creating multifamily developments with no more than 51 percent of units dedicated to lower-income people—sometimes demolishing viable single-family tracts to put in multiple units with "concrete front yards."

GOVERNMENT PROGRAMS

An assortment of government-sponsored programs are out there for institutions seeking CRA-related niches that rivals may not be in, or that offer a small bank a chance to throw some weight far beyond its relative size. Bankers involved with some of these efforts talk of having dominant market share, at least in their home geographic area. Often, it seems, that's because competitors either aren't interested or haven't made the necessary commitment in time or energy. But once again, participation in these programs alone can't guarantee a strong CRA record; they are supplemental strategies for institutions already pursuing broad-based community reinvestment policies.

SBA: Getting Guarantees

The Small Business Administration, while a known commodity to many lenders, is getting renewed attention these days because of CRA. In several merger-related decisions, regulators have made it clear that they wanted the affected bank to do more SBA lending, even if the bank has its own program that addresses small-business needs. Recently, government officials "seem to be turning up the burner" on SBA lending, according to Security Pacific Corporation executive vice president Irving Margol.

An independent federal agency around since 1953, the SBA offers participating lenders guarantees on up to 90 percent of the value of a loan. Banks can use that guarantee to leverage their returns dramatically. Selling those loans in the secondary market can bring gross yields of more than 30 percent on a bank's money, with yields rising as service fees increase. Even at the rock-bottom service fee of 25 basis points, yield would be 12.25 percent if interest rates are at 10 percent.

Most lenders in the SBA network are banks, but thrifts, credit unions, insurance companies, and development companies are also on its rosters. Guarantees will be made on loans up to $750,000, but the average SBA loan is closer to $100,000, and most SBA lenders have fewer than 10 outstanding loans, said Tim M. Thomas of Boatmen's First National Bank of Kansas City in a 1990 paper on SBA programs.

Like other government guaranty agencies, the SBA has been buffeted now and then by fraud, usually involving a contractor who was doing a goodly volume of business with the agency. But misdeeds aside, any renewed push on SBA isn't going to sit well with lenders who have avoided the agency because of the paperwork involved with loan applications and the delays that come as loans get shunted through the agency apparatus for approval. This approval process can take two to three weeks. "It is considered a paper nightmare by those people who would be doing the work," Wells Fargo Bank executive Steven Hall told a CRA conference in California in 1990. Moreover, lenders say that additional staff and training are needed to cope with the SBA's requirements.

SBA's bread-and-butter lending program is generally referred to as 7(a) (the number of the relevant section of the Small Business Act). Through this, SBA loans can be made to small businesses that cannot borrow on reasonable terms from conventional lenders without government assistance; in a city of more than 200,000 population, a borrower must be turned down by two lenders before applying for an SBA loan.

Strict eligibility rules apply. While too numerous to describe in detail here, they basically disallow SBA loans (1) to borrowers who could reasonably find money elsewhere; (2) for speculation; (3) to nonprofit enterprises; (4) for the acquisition of investment property; and (5) to reduce existing lender exposure. While the SBA defines a small business as "one that is independently owned and operated and is not dominant in its field," it buttresses that definition with a laundry list of size requirements by industry.

The lending institution has the responsibility for analyzing the potential borrower, the way it would without any SBA presence, and forwarding its analysis to the agency with the application. In the most common 7(a) loan, the lender makes and disburses the entire loan, with the SBA executing an agreement to purchase an agreed percentage of the unpaid balance in the event of default. Loans over $155,000, at least in 1990, could get a maximum guarantee of 85 percent. The lender pays the SBA a one-time fee of 2 percent of the total guaranteed by the agency.

SBA loan rates are carefully regulated. In 1990, the maximum allowable interest on guaranteed loans of less than seven years' maturity was 2.25 percent above minimum New York prime, and 2.75 percent above base prime for maturities of seven years and up. Limits on fees must be approved by the agency as well. Some banks hike their interest rate protection by originating the unguaranteed portion of the loan, which cannot be sold, with a variable rate.

Happily for lenders, an active secondary market for SBA loans exists. The guaranteed portion carries the full backing from the federal government, and lenders can sell loans directly to a wide variety of other institutions and fiduciaries. This secondary market, then, offers liquidity, servicing income, and increased yield through leverage.

Hundreds of institutions around the country are approved SBA lenders; they range in size form very small to behemoths. The agency divides participants into three groups: participating lenders, who must submit applications for approval by the SBA, usually within 10 days; certified lenders, who have a track record with the agency and are guaranteed a response within three days; and preferred lenders, who meet SBA standards and demonstrate high origination volume. Preferred lenders can approve SBA loans without prior documentation, guaranteed up to 80 percent of loan value.

Trust Company Bank of Atlanta is a certified SBA lender that uses its SBA ties to make credit available in its Minority Commercial Loan Program. In place since 1969, the program is aimed specifically at minorities and offers more flexible loan terms, lower rates, and less restrictive collateral and ratio requirements than conventional small business loans, the bank said. Boatmen's National Bank in St. Louis, a preferred lender, said it can determine "eligibility, creditworthiness, loan structure, loan monitoring service, and collection" for all its SBA loans.

The SBA program has proven that smaller banks can compete with their big brethren. Truckee River Bank, a community institution in northern California, is the state's largest SBA lender, making only real estate-secured loans. South Shore Bank in Chicago, one of the city's smaller institutions, has been among the largest SBA originators in the Midwest.

Some of California's biggest banks, including Wells Fargo and Security Pacific, say they have their own small-business programs and don't feel compelled to work through SBA. Wells executive Steven Hall told a CRA conference that 7(a) loans are a good example of a product his bank didn't feel it could deliver as well as others might, adding that mention of the program has been eliminated from the bank's CRA statement.

Security Pacific took some heat from the Fed in 1989 in an acquisition-related decision affecting San Diego because the bank has not been a major SBA lender, preferring to do conventional lending to that market through its retail division. Security Pacific argued that the SBA loan market in San Diego was dominated by small local lenders who were serving the market well. But it agreed to establish a community development center in San Diego to handle SBA and similar types of lending, to be headed by the persons heading SBA lending at the bank. It also promised to provide training on SBA to branch managers and loan officers.

Wells Fargo's Hall said the bank is one of the two or three biggest lenders through another SBA program, known as 504, aimed at long-term asset financing for proprietorships, partnerships, or corporations—development companies, in SBA parlance. Since these entities must have a net worth of less than $6 million, many tend to fall within the moderate-income confines of CRA. The SBA will finance up to 40 percent of project costs, secured by a second lien on proposed real estate property; the lender finances 50 percent through a separate loan, secured by a first lien, and the business must provide at least 10 percent.

Bank financing can be blended with SBA programs. The Bank of Boston operates a regional loan fund in southeastern Massachusetts that provides economic development loans at 2 percent below the bank's base lending rate. These can be made in conjunction with conventional financing or with SBA loans, the bank said.

Pressure from regulators could well boost the level of lender activity with SBA. So will the emergence of start-up community development banks like Community Capital Bank in New York and the Development Bank of Washington (D.C.). Officials at both banks say they intend to become active SBA lenders. In its offering circular, for instance, Development Bank said it "intends to maximize fee income by continually selling a portion of its SBA loan portfolio, while retaining servicing rights and minimizing risk."

Another spur to SBA lending could be higher rate caps. The SBA, in an effort to induce more bank lending, said late in 1990 that it planned to boost the cap on loans of less than $25,000 by two percentage points and those on loans of $25,000 to $50,000 by one point.

A rash of SBA loans may not thrill community groups, some of whom may see SBA lending as a way for an institution to pigeonhole small loans it would prefer not to make. A diet of SBA loans can cause problems for small businesses down the road, said Tom Fox of the Normal Heights Community Association in San Diego. "The problem that SBA created— and the SBA program was not that bad in itself—was that it was difficult for a small business to expand its local base because it never developed a relationship with a local bank," Fox said. "When all small businesses get funneled into SBA, they don't have a local banker."

Other Programs for Small Business

Authorized under the Small Business Investment Act of 1958, small business investment companies (SBICs) are, in effect, venture capital firms licensed by the SBA. Bank holding companies and national banks are authorized to own or invest in SBICs; state-chartered banks need authorization under applicable state law.

"Like bank CDCs, SBICs represent an exception to prohibitions against bank investments in real estate or business ventures," the Comptroller's office noted in its booklet, *Community Development Finance: Tools and Techniques for National Banks*. It added that "typically, SBICs act as venture capital investors, supporting small-business expansion through a combination of longer-term debt, equity investments, and management counseling." There are more than 600 such companies in the nation, about 70 of which were bank owned or bank controlled, the OCC said.

"SBICs are privately capitalized and obtain financial leverage from SBA," the agency noted in a brochure. "They are intended to be profit-making corporations. Due to their own economics, most SBICs do not make very small investments." They do make straight loans as well as equity investments, and many also provide management assistance.

One particularly compelling feature about SBICs is that they can borrow directly from the federal government at the same rate Uncle Sam pays when it borrows. They also offer tax breaks that banks cannot take advantage of. A subgroup within the SBIC family is the Minority Enterprise Small Business Investment Company, or MESBIC, which will be taken up in the next section.

Yet another appeal of bank SBICs is their ability to sink far more equity in a venture than the parent bank or holding company legally can. This feature created something of a stir in 1989, when the Federal Reserve apparently quashed a proposal by Citicorp Venture Capital—then the nation's largest SBIC—to acquire a unit of RJR Nabisco through an SBIC. The SBA permits investments of up to 50 percent in qualifying ventures.

In fact, SBICs at a number of major banks have been used to make equity investments in nonbanking concerns with potentially rich returns—a notion far removed from community reinvestment. This strategy has been actively pursued by Citicorp, Bankers Trust New York Corporation, First Chicago Corporation, and Chase Manhattan Corporation. Citicorp even created a second SBIC in 1989 to enhance its investment opportunities. This kind of "loophole banking," as some have dubbed it, is clearly not what the regulators had in mind when they cited in their joint statement on CRA those institutions that had "funded a small business investment corporation or created a minority small business investment corporation."

While most SBICs have been formed by urban banks, Southern Development Bancorp, an offshoot of Shorebank Corporation, the enterprising Chicago-based community development lender, has organized an SBIC in Arkansas that it calls Southern Ventures, Inc. This makes investments in locally owned companies in rural areas in the state, using SBA-guaranteed debentures to help leverage its lending.

Another government-sponsored program for small business is being run through the Farmers Home Administration, which is providing loan guarantees of up to 80 percent for revitalizing rural economies. Run as a public-private partnership, in Iowa this program is a joint effort between the National Rural Development and Finance Corporation (NRD&FC) and the Iowa Department of Economic Development.

One bank that is tapping into the program is Bankers Trust Company in Des Moines, which was the initial designated lender. Using the FmHA guarantees, Bankers Trust expects to generate more than $3 million of long-term loans for such purposes as buying fixed assets, lending for working capital and inventory, and expanding light industries. A preference will be given to operations showing a potential of creating stable jobs. "In addition to eligibility, applications for financing will be evaluated on the impact of each business' loan on the surrounding community," said bank executive vice president Tom Smith.

The NRD&FC will screen applicants, negotiate the terms of the credits, and monitor the loans, meaning that the program offers the bank the ability to do considerable good for its local community without considerable trouble.

Federal Housing Programs

As money once earmarked for Great Society programs dried up in the 1980s, community groups turned increasingly to the private sector—a situation bankers know well. But considerable federal housing money is still available for lenders willing to take the trouble to locate it and go through the necessary channels. Funding is distributed through a host of programs; in a paper to members, the Federal Home Loan Bank of Atlanta listed more than 30 under the Department of Housing and Urban Development and the Federal Housing Administration.

Urban bankers should be aware that other federal dollars are available through Community Development Block Grants, given to entitlement cities to stimulate housing and economic development, and through Housing Opportunities Development Action Grants, which assist development in lower-income communities and provide money to first-time home buyers. Cities can use the block grants to make rehabilitation loans and grants, pay interest subsidies, guarantee private loans, create reserves, and pay bank fees. Subsidized rent programs have been dwindling, but HUD still makes money available through its Section 8 Rental Assistance Program. These subsidies can be incorporated into public-private partnerships for rental programs, especially in major cities.

While some community development manuals list Veterans Administration mortgage programs as possible pieces of an institution's CRA efforts, experts say there are very few VA lenders and little potential to develop more. VA programs "are basically irrelevant now," said Charles Grice of the Community Reinvestment Institute in San Francisco. "The VA covers less than $71,000. In California, that gets you a parking space."

Two federal housing programs in particular are worth detailing. Both appear to be paying dividends for the banks that are involved, and the programs could be replicated widely.

FmHA 502 SFH Housing Loan Program
This Farmers Home Administration program is directed at rural communities with populations under 10,000, though it can be used in certain circumstances in small cities up to 20,000 population. Monies are made available for buying, erecting, improving, or rehabilitating rural homes. Eligibility is based on income and inability to obtain a loan at a rate that the borrower could be expected to handle.

The loans can be made for up to 100 percent of appraised value of the site and the home; maturity can run to 33 years, and in special circumstances, 38 years. The FmHA will secure the loan with a mortgage, and the borrower pays only standard legal expenses, no other fees or points. The interest rate can be as low as 1 percent.

It was exactly this combination of extremely low interest and long term that drew Towner County State Bank in Cando, North Dakota, to the FmHA program. The bank was seeking a product it could use to make housing affordable for workers at a local pasta-making plant; many of those workers, unable to buy a house in Cando, were living up to 60 miles away, according to bank president Terry Zeltinger.

"Very few of these loans were being made in our area because the FmHA personnel were too busy with agricultural lending, servicing, restructuring, and collecting," Zeltinger told *ABA Bank Compliance*. But bank officials persuaded the agency to send a specialist to Cando to explain the program, and the bank went forward with a program it believes will fill an important credit need and help the town and its businesses grow.

FHA 203(k)
This Federal Housing Administration program has a very specific target: home rehabilitation. It provides single-loan funding for borrowers to acquire or refinance, plus rehabilitate, one- to four-family homes, then creates a 30-year fixed-rate mortgage with a down payment as low as 3 percent—or even zero down payment where certain subsidies exist. The total rehabilitation must be at least $5,000, and the appraised value of a home at loan origination is based on post-rehabilitation improvements.

While the program has been around since 1961, it has been collecting more cobwebs than applications; fewer than 500 loans were made under it in 1989, said a banker familiar with the program, and fewer than 5,400 had been done in its history through mid-1990. But that inactivity appears to be dissipating.

Security Pacific Bank Washington has set up a 203(k) program in two Washington cities, Aberdeen and Yakima. In the former, Security Pacific teamed up with the U.S. Department of Housing and Urban Development and the Aberdeen Neighborhood Housing Services (NHS), a nonprofit intermediary, to create a joint venture for affordable housing. In Yakima, a local office of housing and neighborhood conservation acts as the HUD consultant and subordinate lender.

The Aberdeen NHS office provides additional funding needed to ensure completion of a project and pays the downpayment and closing costs as well, if necessary. These NHS funds are secured by a second deed of trust on the property, with payment deferred until the property is sold, said SPBW vice president Judy Reed. The partnership approach has "created housing opportunities that none of us could have offered independently," Reed wrote in *Community Investments*, a newsletter from the San Francisco Fed. "Using the FHA 203(k) program to build a healthy community is both true to the spirit of the Community Reinvestment Act and good business for Security Pacific Bank Washington."

The 203(k) program is a centerpiece of the community development lending at Theodore Roosevelt National Bank in Washington, D.C. A new bank in 1990, Roosevelt's focus is "100 percent on CRA," primarily on affordable housing, said its president and chief executive, Harold J. Fisher. Fisher said he has set up a brokerage operation that brokers loans to 27 banks; he said the FHA mortgages are sold two days after closing. While regulators were skittish about the brokerage concept, he said he pointed to wording in the regulations about "arranging" loans and persuaded them to go along.

While his is far from a conventional bank—he said it makes 50 percent to 70 percent of its revenues in fee income from its brokering activities—Fisher extols the 203(k) program, saying it is far more profitable than conventional mortgage lending. "We don't do it because it's do-good," he told a Consumer Bankers Association conference. "It's good business. But it's hard work. This is not an easy program."

"I'm convinced this (program) is a good tool for dealing with Community Reinvestment Act requirements," Paul Scherer, president of Statewide Funding Corporation in Albany, New York, told *Mortgage Banking*. Statewide made half of all the 203(k) loans extended in 1989, pooling the mortgages for sale to the Government National Mortgage Association. HUD has recently been making a special appeal to sign up lenders for the program.

A number of other HUD programs are open to lenders interested in pushing affordable housing. Section 203(b) provides mortgage insurance to finance home ownership, refinancing, or construction of one- to four-family homes in urban and rural areas. HUD insures loans made by financial institutions for up to 97 percent of the property value, for terms up to 30 years. Other programs targeted at first-time homeowners include: Section 234(c), providing federal mortgage insurance for construction or refinancing of condominium housing; Section 245(a), insuring mortgages to finance early homeownership for households expecting their income to rise significantly; and Section 251, an adjustable-rate mortgage insured by HUD. Local HUD offices are set up to answer lender questions on these programs.

Speaking of the FmHA and FHA programs, as well as SBA, the Comptroller's office noted: "Bank familiarity with, and confidence in, these and other federal programs also has made them generally accepted and appropriate tools for enhancing bank capacity to participate in community development finance."

State and Local Agencies

The widening gap between demand and federal support for housing has been filled in part by state and local housing finance agencies. While some are feeling serious constraints, many are ready and willing to work with lenders and nonprofits to boost affordable housing and economic development, particularly if that development is related to small business. State governments also have created loan guarantee programs for community development credits.

State housing finance agencies sell tax-exempt or taxable bonds to raise money for community development finance, then make the money raised available to borrowers at below-market rates. Financial institutions buying or underwriting such bonds get CRA credit. Bank of Boston trumpets its support for the Massachusetts Housing Finance Agency in its CRA statement, noting in 1990 that "in the past two years, the bank participated as co-manager in the underwriting of $705 million of MHFA bonds that helped to produce low- and moderate-income housing and facilitated mortgages for hundreds of first-time home buyers." First Nationwide Bank said in its CRA statement that it has originated more than $1 billion for affordable housing through single-family and multifamily tax-exempt bond issues in California and Florida.

Trust Company Bank of Atlanta noted in its CRA statement that it coordinated the issuance and sale of construction bonds issued by the DeKalb County Housing Authority to develop 156 homes in a local subdivision. That bank also buys between $1 million and $2.5 million in bonds each year from the Georgia Residential Finance Authority, which uses the funds to provide low-interest loans.

While programs and financing availability vary widely, state programs "provide an excellent opportunity to enhance lender participation in local housing programs," both for single-family and multifamily units, said the Federal Home Loan Bank of Atlanta. Some state housing agencies administer the low-income housing tax credit programs discussed in Chapter 5. Others have "loans to lenders" programs in which the housing finance agency uses bond proceeds to lend money to financial institutions, which in turn make loans for housing. Participating banks and thrifts earn a spread over the rate charged by the state agency and frequently collect loan origination fees.

Other programs are set up as mortgage purchase or direct tax-exempt loans. In the former, lenders originate credits at tax-exempt equivalent rates, and the state or local agency immediately purchases the loans using monies from tax-exempt bond sales. In direct loans, financial institutions loan money directly to the government agency; interest earned on this money is tax exempt and usually at below-market rates, and the agency usually passes the earned interest on to the bank.

In addition, "Many state housing or economic development agencies have created new initiatives using budgeted authority or unencumbered income and reserves from other housing and community development financing programs," the Comptroller's office noted in its *Community Development Finance* booklet. "In some cases, these new programs provide loans and grants to local government agencies, which use them to establish revolving, below-market-rate loan funds with participating banks."

At least 16 states and 24 cities administer housing trust funds designed to make public capital for housing more available, according to the Center for Policy Alternatives. Some of these programs are structured as revolving loan funds; others are nonrenewable. In North Carolina, such a trust fund provides administrative grants, loans for predevelopment costs, technical assistance, and financing.

A number of states also have set up linked-deposit programs, in which insured or collateralized deposits are placed with participating financial institutions that agree to make certain types of loans meeting state criteria.

"Generally, linked-deposit programs are designed to assist small or minority businesses, particularly those with the potential to create or retain local jobs, or to help develop or rehabilitate low- and moderate-income housing," the OCC noted. "Others have focused on agricultural lending."

The federal CDBG program mentioned earlier has been providing up to $3 billion a year in outlays and has become a popular vehicle for providing interest-rate buydowns for needy homeowners. Sometimes this grant money is used as noninterest-bearing compensating balances—that is, linked deposits—for loans made by financial institutions; in exchange for the balances, the institutions agree to reduce loan rates to the levels required by the buydown program.

In one example cited by the Comptroller's office, 24 private lenders in Dallas committed $4 million for a home improvement loan pool at favorable rates. The city then agreed to deposit $500,000 in CDBG funds in an account to guarantee individual loans made under the program. And in Contra Costa County, California, Great Western Bank makes rehab loans on a participating basis with local governments, through CDBG funds. The thrift is also servicing similar loans originated under a Los Angeles CDBG program.

In Ohio, the state treasurer's office has had a linked deposit plan since 1984 supplying hundreds of millions of dollars in low-cost funds to banks qualified as state depositories. In the program, designed to create and retain jobs, the small business seeking a loan would deal with a private lender, which evaluates the request and submits an application to the treasurer for a linked deposit, the OCC said. In Maryland, Baltimore Financial Federal participates in a linked-deposit program with the Enterprise Loan Fund (ELF), a unit of the Enterprise Foundation. In a recent rental rehabilitation in Baltimore, that program enabled the ELF to make an 8 percent, $455,000 first mortgage for one project.

Quite a number of states have passed linked-deposit legislation in recent years. In a report on 1989 state economic initiatives, the Center for Policy Alternatives listed five states in which linked-deposit programs were adopted, expanded, or reauthorized—Alabama, Iowa, Louisiana, Missouri, and West Virginia. Legislation creating such programs has been introduced in several other state legislatures.

State pension fund monies are also proving a good source of longer-term bank financing for community development. In Colorado, long-term pension fund deposits are being employed to match-fund long-term loans to small businesses that have no access to national capital markets, the

Comptroller's office said. Begun with a $10 million commitment from the state fire and police pension association, the program has been seeking participation from other major state and local government pension funds.

Then there are state loan guarantee programs, which can cover a host of community development purposes. The Maryland Housing Fund will insure banks up to 100 percent of principal on loans made to certain disadvantaged borrowers, the OCC noted, and the fund also allows the borrower to finance all closing costs. In New Jersey, a guarantee program for small business will cover up to $1 million for fixed loans or fixed assets, and up to $600,000 for working capital loans, the Comptroller's office said. A loan guarantee program in California aimed at small-business development will provide guarantees of 90 percent of the loan amount, up to $350,000.

City or other municipal programs are seldom as large as state efforts but can be significant sources of additional equity or gap financing. Bankers should certainly be familiar with their local city hall representatives and ask to be kept abreast of any new financing programs affecting community development. Federal grant money administered through cities, such as the CDBG funds mentioned earlier, has been used widely by lenders to create "patient equity" that turns marginal projects into sound ones.

Cities as large as New York, Chicago, and Los Angeles have an array of programs to promote small business and low-cost housing that seek financial institution and foundation support. Smaller cities may also be working on a number of fronts. Sacramento, California, for example, runs a variety of programs through its Housing and Redevelopment Agency and its Office of Economic Development.

At the municipal level, housing is often the most obvious government-supported activity. The Bank of Boston is participating in three different programs run by the City of Boston in rental rehabilitation, buildable lots, and abandoned housing. In New York, a number of major banks are participants in programs run by the city's Department of Housing Preservation and Development.

ENHANCING MINORITY OPPORTUNITIES

Given the high percentage of blacks, Hispanics, and other minorities in the nation's poorer neighborhoods, money directed at minority ventures usually falls under Community Reinvestment Act guidelines. Increasingly, banks and thrifts are likely to find that systems are in place—or can be readily formed—to ease the task of putting minority development credit in the hands of those seeking it.

Nonprofit intermediaries can help put together minority borrower and lender; quite a few banks have submitted loan packages to these intermediaries. Other institutions are working directly with investment companies that provide financing to minority businesses. Still others are approaching minority businesses through local churches. And banks can score points with CRA examiners by working with one special class of "minority"—women seeking small-business loans.

BBICs, MESBICs, and Development Loan Programs

Increasingly, financial institutions are taking programmatic approaches for lending to minority enterprises through investment companies or collective loan funds. These come under a number of different names—minority business investment companies, minority enterprise small business investment companies, black business investment corporations, and development loan funds.

BBICs

Perhaps the best-developed of these programs is in Florida, where there is a statewide network of black business investment corporations (BBICs) that has drawn attention from other parts of the country. The BBICs, which technically are community development corporations, are making loans, issuing guarantees to participating banks, and investing in startups. As of mid-1990, the Black Business Investment Fund—the parent of the BBICs— was getting about 40 percent of its capital from financial institutions, and each of the six investment companies operating in 1990 was essentially owned and controlled by financial institutions.

The local BBICs cover communities with about two thirds of the state's black population, Cleve Warren, executive director of the Black Business Investment Fund, told a CDC conference in spring 1990. Each has received at least $500,000 in capital—but not more than $1 million—and the capital is available only if the BBICs can persuade local banks to invest a matching share. Three major Florida banks—Sun Bank, Barnett Banks, and Southeast Bank—are supporting each of the BBICs.

Warren was careful to define the program by what it is not: Not an easy money program, not a below-market-rate program, not a vehicle for refinancing debts or making loans that banks have concluded make no economic sense. While some money may be loaned below market, rates are based on risk and can be made at market. The credits are larger than bankers might guess—$57,000 on average, though one or two of the investment corporations have micro-loan funds lending as little as $500 to individuals.

As a rule, Warren said, the BBICs try to remain small players in any transaction and let the banks carry most of the load, though there have been instances where the minority corporation had been the full lender or an equity investor. And though some banks have been content to remain passive investors, others have participated in managing the BBICs, he said.

While BBIC boards include representatives from the community and local government, bankers constitute the majority and make the financial decisions, said Judy Jones, the current executive director. If a bank already has a CRA officer dedicated to such activity, the boards seek to ensure that such a person be the bank's representative on the loan committee.

Unlike some other programs described in this book, the nonprofit BBICs do not generate a return to banks investing in them. These investments would be carried as "other assets," and institutions would get their contributions back only on dissolution of the investment company.

The BBIC program, which got rolling at the end of 1987, has drawn inquiries from several other states, Jones said. But when she talks about the program, the word *struggle* comes up often. "We've had various experiences with financial institutions. It's a growth experience for both of us," she said. "The important thing is that these institutions address the need that is out there. It's not easy. It's a struggle to get banks to break out of that [traditional lending] mode."

Some of the participating institutions "want to do things as they've always done," Jones added. "I think we still have a long way to go. Some are really struggling with us, but for others, [the BBIC] efforts are really CRA." To really make a difference, the scale of lending needs to be much greater, she said. A banker who has worked with the program, however, said his institution is doing as much as it feels comfortable with. He is hoping other banks or financial entities will join up to spread the BBICs' reach.

Thrifts, credit unions, foundations, and insurance companies are also permitted to work with BBICs'; in Jacksonville, three insurance companies are the primary investors in the local venture. Jones said efforts have been continuing to line up other nonbank investors.

MESBICs and More

Minority small business investment corporations exist as creatures of the Small Business Administration, whose related SBIC programs were detailed in the previous section. As one would expect, MESBICs are SBICs dedicated to serving minority businesses. These entities "focus exclusively on debt and equity investments for small businesses substantially owned by persons of racial minorities and other disadvantaged groups," the OCC noted, adding that while few banks have actually set them up, other institutions are supporting nonbank MESBICs.

That support can be substantial: Manufacturers Hanover Trust Company gave $25 million as part of a two-year revolving credit facility to a MESBIC in New York. But most investments are far smaller. Trust Company Bank in Atlanta invested $75,000 to help form a local MESBIC, of which one of its first vice presidents is a director.

The Massachusetts Bankers Association was busily creating a couple of structural approaches in that state in 1990—a minority enterprise investment corporation, to finance bridge loans and equity gaps facing minority businesses, and a MESBIC. The former would make loans in the $2,500 to $250,000 range, and work with existing finance agencies; it would focus on "community impact projects" such as small-business incubators—programs dedicated to giving small businesses the technical know-how and financing they need to begin. The latter entity would get $2 million from the former to start, an amount to increase to $5 million as needed.

One small institution with a MESBIC is Shorebank Corporation, the inventive community development lender in Chicago. Shorebank calls its MESBIC the Neighborhood Fund. Licensed by the SBA, it provides long-term subordinated debt and equity investments to small neighborhood businesses. It lost a substantial amount in 1989 but was expected to be profitable for the whole of 1990.

In some locales, banks are supporting organizations that do much the same task as MESBICs, though the structure may differ somewhat. In Louisville, Kentucky, several institutions are supporting a Minority Business Development Loan Program, which provides minority-owned small businesses with loans up to $75,000 for five years at low rates. The program was organized in conjunction with the local Office of Economic Development.

In Sacramento, California, lenders interested in making loans to minority businesses can turn to the Sacramento Minority Business Development Center. It offers management and technical assistance to new and existing businesses, plus loan packaging; MBDC analysts seek out lenders to review completed loan packages and make presentations to financial institutions on existing credit needs. In St. Louis, a number of banks participate in the St. Louis Small and Minority Business Revolving Loan Fund.

Minority Vendor Programs

Buying supplies from minority vendors has become an increasingly popular means of augmenting bank CRA programs. These purchasing programs can be set up through individual bank agreements or through a more structured approach that uses third-party facilitators.

Minority vendors have a couple of historic hurdles to clear when dealing with any major industry, including banking: They are often small players in businesses dominated by scale, and buyers are often won over by sales representatives from established (and often huge) suppliers. Banks wouldn't ordinarily know of small minority-owned firms, so any surge in their use will have clear CRA overtones. But those efforts are likely to get considerable positive press.

That was true in North Carolina, where First Union Corporation set up an ambitious program in 1990 to dedicate at least 8.5 percent of its general vendor services to minority-owned businesses by the end of the year. Local newspapers gave the announcement lots of space, and interested vendors deluged the bank with calls. First Union has been navigating toward its goal with the help of a network of minority and women business owners. It also pays visits to minority recruiting offices and minority trade shows, according to spokesman Jeep Bryant.

Consistent with the beefed-up documentation efforts spreading through the financial industry because of CRA, First Union is paying more attention to monitoring its minority vendor practices. "There's a feeling here that we've been doing a good job working with minority businesses in the past, but we didn't do a good job tracking that," Bryant told *American Banker*. Government agencies have extensive contact lists and can be a valuable resource for institutions interested in giving more business to minorities, he added.

A minority supplier program in place at a California bank, however, has put a number of major institutions there on edge. California First Bank, the Japanese-owned institution that bought Union Bank in 1988, agreed as part of a sweeping pact with community groups that it would buy 20 percent of its supplies from minority vendors over a five-year period. "We suffer a little bit in California" from that agreement, Bank of America's Donald Mullane told a 1990 CRA conference, adding that approaching that 20 percent goal is a "really tough thing to do."

Almost three dozen banks around the country have turned to a third party, the Business Consortium Fund (BCF) operated by the National Minority Supplier Development Council, to submit loan packages for minority vendors. The BCF program, begun in 1987, made more than 100 loans in its first three years. Carefully structured, the program is limited to certified minority suppliers and certified lenders and is meant to deliver working capital loans to suppliers holding a contract or purchase order. Loans must be between $50,000 and $250,000, for a maximum of two years, and are made at prime.

Bankers have control over the credit decision process and receive borrowers' payments directly. But lenders are limited to a 25 percent participation in every loan, with the rest taken by the BCF or a related entity, perhaps operating under a different name. Atlanta's Trust Company Bank, for instance, is a charter member of a local BCF venture known as the Atlanta Regional Minority Purchasing Council.

One banker involved with the BCF program, Luis De Jesus, vice president of minority-owned New York National Bank, told *Minority Supplier News* that his bank has been "pleased with how the BCF meets the need for working capital and the need for contract financing." One vendor in the program said it has proved particularly valuable because it fills a gap below the $100,000 level, above which financing for subcontracting projects is much more widely available.

Nurturing Entrepreneurs

Many would-be minority entrepreneurs are being handled through the BBICs and MESBICs and development loan funds mentioned earlier. But financial institutions are also handling the needs of women and ethnic minority entrepreneurs as part of specialized lending units concentrating on startups and venture capital. Some, surely, are not giving themselves CRA credit for doing so. Other institutions have made gifts to organizations working specifically toward finding capital to nurture these fledgling ventures.

"I guess I would view it as such as something of an untapped opportunity, though I'm not sure (women-owned businesses) have been neglected," said Frederick Manning, community affairs officer at the

Federal Reserve Bank of Philadelphia. He does view the area as a CRA niche, but one not remotely the size of affordable housing or lending to ethnic or racial minorities.

First Bank System in Minneapolis, for instance, has been helping support Chart/Wedco, a Minnesota firm providing loans of last resort to women entrepreneurs. The company, which also gets some state grant money, made $900,000 in loans in 1989—an average of $10,000 per credit—and claims to have started more than 800 businesses in the six years from 1984–90.

But the company's founder, Kathryn Keeley, told *American Banker* that she thinks banks need to generate new products to better serve women entrepreneurs. "Much of banking is set up for the big hit. Women tend to have incremental business plans," she said, adding that most women-owned businesses her firm has worked with borrow $10,000 to $25,000 at first, then come back for more.

Keeley also argues that banks need to reevaluate the way they assess women entrepreneurs as borrowers. "Women are particularly active in rural communities. They create jobs for themselves and want to stay where they live," she said. "They have a different kind of collateral [from buildings and equipment]. There needs to be more character-based lending"—a charge that already echoes through a lot of lower-income communities. She adds that women are likely to reward a bank that gives them a loan with other relationships.

One Minnesota banker voices some concerns about lending to women-owned businesses that a lot of fledgling enterprises hear. "The loans could be riskier; women often have less work experience . . . They are often more costly to put on the books and require a lot more time on the banker's part," William Sands, president of Western State Bank, told *American Banker*.

The Native American Dilemma

One sizable minority group that has shown up on few bank radar screens is the Native American. They want credit for a range of commercial and home-related projects, but the demand is slight in relation to other minority groups. In addition, few banks are located near sizable Native American populations, which are with few exceptions in remote, undeveloped areas.

Native American communities are generally very low income, poorly skilled, and unschooled in banking matters. Moreover, government workers familiar with Native American behavior patterns say that generations of government support have failed to instill saving or investing habits on most reservations—hardly an inducement to bank financing. Asian ethnics such as Chinese and Vietnamese, in contrast, are better educated, more financially astute, and accustomed to operating small businesses. In the near future, while most tribal situations are obvious CRA targets, Native Americans are the minority group least likely to gain from CRA-related lending.

First Interstate BancSystem, the subject of a CRA-related protest in Montana involving a reservation, has maintained that only 5 percent of the affected bank's deposits and loans come from the Northern Cheyenne Indian Reservation. Wallace McRae, the bank's chairman, told *American Banker* that the bank has received virtually no applications from Native Americans, even though the reservation has no competing banks or credit unions.

But there are moves afoot to increase the number of entrepreneurial ventures owned by Native Americans. An advocacy and training group, the National Center for American Indian Enterprise Development in El Monte, California, works to create success stories. Both Security Pacific and Wells Fargo have helped underwrite the center's operations from its three western offices. The center tries to counsel the entrepreneurs, assess its financial projections, and line up financing, public or private. Collateral can be a major problem, especially in tribal situations where land cannot be used as an asset, said the center's president, Steven Stallings.

Going to Churches

In many black neighborhoods, the church plays a large, sometimes central role in the lives of parishioners, and church leaders are often active in community betterment issues such as housing and rehabilitation. Black churches are well represented in local and national activist groups. For these good reasons, a few banks have chosen to focus on these black churches as a major entry point for community reinvestment.

Most often, that has involved liaison work with church leaders and credit education; banks in cities around the country have held seminars to educate church parishioners about available credit. Riggs National Bank in Washington has been doing so on a weekly basis, holding Saturday seminars with accountants and tax experts to help would-be borrowers understand what the bank looks for in extending credit.

"We targeted the churches in part because they already do lots of outreach," Richard L. Turner, a vice president and community lender at

Riggs, told a Consumer Bankers Association CRA conference. "Churches also tend to be very liquid." He added that churches in the Washington area seek loans for housing, day care, and other social welfare programs.

National Bank of Detroit has found religious leaders a vital stabilizing force in struggling neighborhoods. NBD in 1987 set up the Family Development Fund, spearheaded by an ecumenical clergy group, that offers grants to congregations for basic necessities such as food and shelter, as well as for training and education.

A handbook describing various housing projects undertaken by churches has attracted widespread attention. Called "Building on Faith," it was issued by the Washington-based Churches Conference on Shelter and Housing; among the handbook's sponsors are Riggs, American Security, Signet Bank, and the Mortgage Bankers Association. The church group provides technical assistance to interested congregations, and the banks have sent personnel to conference-sponsored forums to talk about financing.

There is a "halo effect" from working with church leaders: Parishioners tend to follow with deposits of their own. Riggs has signed up hundreds of church members for checking and savings accounts after it did business with church elders, Turner said—a nice payoff for a bank willing to make lenders available to religious leaders in the community.

Churches also have considerable credit needs for building or rebuilding that banks can tap into. BancOhio National Bank provided financing to a local church to complete expansion and renovation, nearly doubling the seating capacity. The pastor said he would "recommend them to anyone." Harold Fischer, president of Theodore Roosevelt Bank in Washington, D.C., said his small bank has made a number of loans to build or rebuild church steeples.

But Turner warns that church loans can be time consuming and difficult to piece together. The average deal for an acquisition loan takes three months to complete, he said, and construction deals can take 18 months or longer. Most of Riggs' church loans are long-term (five years or longer) credits at fixed rates, he added.

WHOLESALE AND SPECIALTY BANKS LEARN TO COPE

Since home mortgages, rehabilitation loans, and small-business credits are the building blocks of most community reinvestment lending efforts, the new CRA pressures have been particularly confounding for specialty banks—wholesale banks serving major corporations, boutique banks targeting doctors and lawyers, credit card banks, and foreign-owned institutions without substantive branch systems. But the regulators have taken no prisoners: Each of these banks has "the same continuing and affirmative obligations as a 'full-service' institution to meet the credit needs of its entire local community," the agencies said in a joint statement in 1990.

Having said that, the agencies aren't sleeping easily, either. In interviews, regulators admitted to lingering uneasiness over enforcing common standards on major retail banks and wholesale institutions that do no mortgage lending whatsoever. The FDIC planned to revisit the issue early in 1991 to compare how specialty banks have been assessed in various areas around the country, said Janice Smith, head of the community affairs department. "There's been a continuing dialogue as to what, if anything, these banks should do," David Teitelbaum, an attorney with Morrison & Foerster in San Francisco, told *American Banker*.

Still, specialty banks are not finding much leniency. The agencies released joint guidelines early in 1990 for their participation in CRA, a clear signal that they would be held to a defined standard. A New York attorney said his clients are confused and upset as the ground seems to be shifting under them. One wholesale bank client got a 5 under the old rating system shortly before the July 1990 change, he said, even though in previous years the bank had been exempt from CRA. "The regulator in this case just changed its mind," the attorney said.

One of the most celebrated CRA decisions of recent years involved Continental Bank Corporation, the Chicago giant that has transformed itself in recent years into a wholesale bank. In the wake of that 1989 ruling, a host of interpreters warned specialty banks that they needed to take a crash course on CRA whether or not they were planning any acquisitions.

Craig Ulrich, the late vice president and general counsel of the Consumer Bankers Association, contended that banks should be exempt from compliance when they are not deposit-gathering franchises, but the odds are very long indeed that the agencies will reregulate the issue to ease the burden, others say. Most likely there will be some additional fine tuning and guidance as to what activities are best for specialty institutions.

Complaints have been widespread that the interagency guidelines give specialty banks a particularly high hurdle to clear. They were not written with a wholesale bank in mind, said Christopher Williams, a vice president with Morgan Guaranty Trust Company in New York. "There are few hints of leeway where a wholesale bank can squeeze in," he told *American*

Banker. Attorney Warren Traiger argues that as written, it is not clear that a wholesale bank can get even a satisfactory rating.

But the regulators have laid out some clearly acceptable activities for nonretail banks in the CRA arena. These include:

- Providing permanent mortgages to nonprofit developers of low- and moderate-income housing.
- Contributing to loan consortiums supporting affordable housing or small-business development.
- Providing technical assistance to community group borrowers.
- Buying state and local housing mortgage revenue bonds or industrial revenue bonds.
- Providing grants to community groups seeking to educate residents about credit needs or housing rehabilitation.
- Supporting community development credit unions.
- Establishing community development corporations to finance housing.

Just as with retail banks, regulators want to see signs of proactivity. "The fact that wholesale bankers use intermediaries does not imply that they 'know little about how to make loans that individuals need,'" wrote former Federal Reserve community affairs manager James W. Lowell in a 1990 letter to *American Banker*. "And it doesn't mean that wholesale bankers should sit back and wait for the deals to come to their doorstep."

Wholesale Banks Find the Avenues

Although several of the nation's biggest wholesale banks are no strangers to community reinvestment, they have been scrambling lately to find new investments and structure new programs that meet the intent of the revamped CRA law. In 1990, Bankers Trust Corporation recruited a neighborhood housing advocate from Brooklyn, Gary Hattem, to head its community reinvestment program. And Chicago's Continental got approval for a new community development corporation and named a prominent black private banker within its ranks, Charles Brummell, Jr., as president.

Hattem emphasizes the bank's push for partnerships with nonprofits. Bankers Trust will often interact with a group that may not yet be ready for a loan, trying to develop its debt-carrying capacity, he told a Consumer Bankers Association conference. The bank also has had larger nonprofits guarantee loans for smaller ones and has utilized private bank collateraliza-tion for nonprofits' loans. "You can't burden them with the debt without investing in the organizations themselves," he said.

While he believes it can be "a good idea" to join with other institutions in a concerted approach to a reinvestment program, Hattem said Bankers Trust is interested in high-profile projects and will often do things alone so as not to share the spotlight. "We don't try to assist everyone, but define a niche and go after it," he added. It can't hurt Bankers Trust to have one of the nation's foremost civil rights figures, Vernon Jordan, as chairman of a board committee on public responsibility.

Continental's CDC, approved by the Comptroller's office early in 1990, seeks to revitalize lower-income areas in Chicago and surrounding Cook County. Its mission includes providing ideas and financing that will stimulate jobs as well as housing, focusing on the same providers retail bankers are after—small business, developers, and nonprofit community groups.

Since the adverse ruling on its Arizona deal, Continental "has been extremely active in trying to find out what credit needs there are" in local communities, said the Woodstock Institute's Jean Pogge. Still, she main-tained that "Continental has never been a major reinvestment actor" and dismissed the $1 million capitalization of its CDC as "peanuts." She added, "There's no reason why Continental couldn't be a depositor or an investor [in community-oriented institutions]. Taking a less-than-market return would certainly be cheaper than setting up a retail lending arm."

But Continental did take a number of steps in 1990 to beef up its CRA programs. In addition to setting up the CDC, it formed a community business team that focuses on lending to smaller (and most likely, less creditworthy) entrepreneurs. Between the two units, Continental had ap-proved 17 transactions for $5.5 million as of early December 1990, said Fran Grossman, executive director of the CDC. The bank contends that it had been handicapped because "there was no model for a nonretail bank to serve the needs of its community," Kurt Stocker, chief compliance officer, told *American Banker*.

Morgan Guaranty has a couple of subsidiaries, a charitable trust and Morgan Community Development Corporation, that have developed a working relationship with a number of community groups in New York. The bank also bought $150,000 in capital stock and acted as the escrow agent for Community Capital Bank, a startup in Brooklyn that will be profiled in the next chapter. But the simple fact that Morgan is fair game for community activists under CRA causes one New York attorney to roll her eyes. With its aristocratic lineage and aura of discreet money. Morgan has never catered to anyone of modest income. So, in her view, approaching Morgan is a lot like going to Brown Brothers Harriman, the ultra-genteel investment bank that services the carriage trade on Park Avenue and Palm Beach. Brown Brothers, certainly, has never had to concern itself with CRA.

Grants, Loans, and Gifts

The big wholesale banks are conspicuous givers to a number of reinvestment intermediaries like the Community Preservation Corporation in New York and the National Equity Fund, both profiled in Chapter 5. Bankers Trust, in fact, has loaned the National Equity Fund's 1989 New York Equity Fund—structured as a limited partnership—$15 million at 9 percent interest through 1996.

Several of these intermediaries have fine track records and effectively satisfy certain CRA objectives for wholesale institutions, says attorney Traiger. But while he mentions no names, he adds that "some of the best intermediaries are oversubscribed. There's clearly too much money chasing too few good programs."

One smaller intermediary drawing increasing attention is the National Federation of Community Development Credit Unions. The New York-based nonprofit, which will be examined at length in the next section, funnels institutional money to small credit unions in lower-income areas and has drawn support from Bankers Trust and Morgan. In addition to $300,000 contribution at below-market rates, Morgan has also provided grants, in-kind gifts, and loans to the group and to individual CDCUs, according to the federation.

Bankers Trust gave the National Federation $100,000 in interest-free deposits in 1990 and also made a $10,000 contribution to help with administrative costs linked to the deposit program. "Through a competitive process, we expect to see the funds deposited in credit unions located in low-income neighborhoods throughout New York City," said John W. Kelly, a senior vice president at Bankers Trust.

But some wholesale bank initiatives are independent of funneling support to intermediaries. In August 1990, Bankers Trust announced it would provide $500,000 in grants to help community organizations involved with New York City's Special Initiatives Program (SIP). The funding was aimed at boosting the ability of those groups to manage newly renovated housing for formerly homeless families and to deliver social services to these resettled families. In a later phase, the bank planned to pay for a technical adviser to support the efforts of SIP building managers.

IBJ Schroder Bank and Trust Company in New York, a wholesale subsidiary of a foreign (Japanese) bank—and so the subject of a double CRA whammy—has made a host of donations and gifts to community groups involved in activities ranging from job training and social services to economic development and housing. It has also given away surplus furniture, computers, and other supplies.

These types of contributions "are the only ways wholesale banks can possibly comply with CRA," IBJ Schroder vice president Eric Tarlow told *American Banker*. "We have no branches, no ATMs, no small-loan officers."

Boutiques Get No Breaks

So-called boutique banks, specialty institutions that mushroomed in the 80s to serve affluent professionals, are finding community reinvestment a hair-raising challenge. While many of these institutions are chartered in well-to-do suburbs, their service areas usually include more down-at-the-heels neighborhoods where they ordinarily do no lending. But the regulators are not letting them off the hook. "We envision a community as having no holes in it," Clinton A. Poole, deputy comptroller with the OCC in Atlanta, told *American Banker*. He added that he would tell such banks, "You weren't given a charter just to serve upper-income people. You were given a charter to serve people, period."

But banks doing business with the country club set have a reason for being a mite teed off. They are being asked to create programs and direct money to groups with whom they have no routine contact and that they are not organized to serve. "CRA presents a special challenge," Grant R. Essex, president of Chattahoochee Bank in Atlanta, told *American Banker*. "There's no way to say it doesn't apply to us, and there's no way to play games with it and pretend" that you are complying.

Another Atlanta boutique, Vinings Bank and Trust, was stung by some CRA criticism early in 1990 and later put together a detailed CRA plan. "I would have to say we did not pay proper attention to our CRA responsibilities, but I feel we are now," president A. Anderson Huber told *American Banker*. The bank, founded in 1987, got its new religion after an examination by the OCC.

It isn't just newer institutions that have been dragging their heels against the pull of the new CRA. "We've had some tense discussions" with several private banks, some more than a century old, said Georgeann Abbanat, deputy commissioner at the Massachusetts Division of Banks. "We've had some of them say, 'That doesn't apply to us.'"

Also wrestling with CRA obligations are ethnic banks that cater to specific groups. In Los Angeles, some Asian-oriented banks have come under pressure for passing over Hispanics and other minorities. One Asian bank in east Los Angeles did respond to complaints by instituting an outreach program in its local Hispanic community, said Mark Aldrich, an attorney and principal with the Irvine, California, Bankers Compliance Group.

But Aldrich said some ethnic banks still don't seem to understand that CRA entails fulfilling obligations to a geographic service area. "Some of the [violations] I've seen have been so blatant, like one bank that thought it only needed to serve the [East] Indian community," he said.

Credit Card Banks Grope for Answers

Credit card banks, which flourished in states like Delaware and South Dakota in the 1980s because of favorable regulation, are as perplexed by CRA as any of the specialty banks. Created to house and fund credit card activities and products for their parent companies—usually money center or large regional banks—they are nonetheless chartered in (and responsible for meeting credit needs in) this handful of states.

A dozen or so credit card banks in Delaware have been meeting to compare notes and try to come to grips with the $64,000 question: What are we supposed to do? Clearly a new level of effort is required, but officers at some of those banks say regulators are not giving any solid clues about what they would like to see apart from guidelines issued to wholesale and specialty banks in general. "They have no local community, but they do have a responsibility" to meet CRA. "We're trying to educate them, and us [regulators]," said FDIC consumer affairs director Janice Smith.

And, there's the banking framework in the state to contend with. Because of the way credit card banks in Delaware are chartered, they can do nothing that could be considered competition for local banks, noted

Beatrice Stubbs, an officer with First USA Bank in Wilmington who has been working the CRA compliance beat. "CRA's focus is predominantly on housing and small business, which we are definitely prohibited from doing," she said. "Up front, this means that it's impossible to comply with the law as written."

Defining the local community presents another thorny problem when a bank's "service area" is the nation and it cannot compete in its home state. In Delaware, Stubbs says some credit card banks have defined a city or county as their community, others the entire state.

At a prior CRA examination in 1988, one Delaware banker said, examiners seemed content that the bank "did the technical things—had the statement and the map and all that." But expectations are clearly higher now, he said, and credit card bankers are looking over a similar array of intermediaries, consortiums, and loan pools that wholesale banks have been screening.

Stubbs said there is a "whole gamut" of CDCs and community reinvestment corporations, as well as nonprofits, that the Delaware banks are examining. Some in this gamut are particularly active in developing lower-income housing. "We're exploring all those things, but it's a difficult call because we are attempting to be very proactive, and we have no past experience to guide us," she said. And it isn't just her bank. "None of us knows what to do. The feeling I'm getting is that regulators are unsure," she added. "If they knew a little better [what they wanted], they could give us better guidance."

While a handful of the credit card banks were involved in examinations in late 1990, no ratings had been released and no one had lessons to share, she said. "If anyone had that kind of information, we'd all be a lot better off," she sighed.

Foreign Banks: In for a Pound

The Land of Opportunity is also the land of responsibility, at least as far as community reinvestment is concerned. A foreign-owned bank, wholesale or retail, chartered in the United States and getting federal deposit insurance, is subject to the same ground rules that domestic institutions are. And like their U.S. counterparts, foreign banks have been rushing about lately to find appropriate vehicles for meeting their CRA obligations. Some of these have included equity investments in intermediaries, contributions to loan pools, and grants to housing or small-business groups.

The confusion among foreign-owned banks, many of which are wholesale institutions, is unsurprising, said Daniel M. Leibsohn, president of the Low-Income Housing Fund, a community development loan fund in San Francisco. "Some may not understand the regulatory or political environment they are dealing with," he told *American Banker*. "There isn't anything like this where they're from."

The reinvestment process has gone more smoothly in some areas than others. In New York, home to the nation's largest concentration of foreign banks, a number of institutions have made high-profile contributions to intermediaries or community development groups. IBJ Schroder, as noted earlier, has had an active donation program directed at hard-pressed non-profits, and it has provided $500,000 toward a revolving loan pool for the Neighborhood Housing Services of New York City.

Schroder's contribution and $20,000 corporate grants from four other Japanese banks were saluted by Francine Justa, executive director of the New York NHS, in an article in *New York Newsday*. But she left no doubt that she considers them fully accountable to the CRA standards set for domestic banks. "Although they may not have branches in Queens or Staten Island, they are, nonetheless, part of the larger New York community and required to reinvest in that community," she wrote.

The Canadian Imperial Bank of Commerce, like Schroder a wholesale bank, also contributed to the NHS. And it gave $25,000 toward the initial capitalization of Community Capital Bank, the start-up that will be examined at length in Chapter 3. "We saw this as a very good vehicle and a very credible effort to do things across the city," said vice president Gerry Parisella. He added that the new CRA regulations had spurred CIBC to review its commitments to poorer neighborhoods in the Big Apple. "I think, quite frankly, that the fact that the rankings will be made public has provided tremendous incentive to look more closely at what you have done and what you are currently doing and plan to do in the future," Parisella added.

Speaking of commitments, Mitsubishi Bank Ltd. made a big one late in 1990. The huge Japanese bank agreed to provide a $108 million letter of credit backing a proposed 522-unit apartment building in Manhattan, 20 percent of which will be set aside for modest-income residents. The developer's construction and permanent financing actually is coming from bonds issued by the New York City Housing Development Corporation and secured by the letter of credit. Mitsubishi officials said the developer's track record with so-called 80/20 buildings and the incessant demand for rental housing in New York attracted it to the deal, which has a clear CRA linkage.

But from California, with the largest concentration of Japanese banks, comes the tale of a bank that has had more than its share of CRA-related trouble. Mitsui Manufacturers Bank, a business-oriented institution in Los Angeles that once was virtually canonized by author Martin Mayer for its savvy lending policies, was under steady assault in 1990. Community activists sought to torpedo a planned alliance between its Tokyo parent, Mitsui Bank Ltd., and Security Pacific Corporation, as well as the merger of Mitsui with Taiyo Kobe Bank Ltd., a deal that would include acquisition of a small trust company in New York. Sixteen protests against Mitsui Manufacturer's record were filed with the Federal Reserve Board, which agreed in March 1990 that Mitsui's CRA record was indeed inadequate.

When Security Pacific tried to buy a 20 percent stake in Mitsui Manufacturers, that, too, was held up by the Fed. The big Los Angeles banking company then asked the Fed to wait until late in 1990 to process its application in hopes of negotiating an accord with community groups.

Mitsui Manufacturers, a $1.4 billion bank that targets middle-market companies, has been scurrying to cover its flanks. Late in 1989 it hired its first CRA coordinator and became a founding member of the California Community Reinvestment Corporation. Early in 1990 it joined the Low Income Housing Fund of Northern California, and later its southern California counterpart. Then, in September, Mitsui joined the Savings Association Mortgage Company, another big California consortium targeting money for low-income housing. Its chairman joined the "campaign leadership cabinet" for the Union Rescue Mission's fund-raising drive to raise $16 million for food and shelter for the homeless.

"Prior to the fourth quarter of 1989, you could fault the bank for its CRA record," president Jerry W. Johnston told *American Banker* in September 1990. "We are very pleased with what we have done in the last year." He added that "the parent bank is very interested in tracking our CRA performance."

Others are not so pleased and have made their displeasure known—a public relations nightmare for any bank, but perhaps particularly so for the vaunted Japanese. Gilda Haas, a spokeswoman for the Communities for Accountable Reinvestment in the Los Angeles area and a prominent activist, said the group was not satisfied with the bank's progress. She downplayed a Mitsui contribution to an economic development fund in

West Hollywood, saying, "They put in $15,000, and it took them a year to commit." Robert Gnaizda, a member of San Francisco's Greenlining Coalition, charged that Mitsui Manufacturers "has no CRA record."

Some observers speculate that Mitsui has come under particularly rough treatment by activists because it is a Japanese-owned bank. As such, the theory goes, it has vast resources, and any major commitments—like those involving Union Bank a few years ago—would run up a conspicuous flag, plainly evident for other Japanese banks trying to add to their California holdings. "It's a deep-pocket phenomenon," Johnston told *American Banker*, referring to the chorus of protests. "The activists see the $200 billion-plus asset base of Mitsui and can't understand we're just a $1.4 billion bank."

But Haas minimizes the Japanese connection. "We just want them to invest in our communities," she said, noting that her group has been pressuring domestic banks like Security Pacific to do the same. Early in December 1990, Haas said she had agreed with Mitsui Manufacturer's Johnston to set up a dialogue about an eventual agreement; this came after almost a year of what she termed "really bad communication." She added: "We're making them accountable, but they're supposed to be accountable anyway to CRA."

HELPING COMMUNITY DEVELOPMENT CREDIT UNIONS

A small-but-growing number of banks and thrifts are working to provide basic banking services to poor urban and rural residents through contributions to community development credit unions. These special-purpose credit unions are frequently the only link to the banking system in blighted areas where banks have no offices or have closed branches; most are tiny, bare-bones operations that until recently have not even offered checking accounts. Still, they are regulated by state and federal authorities, and more than 9 in 10 are federally insured. The rest are backstopped by state or private funds.

Bankers are scarcely eager to help the credit union movement, which has been striding onto bankers' turf as a rival for deposits and retail loans. But community development credit unions (CDCUs) aren't exactly competition for most banks. About 100 strong, they are serving "the bottom stratum of the depository marketplace," says Clifford N. Rosenthal, executive director of the National Federation of Community Development Credit

Unions in New York, the nonprofit financial intermediary and technical assistance organization that funnels money and support to CDCUs. "We're in neighborhoods banks don't want to be in," he said.

From New York's East Harlem and the Bronx to North Philadelphia and South Chicago to rural areas in Kentucky, North Carolina, and Arizona, community development credit unions are serving a mostly minority clientele, as many as 40 to 50 percent of whom may be public assistance recipients, according to the federation. The institutions remain primarily an urban phenomenon, though one of the nation's largest, with about $23 million in deposits in 1990, was on the Navajo Reservation in Arizona. But most are much smaller. A typical CDCU has between $500,000 and $1 million in assets and between 500 and 1,000 members, according to the National Federation.

CRA pressures have been the spur for a lot of bank and thrift contributions to CDCUs. These contributions are primarily in the form of noninterest-bearing deposits and grants, sometimes in exchange for the institution closing a neighborhood branch; the regulators have recognized this assistance as a bona fide CRA activity. One example, according to the FDIC, is "the provision of technical assistance or stable deposits to fund the credit union's lending." Some other forms of help: capital grants, donations of buildings and equipment, and access to bank training programs.

Assistance to CDCUs clearly falls under the general heading of community development that is factored into every CRA examination. Two of the questions on the FFIEC's "examination checklist" apply directly: "Has the institution taken action to minimize the impact of branch closings?" and "Does the institution participate in investment in local community development and redevelopment projects or programs?"

A certain level of support for CDCUs is the direct result of CRA challenges. The Bank of New York, challenged during its bitter takeover battle for Irving Trust Corporation, agreed to a request by ACORN to make deposits in a startup credit union in East New York. Others have been more indirect. In Delaware, the People's Settlement Federal Credit Union went to a number of banks and reminded them of their general obligations under CRA. For its efforts, the credit union got $300,000 in deposits from local institutions, allowing it to expand its line of loan products and attract new members.

And in Chicago, a CRA challenge at the Austin Bank spurred a $100,000 certificate of deposit investment in the Austin/West Garfield Federal Credit Union. The credit union also got a similar-sized CD from

South Shore Bank, the community development leader that will be profiled in the next chapter; both are rolled over annually at below-market rates.

But increasingly, Rosenthal sees banks becoming proactively involved. Voluntary support has come from money center and wholesale banks in New York, retail banks in cities like Philadelphia and Charlotte, North Carolina, thrifts in Phoenix. "It reflects, I think, increasingly enlightened self-interest on the part of these banks—a recognition that, whatever the banks may think about the credit union industry in general, CDCUs represent not a competitive threat, but a potential resource for solving some of the most difficult problems of unbanked communities," he said.

Some two dozen banks and thrifts have supported CDCUS in the last several years, the federation says. Among those it cites for their contributions: Chemical Bank, Morgan Guaranty Trust Company, and IBJ Schroder in New York; Philadelphia National Bank and Fidelity Bank in Philadelphia; Central National Bank in North Carolina; Chittenden Bank, Bank of Vermont, and Howard Bank in Vermont; First National Savings in Phoenix; and South Shore Bank and Austin Bank in Chicago. These and other institutions "are coming to realize that this is a relatively painless way to reach a low-income community without having to retail it," Rosenthal said.

First National Bank of Chicago, the most retail-oriented of the city's big banks, has been talking with a church-based credit union league on the city's south side with an eye toward offering them deposits or other financial support, said the Woodstock Institute's Jean Pogge.

A Little Goes a Long Way

Minute as most of them are, particularly in their start-up stages, community development credit unions don't need bushels of money thrown at them. Rosenthal notes that they have no capital requirements, but do need to demonstrate commercial viability and community support. A typical goal for a beginning operation is to have an operating budget of $30,000 to $50,000 in three years. Most are single-office operations staffed by a handful of people with low salary scales; private bankers need not apply. They can even be run on a volunteer basis, Rosenthal says, "but then the level of service is very low." The Woodstock Institute's Pogge said a start-up credit union on Chicago's West Side "is hard to run for many reasons. It's too small to pay for the staff it needs."

Products are few and straightforward. Most CDCUs concentrate on passbook savings and small CDs, and their low overhead helps them give borrowers a rate break on most loans. At the Lower East Side Federal Credit Union in New York, for instance, a recent study found that the median loan was $1,700, and that rates were generally under 13 percent. Monthly installments were less than $100 for 64 percent of the borrowers, and the chargeoff rate was less than 1 percent. "We're talking about small-scale loans that people just need in their daily lives, maybe to buy furniture, or if they have gotten in debt," the credit union's manager, Linda Levy, told *American Banker.*

Many CDCUs already have outside benefactors in the form of churches or foundations, and often the $50,000 or $75,000 these charitable groups give is all that keeps the credit unions alive, Rosenthal said. Hence his interest in finding more bank and thrift contributors, particularly outside the Northeast and Southeast, where the heaviest concentration of CDCUs is found.

For major banks, the dollars directed to CDCUs might be a very small fraction of their community reinvestment budget. On an easel chart in Rosenthal's office in September 1990 was a listing of contributions from New York banks, mostly in the form of no-interest loans: Chemical, $250,000; Bankers Trust Company, $100,000; Morgan, $300,000. In its CRA statement, Chemical listed the contribution and said it was being used as a capitalization pool "to make federally insured deposits in startup credit unions in New York and New Jersey."

Several banks in North Carolina have given sizable sums to the Self Help Credit Union in Durham. NCNB Corporation and Central Carolina Bank have each given $100,000, according to credit union manager Bonnie Wright, and First Union Corporation has made a smaller no-interest deposit and "provides us with a lot of informal technical assistance." A couple of smaller banks have contributed to a local capital campaign, she added.

The credit union, with $27 million in assets late in 1990, concentrates on rural areas and targets "people too often underserved by the financial industry," according to a brochure. It has made loans, for instance, to an 80-employee cooperative apparel factory employing mostly low-income women and to a farmer needing money for cucumber-sorting equipment. Self Help "does a commendable job of development in chosen areas with minimal resources," said L. M. "Bud" Baker, Jr., president of Wachovia Bank and Trust Company, another contributor.

Contributions to CDCUs need not be six figures; for smaller institutions, the donations might be $20,000 or less. The Bank of Vermont, for example, gave $15,000 to the Burlington Ecumenical Action Ministry to develop a plan for expanding the Vermont Development Credit Union. The grant "will enable us to lay the foundation for expansion properly," said Caryl Stewart, the ministry's executive director.

Bank of Vermont has offered the credit union some consumer lending training and has held seminars at a local branch to help residents better understand the credit process, said bank president John T. Ewing. "We think that, ultimately, they can deal with that part of the market a lot better than we can," he said. "Their clientele wants very small loans, for buying a refrigerator or for escrow. That's difficult for banks to do."

Chittenden Bank gave the nascent credit union $30,000 for expenses and a $100,000 deposit at 3 percent. Moreover, it is providing technical assistance through the services of a loan officer and the bank's asset/liability manager. Still, Rosenthal finds more than altruism at work in Vermont: CRA pressures played a part, and there was some general resistance to the idea, he said. "Any sizable commercial bank in New York would have to have its head examined to regard us as a competitor," he said. "That's not true in Vermont."

Replacing the Branch

In neighborhoods where banks find branches to be economic albatrosses, CDCUs have obvious appeal. An institution can garner a significant amount of community good will and CRA credit at a lower cost by supporting a CDCU than it could by trying to keep an unprofitable branch on life support.

Chemical, for instance, closed a branch in the Tremont section of the Bronx in 1987, leaving a local check-cashing storefront as the only financial intermediary in the neighborhood. But rather than beat a retreat, Chemical turned the building over to the Mid-Bronx Desperadoes—an unlikely, but real, name for a coalition of nine church and civic organizations. The group then vowed to turn part of the building into a community credit union.

Besides giving the National Federation the no-interest loan, Chemical agreed to pay $15,000 a year to cover maintenance on the building. Community credit unions "provide a very important service, and we're interested in strengthening that service," Robert Rosenbloom, a senior issues analyst at

Chemical, told *City Limits*. The federation's Rosenthal saluted the bank for working out a deal before it faced a CRA challenge over the branch closing.

Manhattan's depressed Lower East Side was the site of another bank-CDCU transformation. Manufacturers Hanover Trust Company left the area in 1984, but said it would support a successor institution. Yet the hunt for a successor proved fruitless, Rosenthal recalled; even small ethnic banks demurred. After 18 months and still no new institution in sight, community groups filed a protest in 1985 against Manufacturers Hanover for a branch closing.

The bank eventually agreed to pay $150,000 to rehabilitate the building and offered a purchase option at an attractive price. It also allowed a start-up credit union, the Lower East Side operation mentioned earlier, to use the office rent free for three years, and put $100,000 in a no-interest, 18-month deposit at the CDCU as seed money. As of mid-1990, the credit union had made $2 million in loans, even though more than half of all borrowers had no record with a credit bureau and 48 percent did not even list a bank reference on their credit application—clear evidence that the credit union was serving the "unbanked."

An unusual CDCU-bank branch relationship is working in Chicago, where customers of the North Side Credit Union can walk into the Bank of Ravenswood to have their checks cashed. The credit union keeps no cash on hand, and the bank cashes the checks for free. The Woodstock Institute's Jean Pogge said she "absolutely" considers such a service to be a CRA-related activity for the bank.

Sophistication on the Rise

Small as most of them are, community development credit unions are turning to collaborative efforts to increase their muscle. The National Federation has amassed a pool of deposits and loans from institutional investors that it turns into a diversified portfolio of deposits in CDCUs around the country. In 1990, the federation was managing more than $4 million in investments from foundations, churches, and financial institutions; as such, it serves as a sort of clearinghouse for banks and thrifts looking to contribute, but not wanting to target any specific CDCU.

Some CDCUs have even banded together to participate in loans. A $55,000 loan to finance the purchase and rehabilitation of an 11-unit, low-income apartment in the Bronx was put together with members of the New York Community Financial Network, a coalition of CDCUs. The loan worked in tandem with money provided by the New York City Department of Housing Preservation and Development. Public money, this from New York State, helped train a core group of lending specialists to help credit unions increase their housing and small-business lending.

Sophistication is taking other forms. North Carolina's Self Help, founded in 1984, is "virtually a hybrid between a credit union and a commercial bank," according to the National Federation. Organized to finance worker buyouts of textile mills and other area businesses, it has expanded its lending to include low-income housing, child care, and minority businesses. In Santa Cruz, California, the Santa Cruz Community Credit Union financed the first co-op conversion of a low-income apartment building, as well as the conversion of a mobile-home park to a low-income cooperative.

Other CDCUs are leveraging their effectiveness by allying with other nonprofits, including housing developers and community development corporations. As these local credit unions become more practiced in specialized lending areas and more knowledgeable about risk, their appeal to financial institution investors should rise accordingly.

An additional incentive for financial institutions considering investments in CDCUs is that most are self-sustaining after they reach a few million dollars in assets, according to the national federation. So a bank's contribution need not turn into an annualized transfusion for the foreseeable future. Funding from blue-chip entities like the Ford Foundation confer additional legitimacy on the CDCU movement. Ford recently gave $1 million in a "program-related investment" to four local CDCU networks and an additional $225,000 to the National Federation to help with marketing, fund raising, and operations.

Pressure, Pressure

Despite Rosenthal's insistence that more institutions are coming forward to help CDCUs, the veiled fist of CRA compliance is clearly at work. It was apparent in Chicago, Delaware, and Vermont, as traced above; it is evident in the support of wholesale and foreign banks in New York. One result, credit union leaders say, is increased willingness on the part of bankers to engage in dialogue—but with an insistence on process and planning that can be foreign to the CDCU culture.

In Philadelphia, Teresa Trudeau, the coordinator of a local CDCU project called PHILCUP, said she has been frustrated by the caution shown by bankers promising support. Philadelphia National Bank is giving her own credit union, Southwest Germantown Association FCU, $12,000 a year to help meet operating expenses, but most bankers seem intent on forcing credit unions to submit plans that show eventual self-sufficiency, she said.

PHILCUP, a joint committee of credit union members and bankers, has been meeting since late 1989. "Without clobbering them over the head, we're saying, 'You know you're not serving the low-income communities. Why don't you just support us?'" she said. While not much happened by late 1990, she noted that the CDCUs have asked banks to help with a three-year, $400,000 capital campaign by soliciting some of that amount from corporate customers. For their part, banks in the area express skepticism over what they see as an informal, often ill-organized process of targeting money at groups with whom they are unfamiliar.

Even in communities without CDCUs, activists are trying to persuade banks to agree to support credit union development as part of broader agreements. Community groups in the Los Angeles area, for instance, have asked Security Pacific to contribute to a startup credit union being sought in the depressed south-central area. But help for the CDCU would be just one element in a wide-ranging series of requests that include cashing of government checks and lending for small business and home improvement.

CDCUs, most of them led by community activists, can be expected to keep on the heat in the 1990s, both in terms of soliciting bank deposits and negotiating for assistance in lieu of branch closings. The latter is a key goal. "We'd like ultimately to be in every area that can't sustain a bank branch," Rosenthal said. Pressure along those lines is being felt in New York City, where the administration of Mayor David Dinkins has publicly stated that it "will attempt to leverage funds of other financial intermediaries to capitalize credit unions in locations where money market banks are closing branches and need is still present."

At a few institutions around the country, however, the idea of government pressure is scarcely a curse. These banks or bank units are dedicated community development lenders who don't have to scramble to do needs assessments or figure out who the local community honchos are; they already know the lower-income market and are busy serving it. We will look at a few of these in depth in the coming chapter.

CHAPTER 3

COMMUNITY DEVELOPMENT LENDERS: FIGHTING THE BLIGHT

A handful of banks or bank units around the country have become crusaders for community development lending in poorer neighborhoods or regions. They welcome the new attention on CRA, at least in the sense that it will force other institutions to take a harder look at their own backyards and put money into capital-starved areas. These committed community lenders believe in the theory that a rising tide lifts all boats.

Two of the banks that will be profiled in this chapter, South Shore Bank in Chicago and Community Capital Bank in New York, are small institutions entirely focused on community reinvestment in struggling neighborhoods. They are staffed by people with a strong commitment to helping the poor; many in these banks spent years working as community organizers or as officers in nonprofit companies in inner cities. Their tolerance for risk and their comfort in dealing with minorities set them apart from most bankers.

As models, these banks are something of an extreme: Banks and thrifts can satisfy their CRA requirements and do a lot for poorer areas without making such a hefty commitment of energy. But this handful of banks represents points of light in dimly lit neighborhoods. As the 1990s progress, more of them are likely to spring up, impelled by the growing clamor to address society's shortcomings and give the less advantaged a chance to share more equitably in the American dream.

Moreover, don't look for bankers at these institutions to downplay their profitability; they trumpet it. South Shore and American Security are getting solid returns, and officials take pains to dispel any notion that what they are doing is in any way charity.

SHOREBANK CORPORATION: SHORING UP
CHICAGO'S SOUTH SIDE

Anyone's reckoning of the nation's top community development lenders will have South Shore Bank of Chicago at or near the top of the list. South Shore has been dedicating its efforts to low-income residents in Chicago's far South Side since 1973, a year when Richard Nixon was still in office and the nation was in the throes of its first major gasoline shortage. South Shore was a pioneer, an activist in poor neighborhoods long before much was happening on this front.

But to profile South Shore's community lending is more complicated than looking at the record of a small commercial bank with an unusual focus. South Shore, with $190 million in assets, is one arm—albeit, a very important one—of a complicated and ambitious holding company, Shorebank Corporation. The holding company also has four other divisions, each related to renewing distressed communities.

What Shorebank is attempting, even on a small scale, is beyond the scope of what almost any other bank has even contemplated. Instead of having to persuade regulators that it is meeting its CRA requirements, South Shore Bank has to convince them that its array of lending policies for the disadvantaged are sound. While things haven't always gone smoothly, bank president James Fletcher said regulators generally "see what we're doing as sort of old-fashioned banking, and they sort of like it." He added that the structure of the holding company has prompted a number of examiners to remark just how different South Shore is.

Different? Consider the other pieces of the holding company. No leasing subsidiaries, no mortgage companies, no credit card operations—the staples of many bank holding companies. There's City Lands Corporation, a real estate development entity that develops and manages residential and commercial real estate for the benefit of low-income people. Then there's The Neighborhood Fund, an investment company licensed by the Small Business Administration; it finances small minority companies with equity investments and long-term subordinated debt.

The other two units are The Neighborhood Institute, a tax-exempt affiliate that operates economic and social development programs, and Shorebank Advisory Services, a consulting firm providing technical assistance on development banking and community enhancement strategies. The Neighborhood Institute itself has a subsidiary, TNI Development Corporation, a for-profit developer of rental and cooperative housing.

Shorebank has tried to cover the map: arranging and financing transactions, developing housing, generating venture capital, consulting on how to do community development, and conducting business training. In doing so, it has broadened the reach of a conventional bank and roped in people who often fall outside the banking system. The Neighborhood Institute, the tax-exempt unit, takes on loan customers that the bank itself wouldn't ordinarily deal with, for instance.

"They do a lot of housing, and they're little differed from City Lands in that almost all of the housing they do, which is with difficult buildings, is done with deep subsidy money from a variety of sources—wherever they can piece together money," Fletcher said. He added that a small-loan incubator program run by the institute represents "the kind of things you just couldn't do inside a bank. They would be classified substandard the day you booked them."

Shorebank sees community investment as a long-term proposition. A good example was City Lands' development of Jeffery Plaza Shopping Center, a nine-acre, $10 million commercial venture in the heart of an inner-city area. Nine years after it began, the center opened in May 1990 and was 75 percent leased from the start.

"Our deals are as complicated as any downtown office building," said Sara Lindholm, chairman of City Lands. And because the transactions involve complex financings with public lenders, "every deal we do takes longer than a project 10 times larger" at a conventional bank, she said.

With the withdrawal of the federal government and the removal of some tax incentives that had helped bring money into low-income redevelopment, Shorebank has been a leader in bringing together various public and private funding sources. Sometimes referred to as "synthetic equity," these sources are not on most bankers' Rolodexes; they include trusts and foundations, state and municipal governments, secondary mortgage agencies, and the Local Initiatives Support Corporation, or LISC.

Shorebank's success has spun off a related holding company venture in Arkansas, Southern Development Bancorp. Overseen by some of Shorebank's board members, Southern Development has a commercial bank and separate arms dedicated to attracting resources and putting them to work. Its bank, Elk Horn Bank and Trust Company, works with largely poor, rural borrowers, but it generated a 0.99 percent return on assets in 1989. In effect, it is a smaller, newer (it had its first full year of operation in 1989), rural version of Shorebank.

Starts and Fits

While Shorebank didn't develop its expertise overnight, neither did it start as a storefront operation with a wish list and only a vague idea of how it would turn that list into reality. Some examination of its beginnings and its philosophy underscore just how unusual the company is.

South Shore Bank, an existing institution, had fallen into decline by the late 1960s, gradually losing deposits and acting "in a caretaker situation until they could get out," Fletcher recalled. The bank's owners petitioned the Comptroller of the Currency's Office in 1972 to move to downtown Chicago, but a local community group resisted, saying a market existed that the bank was not serving.

Enter a group that included Fletcher and a number of people who now have been the officers of the company for many years. They had written a business plan and were looking for "neighborhoods in which to put this grand experiment together," Fletcher said. And so the group put up some of its own equity, took out a loan from the correspondent bank, and bought South Shore in 1973 for what Fletcher recalls was about 1.25 times book value.

Starting with about $40 million in assets, the bank has grown almost five times since then. That's hardly an enormous growth rate considering the explosion of brokered deposits and the real estate boom of the 1980s, but the institution has been consistently profitable, and has a performance record that is the envy of many in its peer group. Its 1989 return on assets of 0.85 percent was its lowest since 1984, and its loan losses have been consistently well below peer group averages. ROA was 1.09 percent in 1988 and a fraction higher in 1985 and 1986. Loan losses were just 0.12 percent of outstandings in 1989, compared to the peer group mean of 0.87 percent.

The bank president says South Shore aims for a minimum ROA of 1 percent and was somewhat disappointed with the numbers from the last couple of years. "While we think those numbers are good, and maybe even surprise a few people, we ought to find ways to make those numbers better," he said. Return on equity has ranged from 12 percent to 17 percent in the past several years; Fletcher says the bank should hit 16 percent consistently.

The loan portfolio stood at about $116 million in summer 1990, with real estate representing about $50 million of that, he said. Most of the real estate lending was in multifamily homes, and about $43 million was in commercial loans, many of them SBA-guaranteed. Many of its single-family loans don't show up on the books because South Shore sells them to Fannie Mae as they are made.

Average loan sizes run about $225,000 in the multifamily portfolio and around $150,000 in what Fletcher calls "the SBA side," the commercial group. Some credits are far larger, near the legal lending limit of $1.7 million, and parts of these loans are sold to other lenders. American National Bank & Trust Company in Chicago, its correspondent, buys many of those participations, he said.

Its lending market is extremely local, though less so than a decade ago. South Shore found that some savings and loans were starting to make loans in its core territory eight or nine years ago; that competition, coupled with a desire to concentrate on multifamily housing, pushed the bank west into Chicago's Austin area. Fletcher said the bank looked at every neighborhood in the city before deciding on Austin, which he said had "enough to get us excited. There is some stability there. There are organizations there that are working hard." The bank has been lending there since 1986.

Some of the mortgage lending South Shore is doing in Austin is being boosted by Fannie Mae, which has agreed to purchase up to $5 million in first mortgage loans. (Fannie Mae's affordable housing initiatives and how they can help lenders will be covered at some length in Chapter 5.) This program is targeted at borrowers making less than 80 percent of the median income for the area; borrowers may supplement their initial down payment with market-rate second mortgages provided by South Shore to buy and rehabilitate eligible properties.

In contrast to its lending strategy, South Shore's deposit-gathering techniques are national. To supplement its local efforts, most of which are in deposit-poor areas, South Shore has a sophisticated direct-mail-order operation that targets socially responsible individuals and groups, including religious orders. These outsiders represent almost half of the bank's deposit base.

"We have some corporations, but that number is smaller than I think it ought to be and should be," Fletcher said. "I'd like to believe that we just haven't done a good job marketing to corporations, especially here in the Chicago area, the metropolitan area."

That Engine Called Development

Fletcher and other Shorebank officials offer a uniform vision of the company as a do-gooder that can turn a profit in neighborhoods where others fear to tread. They say their focus is on areas where their lending can have a visible impact. "We think of places that need credit. Where for one reason or another, the flow of credit into those neighborhoods has stopped or is at a trickle or where we're needed," Fletcher says. "Where what we do will make a difference. Those [places] tend to be in the city. They tend to be minority. So that's the basic selection."

Seeing the deterioration of largely black neighborhoods in the early 1970s, he recalls, "What we said we wanted to do was take a bank, provide credit, and by providing that credit serve that engine called development. By providing that we began to feed into the market economy of that neighborhood, and perhaps by doing that start reversing the trends. That's really what we do." Mary Houghton, president of the holding company, puts it more metaphorically: "At Shorebank, we let people run and see what they invent."

The decision to branch into a number of different umbrella units reflected the limitations of a banking charter, Fletcher said. "Banks don't take equity positions. They can't own and operate buildings. They can't be a developer. Yet we knew we needed a company that could play that role in the process, because there were not a lot of developers beating the doors down in these neighborhoods."

The holding company also gives Shorebank a flexibility that few lenders can match. Largely through The Neighborhood Institute, Shorebank takes on commercial customers that wouldn't draw a glance from major banks: single parents, for example, trying to generate enough off a small business to provide an income for them and their families. "And whether (or not) that parent ever gets beyond that one product and that one little business, I think it's fine. We want to see more of that, not less," Fletcher says.

At bottom, Shorebank puts a lot of faith in its borrowers. "I feel comfortable making a single-family mortgage in Austin to a family that has a work history," Fletcher says. "They don't make a lot of money. They pay their debts. Their options aren't as broad as someone else's options in Winnetka"—a wealthy suburb north of Chicago—"or some place else because their earnings power isn't quite as great. And they happen to be black. But if you work with those families, you learn that they can afford to pay a mortgage. And they will pay it."

Bootstrapping Ma and Pa

A great deal of the housing-related lending South Shore has done has been with small rehabilitation efforts, sometimes called "ma-and-pa" operations because they involve a husband-and-wife team. The bank has relationships with more than 200 of them, lending them the money to buy and renovate old buildings.

"They never borrowed money from a bank before," Joan Shapiro, senior vice president, told *U.S. Banker*. "All of them started doing it nights and weekends. Now about 50 do this full time. They're skilled, savvy businesspeople now."

Fletcher offers a highly refined profile of such rehabbers: "They tend to be 40-plus [in age]. They tend to be a couple. One probably works in some capacity for government, be that local or state or federal . . . It's not untypical to see a policeman married to a clerical-type person at a large company." Again, not the sort of people most institutions would bankroll.

The bank's small business customers tend to be franchises or small manufacturing companies ranging in size from a couple of hundred thousand dollars a year to more than $12 million a year in sales, Fletcher said. Through The Neighborhood Fund, the bank can stretch its dollars to these little borrowers, leveraging every dollar of private capital four times through the SBA. South Shore, which has been a preferred SBA lender since 1986, can make guaranteed loans up to $500,000. The loans carry a maximum interest rate of 2.5 percentage points over prime.

One franchisee that Fletcher mentions approached the bank about a loan for a McDonald's franchise. As the bank was talking to her, an opportunity came along for a different franchise, a seafood chain called Dock's. The bank took a chance on her even though she had little expertise and not much money.

The bank found a location for her and gave her a loan. "So we got what we think is a good credit on our books, the store's doing well, and that money stays here. She's got some people employed here in the neighborhood," Fletcher said. Not only that, he said, but the site was vacant and had been off the tax rolls for years.

But he sounds a note of caution repeated by profitable community development lenders elsewhere: Even banks like South Shore cannot accommodate everyone. Some would-be borrowers just don't look like acceptable risks. While the bank doesn't want to discourage anyone, "That gets to be very difficult," Fletcher says. "How do you spend time with someone when your best guess is you're not going to get a return on that conversation or on that time?" This time question is "one of the tensions that goes on inside our institution all of the time. It's a good tension, I think."

Spreading the Gospel

Shorebank officials have become a resource group for others in the country interested in undertaking focused community development lending in poorer areas. Fletcher said there have been discussions of start-up efforts in Kansas City and in the upper peninsula of Michigan, whose forested hills are a long way from the teeming streets of Chicago. The Michigan situation has more immediacy, he said, because interstate laws would allow Shorebank to own a bank in the Great Lakes State.

Southern Development Bancorp, the spin-off in Arkansas, itself came about as an initiative from the Winthrop Rockefeller Foundation. The foundation approached Shorebank leaders in 1986 with the idea of launching a privately capitalized development bank focusing on new and homegrown businesses; the ensuing corporation drew heavily on the experience, and the personnel, developed at Shorebank. But since the capital came from other sources, Shorebank has no ownership.

Spirit and commitment are as vital as any other pieces of the community renewal process, in Chicago or Arkansas, Shorebank officials maintain. "I believe a large part of the development business is that you get in it and start doing it," said Ronald Grzywinski, chairman of Southern Development and of Shorebank. "You keep your eye on the ball and keep adapting and changing and modifying. You do a lot of handcrafting."

That level of attention to small borrowers who might seem poor credit risks would be anathema to some banks. And risk is clearly going to be one of the dominant issues for banks and thrifts coming into the early 1990s with the harsh light of regulatory scrutiny hot on their desks. Conventional thinkers, feeling this heat, might instinctively recoil from the kinds of lending South Shore does. "A typical banker would never be satisfied with this place," said senior vice president Richard Turner. "In his mind we take too much risk."

Asked why other banks have been slow to follow his bank's lead, Fletcher is blunt. "They have no interest. Their perception of what is safe, sound, and profit-making business doesn't, unfortunately, include for the most part the inner cities."

Patience and persistence paid off for Jeffery Plaza. Because it was so long in the making, "a lot of banks would have dumped it," John Long, a local community leader, told *American Banker*. But South Shore's bankers "tend to be more patient than other people," he said.

"You know," Fletcher said with a note of sadness and frustration, "I am constantly amazed that I meet people in 1990 that run companies or are engaged in businesses who are otherwise bright, intelligent, successful people, who think the world stops at 12th Street (on Chicago's South Side). Nothing south of there but a wasteland."

Knowing the importance of perception, South Shore Bank has been remodeled twice under the current management, a new drive-in bank has been built, a new parking lot put in. "You have to look better than people expect," Fletcher said.

Shorebank accepts its role as an innovator, all the while hoping that bankers elsewhere may heed the call. "We were involved in this effort before there was CRA. We would be involved if there was no CRA," Fletcher said. "We do it because we think someone ought to be in this business. And we think it is a business. We think there's a whole industry called development, and it ought to be explored by more than [just] us."

AMERICAN SECURITY'S CAPITAL EFFORTS

Perhaps no large bank has received more attention for its community development lending in the past few years than American Security Bank, the $5 billion-asset subsidiary of MNC Financial Corporation. And with good reason. Charged with a mission to meet the community's credit needs and remain an "active corporate citizen," the bank has been involved in both traditional and innovative lending aimed at revitalizing neglected neighborhoods in its Washington, D.C., service area.

In the four years following its organization in early 1986, the bank's Community Development Lending Group financed 200 projects in inner-city areas that entailed $250 million in loan commitments. Included were more than 6,500 units of multifamily rental housing, more than 250 home ownership units (most of them co-ops), and about 2 million square feet of retail/commercial space. In many projects, the bank has pieced together partnerships with other financing agents, entrepreneurs, the District government, and the nonprofit groups in the local community that are doing the actual work.

Rather than focus on any one niche, American Security has embraced a wide range of project types: multifamily apartment rehabs, commercial properties, cooperative conversions and condominiums, retail and neigh-

borhood service centers, community facilities such as churches, and transitional housing. Money has been targeted specifically at areas attempting to
revitalize themselves. The bank stresses proactivity: actively trying to
determine community needs, then meeting them if the numbers on the loan
documents add up.

As the lending group has grown in size—it had nine members in 1990,
up from one at the outset—and importance, its energetic leader, Karen
Kollias, has become a national authority on community lending. In addition
to serving on an American Bankers Association subcommittee on community development lending, she has been a visible resource person at
seminars and conferences and has written widely about how banks should
tackle this area.

Kollias, a vice president at American Security, brings the commitment
of someone who used to be on the other side of the table. She spent most of
her 18 years in the field with nonprofit groups and government agencies in
the housing and reinvestment filed, among them the People's Involvement
Corporation in Washington and the National Center for Urban Ethnic
Affairs.

In her widely shared view, community reinvestment needs have
mounted as the federal government's funding pipeline has dried up and
troubled neighborhoods have continued to crumble. Much of downscale
Washington, the areas away from downtown's marble edifices and the
green-lawned Northwest, is poor, mostly black, and torn by one of the
nation's most vicious drug markets. Most banks are giving those areas a
wide berth, but the need for revitalization reverberates like a howl on a still
night.

"There's a great deal of demand for providing community development financing, because there's been so many needs in the neighborhoods
that have been overlooked for a long time that are now very, very obvious,"
Kollias said.

Affordable housing is one; small-business development is another.
Operating out of its fortresslike headquarters on 15th Street in downtown
Washington, American Security has concentrated its efforts in neighborhoods east of the Anacostia River—some of the capital's most blighted areas.
It has done so, the bank said in a promotional brochure about its program,
because "continued effort to preserve and revitalize underserved neighborhoods can result in a sustained cycle of economic development," leading in
time to "higher levels of confidence and stability in the community."

"We've discovered that over the last couple of years, the industry has overbuilt shopping centers, office buildings, and hotels," says Joseph Tockarshewsky, executive vice president and head of the real estate lending group. "Nobody's overbuilt affordable housing. We've seen it as an opportunity, an opportunity that was right in our own backyard."

Philosophy and Practice

American Security's mandate for community lending comes, as the experts say it should, from the top, from Chairman Daniel J. Callahan. In its Community Reinvestment Act statement—a bound, indexed volume that includes a series of maps locating projects the bank has helped finance—American Security says its role as active corporate citizen "affects every aspect of the bank's business, especially decisions concerning where and how the bank 'reinvests' in the community." Safety and soundness remain criteria, of course, but Kollias and her group "have proven that real estate projects in the District's distressed neighborhoods are both achievable and profitable," Callahan said.

Accent the profit. American Security has approached community development lending as a profit center within its real estate division, not as a public relations-driven loss leader. Kollias said the returns on the group's financing, collectively about 1.6 percent on assets, have been in line with the rest of the real estate group's projects. "When structured properly, a community development loan can be as profitable as any other loan," Kollias says. Of the first 160 loans the group made, only 1 went into default.

Ensuring profitability is hardly an easy task. While American Security says it uses the same criteria in community development lending that it applies to other real estate transactions, the emphasis is different. Take the "four cs" of underwriting (credit, character, cash flow, and collateral); most low-income borrowers may be short of the first two, so cash flow and collateral take precedence. Moreover, the bank is willing to look at unconventional sources of cash flow such as reserves, guarantees, or letters of credit, especially if a project's cash flow is likely to be slight in its first years.

Although standard financing is available through the bank's Community Development Lending Group (CDLG), the unit specializes in custom financing. Instead of conventional mortgages, these could include construction loans, land acquisition/development credits, interim loans, and lines of credit. Many of the housing projects the CDLG finances are unoccupied or partially occupied, so the chances are slim that a permanent mortgage will be committed at the same time the bank commits its acquisition/construction loan.

This customization requires experienced lenders who understand how various government and nonprofit sources can mesh to make a project work. "You need staff capacity that understands the development process, and the development process specifically within the different communities," Kollias said, "so that they're comfortable with market comparables and underwriting and the other sources of finance that usually come into play with these types of projects."

Lack of competition was a major factor in determining American Security's commitment to distressed areas, officers say. "There was such a demand, we could make an immediate impact on different areas of the city right away," said Vickie B. Tassan, vice president and CRA officer. She added that the bank was fortunate that Washington has "a strong nonprofit network to use as a development arm." In a promotional video about its program, the bank noted that the weak market for such lending meant it could "cherry-pick" the best potential credits.

In the blighted Knox Hill neighborhood, for instance, the bank learned of the formation of a planning committee examining a number of potential projects. It joined this panel, made up primarily of community interest groups brought together by a nonprofit developer. Subsequently, American Security took some developer customers to the area and got them interested in working there—and in borrowing from the CDLG.

American Security has made the most of synthetic equity, including subordinated debt from public sources. Nonprofit organizations may be able to turn to the Local Initiatives Support Corporation, for instance, which provides equity investments in nonprofit-sponsored projects. Frequently, this type of arrangement means the bank approves subordinate deeds of trust, particularly in cases where projects are developed on previously owned lands or where federal funds are used. This may be an unpopular concept for permanent lenders, but American Security officers say they are comfortable with it.

The CDLG has issued a number of "mini-permanent" loans to developers unable to secure permanent financing because they simply did not have an adequate operating history, Kollias said. These credits provide developers "with construction financing and then a stabilization period with fixed-price financing of at least three to five years to give them the operating history required by a permanent lender," Kollias noted.

In general, she said, the CDLG applies underwriting assumptions that a permanent lender would be making on areas such as interest rate, amortization, loan-to-value, and debt service coverage ratios. The projects it finances generally achieve 1.15 coverage, often considered the minimum desired by permanent lenders. It even makes loans to rent-controlled projects, generally five-year loans that enable the developer to phase in the improvements in the first two to three years and reach a stable rent roll by the end of the fifth year.

Most of the housing-related loans would not make economic sense if they involved new construction, Tockarshewsky said. But the District has an abundance of derelict housing that can be bought at low prices—a situation common in many older cities, and one that stacks the odds in the lender's favor.

Kollias cautions that American Security, or any bank, cannot be all things to all nonprofits. "Given the structure of nonprofits, their financial capacity is not their strong suit, and therefore technical capacity is critical," she says. As a result, the CDLG "has been conservative in the selection of the groups it works with, using development expertise as the measure of capacity." The group has established firm relationships with a number of nonprofit developers to whom it has extended unsecured lines of credit that go as high as $500,000. "For those organizations which have development capacity, the bank has treated them like any other borrower," Kollias said.

Some Specific Projects

While no two projects are the same or are financed just the same way, the CDLG says, bits and pieces of the same type of mosaic may turn up frequently. Two projects of similar size in the same neighborhood provide a good basis for comparison—and some instruction about the variables in community development lending.

In the first, the CDLG provided the loan to two individuals who had formed their own development firm. They used the loan to buy 36 vacant units in three low-rise buildings in a neighborhood pocked with weed-strewn lots and a host of hollowed-out building shells. The developers' own equity and the bank loan were the only financing.

Because of the demand for low-income housing and the availability of rental subsidies for tenants, the project was 100 percent occupied when the rehab was done. The CDLG familiarized a mortgage banker with the developers and the project, and, while the high level of nearby abandonment furrowed some brows, the mortgage banker made a successful case to the Federal Home Loan Mortgage Corporation (Freddie Mac), which bought the loan. With that sale, American Security never had to fund the "mini-perm" loan it had been thinking about making on the project.

The second development involved almost identical parameters—36 units in three buildings. One of the buildings was sold to the nonprofit by the city, and the redevelopment work required gap financing from two other public sources in addition to the bank's loan. As a result, there were three subordinate deeds of trust behind the bank, plus a covenant that required the owner to keep the development available to low-income people. Working with a mortgage banker, the CDLG made clear the various restrictions and why the project was structured the way it was. Armed with that knowledge, the mortgage banker sold a permanent mortgage to the secondary market.

A couple of other projects underscore the diversity of American Security's program. The CDLG financed a shopping center redevelopment in northeast Washington, providing funds to refinance, expand, and complete work at the center, which includes three prominent corporate tenants—Citicorp, Safeway, and McDonald's. The project was sponsored by prominent retail developers, in partnership with an experienced community development corporation.

Financing for a housing development in southwest Washington involved neither a loan nor a line of credit but an equity investment. The 410-unit, multifamily complex known as Oak Park had been more than half vacant for many years and needed extensive rehabilitation. As envisioned, the rehabbed complex would cater to moderate-income families, but 20 percent would be set aside for low-income housing because the District government had provided gap financing.

American Security received approval from the Office of the Comptroller of the Currency in August 1989 to make a direct investment of $955,000 in the Oak Park Limited Partnership. That gave the bank a 55 percent interest in the project. Special authorization for the project came from the Comptroller's Community Development Corporation and Investment Program, which enables national banks to make equity investments that would otherwise not be permitted.

Cooperative Programs

American Security isn't always the sole financial institution involved in specific projects. Together with the National Cooperative Bank in Washington, as mentioned earlier in the book, it set up a loan pool project to widen the availability of financing for housing projects in troubled areas. "The structure and term of the loans generated by the loan pool are different from traditional underwriting guidelines but are not inconsistent with sound credit decisions," the bank said in its CRA statement.

The loan pool format allows the acquisition/renovation phase of a loan to be rolled into the permanent phase with no additional permanent financing fees and no rate adjustments during the 10-year permanent period. Only projects with "significant community benefit" are eligible: tenant-sponsored, limited-equity cooperative conversions; permanent rental housing for low-income families; and transitional housing for families.

American Security also has entered into an agreement with National Cooperative and the Consumers United Insurance Company for coordinated co-op housing finance in targeted neighborhoods. The insurer has been offering predevelopment and acquisition financing, American Security the construction financing, and the Co-op Bank the permanent loans. As structured, this "one-stop" financing program is targeted at developments with at least 20 units and a minimum construction cost of $250,000.

One big reason for the joint venture: cost. Experience with a few co-op conversions showed that "the fees obtained with these loans did not come close to covering the bank's time with the projects," Kollias said. But the bank didn't want to pull out of the market "since this is the primary form of home ownership for low- and moderate-income families in the District."

The bank has also led the way for a $2.25 million loan purchase agreement with LISC, which authorizes the purchase of loans originated and 75 percent guaranteed by LISC. American Security contributed $1 million to the facility and persuaded five other area banks to kick in $250,000 each.

Dividend: Good Will

Appropriately enough, American Security can point to a cause-and-effect relationship between some of its CDLG projects and good will that has generated additional deposits for the bank—a nice payback for any institution willing to take on a little additional time and risk.

Particularly in the case of less seasoned developers who may not have had any ongoing relationships with a lender, a lot of "hand-holding" is required. Banks don't generally approve of such activity because it isn't cost effective, Kollias said, but "by taking the time and interest in some of the small developers and businesses, [American Security] has received a majority of these customers' banking business and accounts. These daily cash balances and interest earned from the loans make money for the bank."

Alice Vetter, president of MUSCLE, a local nonprofit, draws the connection very clearly. "We were grateful to American Security for taking a chance on us, and when we had an opportunity to invest some money, we were able to take a $3 million advance on a development project and put it into American Security," she said. "Then, when we sold an apartment complex that was donated to us for a little under $1 million, we put that money into American Security as well."

Having public officials in your corner doesn't hurt, either. At the ceremonies for the opening of a local shopping center financed by American Security, District City councilwoman Charlene Drew Jarvis said, "American Security Bank has more than surpassed the goal of any bank's involvement in the community."

And those goals have been met profitably, American Security officials insist. "We've learned a lot over the years about community relationships," Vickie Tassan, the CRA officer, told two researchers for the Consumer Bankers Association last year. "One thing we have learned is you don't have to cave in to protestors. You don't have to offer below-market financing or concessionary rates. You can be responsive and responsible and still make a profit."

"We took risks, the developer took risks, but they were reasonable risks," Callahan told the CBA researchers. "Our competition kept their distance. God knows what they thought."

The bank hasn't been timid about blowing its own horn. In addition to the visibility of Kollias and Tockarshewsky, who has been chairing the ABA subcommittee on community development lending, the bank has compiled a binder with press clippings about its CDLG efforts and made the promotional video about its program available to the ABA for distribution. Some banks probably wouldn't welcome that visibility. But most banks would surely welcome a highly regarded community reinvestment lending group that generated anything approaching the profitability and good will of American Security's. Few are even in the same ballpark.

NEW PLAYERS TARGET THE UNDERSERVED

Of the other banks devoted to community development lending at this writing, the most prominent are in three different modes: in the game, checking into the game, and getting suited up. These three, respectively, are Ameritrust Development Bank in Cleveland, Community Capital Bank in New York, and the Development Bank of Washington.

Ameritrust Development Bank

A special subsidiary of Ameritrust Corporation, a major regional bank, the development bank specializes in servicing low- to moderate-income areas. It was started in 1986 by John Kolesar, a priest-turned-banker who became one of the nation's most visible bank proponents of community development lending. Kolesar stepped down in August 1989, but his successor, Charles Thigpen, is a veteran community development banker who has continued the bank's commitment to inner-city neighborhoods.

Late in 1990, the development bank—a full-service bank, not a community development corporation—was carrying about $18 million in deposits and $30 million in loans, according to Thigpen. That gap has been funded by the holding company. About 43 percent of its loans were in residential real estate, 40 percent in commercial real estate, and 15 percent in commercial loans to small businesses, Thigpen told a Consumer Bankers Association conference.

The bank packages loans for apartment developments up to 200 units, Thigpen said. While the development bank does make loans to nonprofits at 50 basis points below market rates, for the most part it eschews below-market pricing. Indeed, Thigpen is adamant about the pricing issue, arguing that reducing the rate on a loan "is to inject artificiality into the economics of the project" and is, in the long term, counterproductive.

Kolesar noted that the Comptroller's Office has looked favorably on Ameritrust's lead bank's decision to scale back its own community development activities in deference to the development bank; in exchange, the lead bank gives the development bank significant back office support and a line of credit. Partnerships with nonprofit community groups played a key role in the success of the Ameritrust unit, Kolesar said. At times, they were the borrowers; at other times, they were the middlemen, bringing together the bank and private developers.

Community Capital

Opened in late November 1990 after a grueling four-and-a-half-year organizational campaign, Community Capital doesn't yet have a record to chronicle. But it has brought a lot of energetic, committed community and financial experts together in a way that brings new promise to blighted areas of New York City. Community Capital offers evidence that investors will support a start-up bank dedicated not to lending to surgeons or law partnerships, but to people living in disadvantaged neighborhoods. Its ambitions, and the attitudes of its leaders, put it on the cutting edge of community reinvestment lending; its success or failure will say volumes about the viability of reinvestment efforts that far surpass CRA requirements in the 1990s.

Community Capital began its life with $6 million in equity capital from 248 investors—corporations, foundations, and individuals—representing 21 states and a wide array of societal groups. Corporate investors included American Express Company, Time-Warner Incorporated, and Metropolitan Life Insurance Company. Four banks also chipped in: Morgan Guaranty Trust Company, Canadian Imperial Bank of Commerce, the Amalgamated Bank, and U.S. Trust Company.

Morgan Guaranty, which served as the escrow agent pro bono, was "tremendously helpful to us," said Lyndon Comstock, the new bank's chairman and the guiding force behind its development. Having one of the most hallowed names in banking on board was also a magnet for other potential investors wary of making a commitment, he said. Morgan, which also plans to buy some of Community Capital's loans, sees the investment as "a way for us to support community lending for which we would not otherwise have the capacity," Hildy J. Simmons, a vice president, told *The New York Times*.

Most of New York's major banks declined to make an investment "because their CRA aims took them elsewhere," Comstock said. The share purchase by Canadian Imperial, on the other hand, attests to the pressures felt by foreign banks operating in the United States who are scrambling to find relevant CRA investments. "We saw an investment opportunity that would address a real need in a local area," said Gerry H. Parisella, a vice president at Canadian Imperial, which kicked in $25,000 toward the new bank.

Community Capital's long road to opening was paved with the kind of potholes many startups have to navigate. It went through a name change: The original proposal was the Bank for Socially Responsible Lending. it met regulatory resistance: Comstock says the New York State Banking Department (the bank is state chartered and FDIC insured) was very cautious and intent on making sure the bank was well capitalized and had a sound business plan. Before its opening, its executive offices were located up a creaky set of wooden stairs in a drafty Baptist church in downtown Brooklyn.

From its office in downtown Brooklyn, not too far from the Grand Army Plaza, Community Capital has grand designs for a local community development lending institution that will focus on small business development and low-income housing. Its market is all of New York City's poorer neighborhoods, not just Brooklyn, Comstock said. But the bank also will have a consumer banking side, offering certificates of deposits, NOW checking, and money market accounts—all with a competitive interest rate. The actual retail operation, Comstock insisted, will be relatively bare bones, with only a handful of tellers and customer service representatives. By April 1991, the bank had collected $5 million in deposits.

The deposit-gathering, Comstock said, will be modeled somewhat on what South Shore is doing. He concedes that many—perhaps half—of the retail accounts will be pulled in from outside the bank's local market, some through a national mailing list of people involved in socially responsible investing. Initially, he said, the bank would be limited to $75 million in assets, though it is targeting only $15 million in the first year. Will there be any $100,000 CDs? Possibly, he said, but "it will not be hot money."

On the lending side, he said, "we're not going with a single-neighborhood strategy. We're going with a citywide strategy." Realistically, that means lending to the boroughs of Brooklyn, the Bronx, Queens, and Manhattan; he expects little demand from solidly middle-class Staten Island. Comstock sees two big and relatively untapped markets for the bank: nonprofit community housing developers and small businesses. Neither area has been big enough to interest major banks, at least in the neighborhoods the bank is targeting, he said.

"I've talked to [the nonprofit developers]," he said, "and most of them feel the attention level is extremely poor at the big banks. They have to wait six months just to be told no. Only two or three are getting an adequate level of service, and where they leave off, that's where we will pick up."

Finding the Niches

Servicing the bank's underbanked market may be little more than giving it more attention. "If you give people any reasonable level of service, I think you'd have people beating down your door," Comstock said. There are probably 250 nonprofit developers in the city, and 30 or 40 have substantial experience, he said, adding, "It's more important for us to know who the borrower is than where the developer is working."

He insisted the lending can be done profitably, and with the help of the Small Business Administration, the risks can be whittled down to very little. SBA programs can guarantee up to 90 percent of individual loans, and he said that New York City appears to have a substantial unused SBA allocation that interested lenders can tap into. Housing rehabilitation loans will probably make up the bulk of Community Capital's initial housing loans, Comstock said, though he expects a shift toward new construction in five years or so as the city turns over its housing stock and developers see the potential in building on vacant lots. When that happens, he predicts a surge in "in-fill" housing, where new buildings are erected next to existing, perhaps rehabbed, ones.

Community Capital is not interested in lending to retailers, Comstock said, but plans to concentrate on light manufacturing, particularly companies with under $10 million in annual sales—small fry that the money centers have historically given scant attention. Food processing has some dynamic elements, he said, with ethnic foods such as West Indian gaining popularity. Refuse removal in landfill-strapped New York and health care, including home health care, should provide plenty of opportunities for lenders willing to make nontraditional investments, he said.

"Companies are being created, and niches are opening up," he said. "We probably wouldn't finance a pure start-up, but we would back someone with a track record who's been in business a couple of years."

Comstock readily admits the bank's lending must be profit-driven. He said Community Capital plans to charge the prime rate plus 200 basis points on most small-business and construction loans—a rate he believes will be acceptable to borrowers and provide the bank an adequate level of return. He points to South Shore's enviably low chargeoff record as evidence that loans in low-income neighborhoods can be good business.

Launched in a time of trial in banking, Community Capital is seeking to prove that despite the general industry overcapacity, some areas remain distinctly underbanked. If banking is going to engage in social engineering, it will be people like Comstock who will be at the drafting table. He is both wistful and combative about the general lack of interest in emulating banks like South Shore. "They are generating a 15 percent return on equity. Why aren't other people copying them?" he asked. He blamed this aversion on the cultural divide between well-heeled professionals and the struggling underclasses, as well as on the "sheep instinct" in banking that deters bankers from pursuing anything that seems pioneering unless enough other institutions are doing it.

Comstock has warm words for intermediaries like the Community Preservation Corporation, but entire neighborhoods are not represented in CPC lending; clearly, there is room for additional housing lenders, he contends. While Community Capital is committed to its retail operation, Comstock said checking and other transaction activities are "very expensive to run out of the bank." The bank may try to work through community development credit unions to extend its reach, he said; in exchange, his bank might be able to help with the operations problems that confront these small credit unions.

But there are skeptics who aren't sure Community Capital is entirely on the right track. An executive with one nonprofit in New York is fairly dismissive of the bank's efforts. "They say they're emulating [South Shore] in Chicago, and they're calling all of New York their marketplace?" he asks with more than a touch of sarcasm, alluding to South Shore's focused neighborhood lending. He adds, however, "I hope they do make it."

Development Bank of Washington

The Development Bank of Washington was still in formation late in 1990, but it is embracing many of the ideas set forth by South Shore, Ameritrust, and others. It will be a dedicated community lender, trying to leverage money pumped in by investors to spur job development, home ownership, and additional housing in the Adams-Morgan neighborhood and other areas east of Rock Creek Park—an area with "the largest and most diverse concentration of Hispanics and other ethnic groups in the Washington region," according to an organizers' brochure.

But the new bank, the first to carry a District of Columbia charter, is also tapping into the discontent voiced by many consumers since the advent of interstate banking—that service and awareness of local concerns have eroded. "In many instances, this type of loss of independence and local orientation, in our opinion, has led to a deterioration in banking services," the organizers argue. The bank was hoping to sell from 400,000 to 700,000 shares at $10 a share, with a minimum order of 500 shares and a maximum of 5 percent of the total shares sold.

The Development Bank's president, Samuel L. Foggie, has been down the road before. In 1964, he founded United National Bank in Washington, also an institution dedicated to serving minorities and low- and moderate-income residents. He retired from the bank in 1989 but was talked into signing on for another stint with the new institution. The bank's chairman, Jerry Apodaca, has more of a political nexus; he is a former governor of New Mexico and has been active in national Hispanic affairs for years. Clearly, the bank will get under way with a good deal more savvy about government and public-private linkages than most start-ups.

Linkages will be the key to a lot of community reinvestment. As we will see in the following chapter, a goodly number of banks and thrifts are turning to pooled lending and other group initiatives and trying to make a difference, particularly in the area of affordable housing.

CHAPTER 4

NEW PARTNERSHIPS FOR HOUSING

HOW BANKS ARE REACHING OUT

A lot of money is being aimed squarely at rehabilitating older housing or building new units for low- and moderate-income people, especially in urban centers blighted by economic decay. Much of that financing will be provided by consortiums and loan pools, as we will see in the next chapter. Banks and thrifts are the primary contributors to these pools, and these efforts have been turning up on a host of Community Reinvestment Act statements.

Not every community or region has an appropriate pool, and not every institution has felt compelled to limit itself to that route. Large or small, institutions around the country are electing to make their own arrangements to funnel money to needy individuals or groups who are trying to address the affordable housing crunch. As the 1990s progress, experts foresee growing ranks of banks and thrifts devising their own projects—often in partnership with nonprofits—and reaping their own rewards. Pressure from CRA will help push this process along, but so will the growing sense of the "social compact for banking" that Atlanta Fed president Robert Forrestal sees developing. Housing the poor, certainly, is near the top of many a social activist's wish list.

Statistics tell a disquieting story. According to one reckoning, home ownership peaked in 1980, at 65.6 percent of the population, and dropped to 63.9 percent by 1989. The growth in real home prices outpaced household income growth, with younger people hit the hardest: by 1988, just 15.5 percent of those under 25 owned a home, compared to 23.4 percent in 1973. Housing finance, one of the major links between financial institutions and the consumer, will be an active area in the 1990s. Banks that can demonstrate leadership—especially with proactive, targeted programs—will be in good stead with borrowers and regulators.

The need is achingly clear. One million housing units getting federal assistance, and a similar number of public housing units, are deteriorated and subject to demolition, said Allen Fishbein of the Center for Community Change. That loss would only create more of a chasm that must be filled. In higher-priced communities, affordable housing is at a particular premium. "Five percent down for an affordable mortgage out here is like 20 percent down in Peoria," says Tom Fox, director of the Normal Heights Community Association in San Diego. "The working class in the middle-income area or below can't get housing."

Fortunately for financial institutions, Uncle Sam is still active on some housing fronts. Helping, too, are local and state governments, sensitive to the housing crisis that is stalking cities and rural areas alike. A growing number of loan, grant, and guarantee programs requiring private-sector (i.e., financial institution) participation allow for considerable flexibility. Tax credits aimed at generating low-income housing, for instance—a product of the Tax Reform Act of 1986—have played a big role in getting scores of projects off the ground.

Some of these trends are taken up, for instance, in publications from the regulators, such as *Community Development Finance: Tools and Techniques for National Banks,* issued by the Office of the Comptroller of the Currency in 1989. In that pamphlet, the OCC noted that some of these federal and state programs offer would-be housing providers such inducements as:

- Interest-rate buydowns.
- Second-position low- or no-interest loans.
- Land and public improvement writedowns.
- Grants to borrowers that are recoverable when property is sold.
- Downpayment or principal reduction funding.
- Loan guarantees, some up to 100 percent.

Still, no matter how much help some of these programs provide, some borrowers just don't look like good bets, at least by the numbers; safety and soundness alarms still ring in bankers' heads. So added flexibility comes into play. Loan-to-value ratios may be extended from the conventional 80 percent to as high as 95 percent; debt-to-income ratios can be raised from conservative to the most liberal federal agencies allow, and banks and thrifts can exceed these in individual cases if applicants have a demonstrated ability to meet a higher ratio.

Once made, housing loans are finding a larger and larger placement pool. In addition to selling them to the principal secondary market agencies, banks interested in taking the loans off their books might be able to find buyers, for instance, in city or county governments that have local mortgage purchase programs financed by local revenue bond issues. Or they could sell them to intermediaries like the Local Initiatives Support Corporation, which, along with some socially concerned investors, has formed private placement mechanisms for bank-originated community development loans.

The Office of Low- and Moderate-Income Housing Initiatives at Fannie Mae, discussed in depth later in this chapter, facilitates the acquisition of single- and multifamily housing mortgages originated by lenders. The promise of such a ready secondary market has helped ease bankers' fears about saddling their balance sheets with what they perceive as riskier loans.

Working with Local Agencies

A good deal of the work being done by institutions, particularly in partnerships with government entities, is being done with community development corporations. Since that approach is only one avenue, it certainly does not preclude banks and thrifts from engaging in such programs whether or not they have a CDC.

Liberty National Bank and Trust Company in Louisville, for instance, decided to work directly in a housing program with the Louisville Housing Service, a subsidiary of the city's housing authority. LHS borrowed $1 million from the bank at 7 percent interest to finance development of 40 condominium units in a rundown area, as noted in a 1989 issue of the *ABA Banking Journal.*

The partnership idea was crucial to the project, Liberty's president, Joseph W. Phelps, told the magazine. "The public housing authority does the bookwork, and they give us their background information on who might be eligible and why," he said. That cuts the bank's risk, he said, adding, "We want to do our share, but we have our shareholders to look after, too."

A related partnership story comes from St. Louis, where Boatmen's Bancshares has established a successful community development loan program. Begun in late 1985, its effectiveness stems largely from the input of neighborhood organizations, bank officials say. "These neighborhood groups are the backbone of Boatmen's Community Reinvestment Program," wrote John L. White, senior vice president for community relations, in *ABA Bank Compliance*. "They have generated loan referrals far in excess of what was anticipated." In fact, the bank reported at the end of 1988 that its target of $50 million in real estate loans had been surpassed by more than 100 percent, with nearly half of those going to purchase or rehabilitation of one- to four-family properties.

Some banks have opted for housing partnerships with nonprofit agencies with a geographic concentration outside the central cities. Central Trust Company in Cincinnati has forged a linkage with Communities United for Action, a community organization with 35 member groups of varied cultural and ethnic backgrounds and income levels. Over five years, ending in August 1994, the bank expects to commit $52.5 million in low-interest home mortgages to borrowers with family incomes of less than $35,000.

Among the concessions the bank will be making: interest rates will be 25 basis points below its market rates; points will be "significantly reduced and in some cases eliminated entirely"; adjustments to the normal ratios of income-to-housing expense have been made; and special consideration is being given to applicants with little or no credit history.

First Fidelity Bank in New Jersey has been working with a local nonprofit, New Jersey Citizen Action, to make available below-market mortgages to people earning below 80 percent of median income. Fixed rates can be as much as 1.5 percent below market, with 5 percent down, no points, reduced application fees, and higher than normal "back ratios" of 33 percent housing and 38 percent total debt.

Bank of Vermont made a below-market-rate loan to a nonprofit group, Lake Champlain Housing Development Corporation, for the purchase of a rental housing development in Winooski, Vermont. The loan will ensure "that 26 units of rental housing will remain perpetually affordable and available to people who have few, if any, other housing choices," the institution said. The bank also made a $500,000 equity investment in another nonprofit housing operation as part of a larger financing package designed to make the renters of 336 units the owners of the property.

In addition, the bank has given a $3 million credit line to the Burlington Community Land Trust, a nonprofit dedicated to keeping affordable housing available to those who need it. The land trust does both rehabilitation and new construction, and controls the equity taken by resellers to make sure prices don't spiral out of the reach of poorer buyers.

Some Programs that Work

A few of the most successful, proactive housing finance programs have already been chronicled in Chapter 3, which examined efforts at American Security Bank and South Shore Bank. A third big success story, also covered in that chapter, is Ameritrust Development Bank in Cleveland. But a more mainstream program at a major bank that commands attention is in place at First National Bank of Chicago.

Through the Neighborhood Lending Program, established in March 1984, First Chicago has provided more than $105 million in residential and commercial retail loans, according to officials there. Kristin Faust, formerly an officer in the bank's Neighborhood Lending Division, told an American Bankers Association conference that the division never lends for more than 80 percent of the collateral value and requires a $1.20 cash flow for every $1 of debt. "We're willing to go the extra step for borrowers, but what doesn't work is throwing your standards out the window," she said. "That's foundation work."

Part of its success, First Chicago officials say, reflects its experience in working with government agencies and private capital to promote rehabilitation or expansion. "We have developed an expertise in structuring public/private partnerships where city, state, and federal funds are used to leverage our own, making what would otherwise be an undoable deal work," said Terrence Young, vice president and division head.

First Chicago officials concede that their community investment efforts were spurred by meetings with local leaders in 1983 that sprang from the bank's acquisition of American National Corporation. The top two credit priorities identified by community organizations: small multifamily housing and single-family housing. Most loans in the first category are between $100,000 and $600,000, though they have gone as high as $2 million, officials said.

In a report on one of its largest loans, First Chicago related how it took on one of bankers' bête noires: single-room occupancy housing. The 12-story building, the Norman Apartments, had 40 percent of its units so designated; the bank noted that "banks generally are very reluctant to loan money for such apartment buildings because they are thought to be filled with transients and 'undesirable tenants.'" But further investigation turned up the fact that most tenants had been there for more than two years and were paying more for weekly rents than they would have paid monthly on a one-year lease—proof enough that it was potentially a viable project.

Moreover, the borrower was a developer, the Oakwood Development Company, to whom the bank had already given three loans. Coupled with the presence of a strong residence manager—working for the developer— who maintained strict rules and 24-hour vigilance, the bank agreed to a $1.8 million, 18-month construction loan that was converted into a 30-year adjustable-rate mortgage when construction was completed in December 1988.

A different kind of partnership is at work in New York, where Chemical Bank has hitched its affordable housing efforts to a grant-based program it calls the Housing Opportunities Program. Begun in 1986, it offers general-purpose grants, recoverable grants, and seminars for community groups keen on developing housing. "The goal really is not to make these groups experienced nonprofit developers, or [have them] do these things on their own," Robert A. Rosenbloom, assistant vice president of corporate social policy, told *American Banker.* "The goal is to have them work with experienced people and know the right questions to ask."

Direct grants are given to handle overhead in support of nonprofit housing groups—money to handle things as basic as paying for electricity or photocopiers, said Cynthia C. Wainright, head of the bank's corporate social policy group. Recoverable grants are, in effect, no-interest loans that go toward such basics as architectural, engineering, and legal fees prior to development.

"I think if you are looking at an urgent need in New York City, housing is it," Ms. Wainright told *American Banker.* "The recoverable grant program addressees a social need in a particularly apt way for a bank. That has been our goal."

Chemical's rival, Chase Manhattan Bank, has a nonrecoverable grant program to advance projects deemed of particular significance to the local communities. Chase gave $50,000 to the Brooklyn Neighborhood Improvement Program, for instance, for rehabilitation of 40 units of low-income housing, and half that amount to another Brooklyn group for rehabilitation of low- and moderate-income co-op apartments.

Affordable Initiatives

Such grant efforts may be just the ticket for some banks with a track record in the grant arena, but most institutions looking to promote housing will be making loans. Some will use government or grant money in partnership arrangements, others won't.

First Union Corporation, the North Carolina-based superregional, in late 1989 unveiled an Affordable Home Mortgage Program aimed at making mortgage loans of $10,000 to $60,000 to first-time buyers with incomes lower than 80 percent of the median income for their county of residence. Down payments can be as low as 5 percent, and can include gifts and even sweat equity. In the summer of 1990, First Union was offering these mortgages at a fixed rate of 9.75 percent, 75 basis points off its conventional rate.

Society National Bank in Cleveland has targeted low- and middle-income residents with its "HomeAssist" program. It features a 5 percent down payment, with the bank committed to matching up to 50 percent of the down payment, up to $1,000, with no repayment needed. While rates are fixed at terms from 10 to 30 years, the conventional debt-to-income levels are adjusted in favor of borrowers.

In New England, Bank of Boston and its Bank of Vermont unit are addressing affordable housing through their First Step Mortgage Program. First-time home buyers making $40,000 or less ($30,000 for a single person) need pay only 2.5 percent down, and the limits on housing expense and total debt to income have been raised to 31 percent and 36 percent, respectively.

Perhaps spurred by competitive pressures, Shawmut National Corporation last year began a fixed-rate mortgage program to supplement its adjustable-rate offerings for low-income home buyers in Boston. The fixed-rate, 30-year mortgage is priced a half-point below current rates and will carry no points at closing. Coupled with the adjustable, which has a rate set at 1 percent below market for the first five years of the loan, the new fixed-rate product is part of an $8 million commitment for low-income home buyers made by Shawmut in January 1990.

Bank of Vermont and its parent also helped launch a new generation of lower-cost rental housing by sponsoring a design competition for affordable housing in Vermont that would be cost efficient, scaled for New England towns, and easily built by local contractors. A contest, cosponsored by the nonprofit group Housing Vermont, generated 122 entrants; a Boston architect won a $10,000 first prize for his design.

Norstar mortgage, a unit of Fleet/Norstar, has been lending more than $50 million annually to affordable housing organizations in New York City. The company claims to be the largest such financing agent in the city. A good portion of its lending is sold to the secondary market, Fannie Mae in particular.

One Norstar executive says other bank-owned mortgage firms should consider following suit. "Mortgage bankers should actively go out and seek builders who are involved in affordable housing and structure the financing or assist in it, counsel buyers, and assist in the mortgage applications," Lawrence Strauss, a vice president with Norstar Mortgage, told *Mortgage Banking*. "Go out to community organizations and put together packages to sell. It's serving a wonderful purpose, providing a home."

THRIFTS AND AFFORDABLE HOUSING

CRA pressures are forcing thrifts, too, to maintain a pivotal role in providing housing to the less affluent. That will be well-nigh impossible for some, struggling to stay alive after years of mounting losses, but regulators will be taking their fiscal health into account. Still, a group of larger, well-capitalized savings institutions has been targeting affordable housing for years and is expected to keep up that commitment in the 1990s. Programs being offered by regulatory agencies such as the Federal Home Loan Banks are giving other thrifts a chance to make some community investment loans without putting renewed stress on the bottom line.

RSVPs for AHP

Thrifts are getting a boost from the Federal Housing Finance Board, whose Affordable Housing Program allows thrifts to advance housing money to persons making 80 percent or less of the median income for the area. Federal Home Loan Banks advance the funds at a subsidized rate; the lending institution, in turn, must pass on the subsidy to the borrower. The AHP advances represent earnings that would normally go to the stockholding member institutions in the form of dividends. Pricing is specific to each project, and financing terms are available from one month to 20 years.

District banks are finding no shortage of takers. "We have the potential to fund $10 million—there's that much interest—but only $4 million in AHP funding is available this year [in our district]," Kimberly Jenkins, associate community investment officer at the Seattle Federal Home Loan Bank, said in spring 1990, when applications for the first round were received. Initial response in New England was "overwhelming, just tremendous," said Susan Tibbetts, the former community investment officer at the Boston Home Loan Bank. But James Yacenda, the CIO at the

San Francisco bank, said the fact that the AHP is structured as a grant program might cut into its popularity with members there.

By May 1, 1990, the deadline for applications for the first round of funding, 433 applications had been filed to build a total of more than 27,000 housing units. In the second round, 462 applications were made in conjunction with proposals to build 25,200 units. When the final first-round selections were made in July, 193 projects had been chosen; thrifts were to be distributing $47.2 million of industry money toward the development of 13,706 residential units, with a total cost of $669 million. In the second round of funding, announced two months later, an additional $31.5 million was allocated. Among the mix of proposed projects: urban homesteading and cooperative housing for the elderly in Illinois, shelters for battered women in Indiana, and elderly housing in Massachusetts.

"The diversity is incredible. I've been in this business 40 years, and I see things [in project proposals] that I've never seen before," said Calvin Baker, community investment officer at the Pittsburgh Federal Home Loan Bank. And many of the projects are being aimed at the very poorest Americans. Of those proposed through the second round of funding, 54 percent of the units were targeted at very low-income people, and that percentage was 65 percent in four districts—Cincinnati, Des Moines, Dallas, and Seattle.

The AHP program garnered very strong support from community groups around the country, said Allen Fishbein of the Center for Community Change—testimony to the "tremendous need for new affordable housing."

Many of the approved projects leveraged other forms of assistance to make their funding go farther, noted Frederick Wacker, community affairs officer at the Federal Home Loan Bank of Atlanta. Of the 193 approved projects, he said, state and local grants were being used in 105; HUD money was being used with 64; bond monies, with 52; tax credits, with 45; and foundations, with 19. And individual institutions were not the only award recipients. The Savings Association Mortgage Company, a California lending consortium that will be examined at length in Chapter 5, got $2.8 million in the first two rounds of AHP funding and plans to leverage that into $31 million in low-income housing loans.

The big individual winner in the first round of funding was First Nationwide Bank in San Francisco, the Ford Motor Company subsidiary. First Nationwide had 16 of its 18 project proposals approved; the thrift will contribute $27 million in loans toward construction costs of $106 million.

Included are plans for low-income housing in Cleveland and construction of very low-income rental apartments for senior citizens in San Jose, California.

Great Western Bank is working through the AHP program to provide $17 million in below-market loans for a proposed 316-unit townhouse project being developed in south central Los Angeles. The effort is part of a public-private partnership that includes the city of Los Angeles and a number of other nonprofit groups, including the Archdiocese of Los Angeles and LISC.

USAA Federal Savings Bank in San Antonio will receive money from the Federal Home Loan Bank of Dallas that will enable it to provide an interest rate reduction on $1.5 million in loans made to a nonprofit development group that will buy and rehabilitate two apartment complexes for rental by low-income persons.

The Bank of Vermont was approved for three of the 13 projects in New England, said its president, John T. Ewing (the institution had been the Burlington Savings Bank until 1983 and remains a stock savings bank). Ewing said that in the AHP program, the bank plans to draw down funds at between 4 and 7 percent, then lend that money out with a markup of about 200 basis points. "We feel the credit quality is there" to do a number of projects, he said.

While a desire to do good is clearly at work, the Home Loan Banks have a fulfillment to meet. Under FIRREA, they are required to donate 5 percent of their net income to the Affordable Housing Program. That contribution will rise to 10 percent or $100 million, whichever is greater, in 1995. Moreover, the district banks are responsible for keeping track of the projects that receive funding; an award clearly has the strings of compliance attached. In instructions, the district banks ask applicants to "provide specific information on how the subsidy will be monitored and reported."

Some sniping at the AHP has come from activists who complain that because the Federal Housing Finance Board is controlled by the HUD, the program is little more than another HUD grant program. While it should be connected to local decision making, "the regions and localities don't have anything to do with making decisions on what projects receive money from the AHP," Peggy Miller, congressional lobbyist with the Consumer Federation of America, told *Inside Mortgage Finance*.

Another sour note revolves around projected funding. A FHFB official predicted that AHP outlays in 1991 could be 10 to 20 percent lower than

1990's $78 million—and that the program would become even more competitive.

A second major program that thrifts can tap into is the aptly named Community Investment Program, a once-voluntary effort that was made mandatory by FIRREA. In addition to providing funds for housing development—the guidelines are less restrictive than AHP, permitting loans to persons making up to 115 percent of median income in the area—CIP advances can be used to spur economic development. There is no legislated limit on the advances, which thrifts can apply for at any time; the cost is the FHLB bank's cost of funds plus "reasonable administrative costs." Begun in 1978, the CIP program had by 1990 accounted for more than $8 billion in loans generating some 570,000 low- and moderate-income housing units.

In New England, the CIP program was repriced in fall 1990 to the Federal Home Loan Bank of Boston's cost of funds, making it even more affordable to member institutions. Home Loan Bank President Michael a. Jessee said the Bank was prepared to issue up to $500 million in advances for the CIP and a sister program, the New England Housing Fund.

In the Atlanta district, funding was set at $250 million in 1990-91. Loans under the program are priced at 25 to 35 basis points below the Atlanta bank's regular rates, depending on the maturity of the financing. Among its accomplishments, the program has financed the rehabilitation of 50 units of Section 8 housing by a minority developer in Florida and a 96-unit residential development with 45 moderately priced units in Montgomery County, Maryland. It also supported the development and financing needs of almost 100 small businesses in the Southeast.

Home Loan Bank funds helped enable Citibank Federal Savings Bank in Chicago to take a big part in a community land trust program set up by Acorn Housing Corporation, an offshoot of the community activist group. The land trust is acquiring and rehabilitating properties bought from the Resolution Trust Corporation, Department of Housing and Urban Development, the Department of Veterans Affairs, and other agencies. The trust then sells the houses to lower-income people at below-market rates.

"We're charting completely new ground here," Brenda Gaines, senior vice president for residential lending at the Citibank unit, told *American Banker*. "What they want is a larger number of affordable houses for their clients. It makes sense to work together." Citibank Federal is providing $565,000 toward a program to fix up and sell 23 residences by mid-1991, with a slightly smaller amount coming from the Illinois State Housing Trust Fund. First Chicago Corporation is chipping in $131,000.

In addition to overseeing funding, some regulators are developing sources and expert advice. In New York, for instance, the Federal Home Loan Bank has developed a computerized data base to match member institutions with community housing providers. Organizers of the project, begun in mid-1990, hoped to introduce the data base idea to member institutions and take it around to small gatherings through the year and into 1991.

Doing Their Own Thing

Like a good number of banks, some healthy thrifts will be trying to carve out a lower-income consumer niche of their own by doing what savings and loans have historically done best—originating home mortgages. Half of all healthy thrifts had an affordable housing program in 1990, according to the U.S. League of Savings Institutions, with underwriting flexibility far and away the most popular way of accommodating lower-income borrowers. A particular concentration in the community investment area is likely to be in mortgages for first-time buyers.

For while some multifamily development is going on, the outlook for any surge in such lending by thrifts is relatively bleak. "Between the qualified thrift lender [test], higher capital requirements, and profits, the multifamily market is pretty much dead in the water," said Frank A. Willis, executive director of the U.S. League's Housing Opportunities Foundation.

Commonwealth Federal, a medium-sized thrift in Valley Forge, Pennsylvania, began an affordable mortgage program in March 1990 aimed at low- and moderate-income initial buyers. The thrift committed $5 million to the program, which offers loans at 50 basis points below prevailing interest rates. Buyers are qualified on the basis of income: households of four or more can be earning no more than $35,000 a year and must have a strong credit history. In addition, the home purchase price can be no more than $69,000.

Commonwealth is making additional concessions, said its chief operating officer, Charles H. Meacham. "We allow principal, interest, taxes, and insurance to add up to 33 percent of the qualified buyer's gross monthly income, versus the standard 28 to 30 percent," he said. "That gives [the buyer] more buying power." The rate is guaranteed for 60 days, he added.

The Pennsylvania thrift is also sponsoring free seminars at local community colleges to help needy first-time home buyers learn the ropes—an idea that a Michigan thrift is making a mandatory part of its home buyer's program. Standard Federal Bank in Troy, Michigan, said it plans to make $5 million of home loans available to Detroit residents making less than $48,500 a year. The thrift's commitment is part of the Community Home Buyers Program, a huge nationwide venture with major backing from Fannie Mae and Freddie Mac that will be examined in the next section. As structured at Standard Federal, potential borrowers must attend a seminar on home buying and owning. At the end of the seminar, attendees get certificates that enable them to apply for a loan.

Renovation efforts are another good target for housing funds. The Dime Savings Bank of New York participates in a number of loan pools, but also bills itself as the only lender in New York City to provide rehabilitation loans to borrowers who have bought one- to four-family buildings at auctions conducted by the city. Working through the Small Home Rehabilitation Program, or SHARP, the Dime said in 1990 it had provided more than $6.5 million in low-cost loans for rehabilitating more than 159 housing units over the previous decade, with another $1.5 million committed to 30 ongoing projects. In addition, the Dime has committed close to $3 million in financing since 1985 to the Harlem Brownstone Rehabilitation Program.

Across the country, in Seattle, Pacific First Federal Savings Bank extended a takeout loan of just over $1 million to help finance a $2.4 million renovation project being carried out in 1990 by the nonprofit Historic Seattle Preservation and Development Authority. It joined with two major banks in the effort, which restored 47 units of rotting and boarded-up housing for low-income renters. An unusual aspect of the project was its focus on preserving housing nearly a century old. In fact, the National Trust for Historic Preservation and other agencies anted up $627,000 in additional financing for the project. Such lending "goes beyond the CRA," Jennifer Blake, a finance specialist with the National Trust, told *American Banker*. "What historic preservation has to offer banks is more attractive projects that they an have some pride in."

Any discussion of affordable housing programs would be incomplete without an examination of what the nation's secondary mortgage corporations are doing, and not just for thrifts. Banks, too, are finding that Fannie Mae and Freddie Mac can be genuine helpmates in generating more affordable housing.

WORKING WITH FANNIE AND FREDDIE

The nation's two secondary mortgage giants are starting to make bigger strides on the affordable housing stage, and growing numbers of banks and thrifts will be looking to their big coattails for help. Fannie Mae and Freddie Mac are separate, federally chartered agencies that have become fierce competitors for mortgage portfolios around the country. This competition, some observers believe, may account for some of their recent activism in affordable housing. So has increased scrutiny from members of Congress who wonder if the corporations' relatively meager capital bases constitute secure dams against a potential flood of obligations. Evidence of increased affordable housing finance, the thinking goes, will help appease Congress and give the agencies more breathing room on the capital issue.

Whatever the source of their activity, the agencies can be angels of mercy for financial institutions wary of carrying big mortgage portfolios on their books. As secondary market kingpins, Fannie and Freddie stand ready to buy portfolios from banks and thrifts, pool them, and sell them to investors, freeing up more capital for the housing finance market. Their influence is widely felt. Since its inception in 1970, for instance, Freddie Mac claims to have helped finance one in eight American homes and more than half a million apartment units. Fannie Mae buys mortgages from some 3,000 primary lenders across the nation.

Because of the quality restrictions historically placed on the mortgages that can be sold in the secondary market, neither has until quite recently bought many low-income housing loans from lenders. But they are starting to make up for lost time. Fannie Mae launched an ambitious low-income housing initiatives program in 1987, and Freddie Mac formed its own dedicated office in 1990. Fannie Mae, especially, has become a major cog in affordable housing programs that are local and national in scope.

Both corporations agreed in 1989 to take part in an ambitious affordable housing program launched by General Electric Capital Mortgage Insurance Companies, or GEMICO. Known as the Community Home Buyer's Program, the effort is designed to help less-affluent households qualify for home ownership by modifying underwriting guidelines and providing a home buyer education program.

Prompted in part by the desire to satisfy lenders' CRA requirements, the program began with four banks and two thrifts and within six months had grown to 130 institutions and more than $650 million in loan commitments, and to $900 million in commitments by October 1990. Fannie Mae and Freddie Mac said they would buy the mortgages from originators wishing to sell; for its part, GEMICO is insuring the loans, on which borrowers may be able to devote 33 percent of the monthly income for housing expenses. Fannie and Freddie also made unusual concessions, waiving customary requirements that borrowers must have cash reserves equal to two months of mortgage payments, and accepting payment records on rent and utilities toward the borrower's credit history.

General Electric has made home buyer education a cornerstone of the program. It has created an eight-hour course focusing on such topics as the economics of buying and owning a home, selection of a home, default, and foreclosure. While battalions of lenders have marched into the program, the push for the program actually came from community groups sitting down with Fannie Mae, Freddie Mac, and private mortgage insurers, said Allen Fishbein of the Center for Community Change.

In this segment of the home market the program "is a huge deal," Charles Riesenberg at First Bank System's community development corporation told *Mortgage Banking*. "These low- and moderate-income folks are first-time home buyers and they don't know anything [about buying a home]. . . This is an opportunity for mortgage bankers to get them into the market."

Talman Home Mortgage Corporation, for one. A unit of the Talman Home Federal, the big Illinois thrift, the mortgage banker is working with the program and an AHP grant to provide more than $5 million in loans to low-income homebuyers. With the grant money, and help from the Illinois Housing Authority, buyers can purchase homes at 8.5 percent fixed rates without any closing costs.

But for all the hullabaloo, the program has proven a slow starter. Only $13.5 million had been closed nationwide by September 1990, according to *Inside Mortgage Finance*. GEMICO chief executive Gregory Barmore said that the weak housing market was hurting originations, and that the people in the program may not have the wherewithal to build savings for a down payment. Martin Levine, Fannie Mae's vice president for low- and moderate-income housing, cited competition form the FHA and its 100 percent financing. "Certain underwriting features have been competition for the program," he told *Inside Mortgage Finance*.

Transforming affordable housing loans into securities marketed by the secondary agencies is easier said than done. "Current secondary market requirements and underwriting criteria may constrain the financing of affordable housing through securitization," the Federal Housing Finance Board acknowledged in a 1990 report. The board said it would pursue new initiatives in this area, but nonprofits like the Low Income Housing Fund in San Francisco are pushing the secondary market players to broaden their guidelines and make a major commitment to buying nonstandard loans.

Daniel M. Leibsohn, president of the Low Income Housing Fund, has proposed that Fannie Mae dedicate $150 million to $250 million to housing projects that are good risks but don't fit the agency's standard eligibility requirements, according to *National Mortgage News*. These could include nontraditional categories such as mixed single-family and multi-family projects.

Underwriting is a sore point with some neighborhood investment advocates, who imply that the preoccupation with the underwriting process has suppressed the secondary market; in turn, that has restricted banks' ability to lend. "I appreciate the need to standardize, but development project credit cannot be standardized," declared the Woodstock Institute's Jean Pogge.

Charles Grice, managing director of the Community Reinvestment Institute, said the scarcity of secondary market avenues is "the biggest problem we hear about" in community development lending. "I hear banks openly complaining about Fannie Mae not easing their pain" by increasing their liquidity, he said, adding that he believes the secondary market agencies could set up approximate standards that would unclog the pipeline. He added that his research group fields a lot of calls from public pension funds. "The markets are not any better for them."

At California's Savings Associations Mortgage Company (SAMCO), a long-established loan consortium, president Doris Schnider was negotiating late in 1990 with Fannie and Freddie with an eye to selling loans to either or both. Saying SAMCO's loans are "well seasoned"—the mortgage companies don't like their loans too green—she added, "It's becoming more attractive, as our volumes are increasing, to have a secondary market to enhance our program with lenders."

Kathy Kenny, deputy director with the San Francisco Development Fund, said she has heard one recipe for seasoning: that Fannie and Freddie prefer to wait until a project has been renting for six months to two years before buying the loan. That way, the cash flow has had a certain time to stabilize.

Fannie Mae Has a Say

Fannie Mae has compiled an impressive array of credits since its office of Low- and Moderate-Income Housing was launched in 1987, committing itself to provide more than $4 billion in specialized financings to assist more than 80,000 households by the summer of 1990.

The corporation put out a 234-page booklet in March 1990 describing its low-income initiatives in great detail. The programs are far too numerous to discuss here, but they fall into four basic categories: public finance activities, in which the corporation works with state and local housing finance agencies; community lending initiatives, in which Fannie Mae buys mortgages from lenders originating single-family and multifamily loans; rental housing equity investments; and a miscellaneous group of initiatives with nonprofits and trade groups attempting to generate more low-income housing. It is the lending linkages that will now be examined in some detail. Collectively, they provide ample opportunity for institutions interested in making community development loans but not keen in keeping them on their books.

Most of the community lending initiatives were local, involving nonprofits and lenders from those communities. Almost 90 percent (33) were aimed at single-family home loans, while 5 were dedicated to multifamily. All of the multifamily programs are at least regional, and two are nationwide. In one of those, Fannie Mae grants prior approval to lenders, then purchases first-lien multifamily mortgages, the proceeds of which are used to finance or refinance rehabilitation. In the second effort, known as Delegated Underwriting and Servicing, Fannie Mae buys multifamily loans ranging from $1 million to $50 million from approved lenders.

A number of nonlenders also participate in some of Fannie Mae's programs. In a home ownership program run by the Community Preservation Corporation, a loan consortium in New York that will be discussed in detail in the next chapter, the mortgages are originated by Norstar Mortgage Company and pooled by Fannie Mae; they are then sold as mortgage-backed securities to a consortium of life insurance companies. This way, developers are assured of permanent financing at a given rate at the time they begin work on a project.

In April 1990, Fannie Mae kicked off a program aimed at helping lenders by creating a similar type of mortgage-backed security for below-market loans. Thrift lenders obtaining below-market advances from their

Federal Home Loan Bank can make loans and then pool them into a "Fannie Mae Affordables" security. This instrument can be kept in the institution's portfolio or sold to the Federal Home Loan Bank to repay the advance. These funds are being tied to the Affordable Housing Program and Community Investment Program covered in the previous section on thrifts' role in affordable housing. In fact, Tom Marder, a spokesman for Fannie Mae, said that the Fannie Mae Affordables program was used in 20 to 25 of the first 100 programs funded under the first round of the 1990 AHP effort.

Ordinarily, assets originated at below-market rates can't be traded at face value. But assurances that the Federal Home Loan Banks will buy back the securities at par will be a real inducement to lenders, said officials familiar with the program. Eligible mortgages are similar to those in the GEMICO program—15- to 30-year fixed loans with a loan-to-value ratio up to 95 percent.

Some lenders in the program foresee solid servicing profits and only an average default rate. "These loans are just as profitable as regular mortgages," Wayne Ferguson, a vice president at Boston Five Cents Savings Bank, told *American Banker*. He said the program should enable the thrift to boost its origination of low-cost loans.

Fannie Mae also has kicked in to a number of local housing programs. In Burlington, Vermont, for instance, Fannie Mae contributed $3 million and took a role as a limited partner in a nonprofit community housing project after the Bank of Vermont put up $500,000 in equity for its own limited partner role. In 1989, Fannie Mae agreed to buy $5 million in home loans from South Shore Bank in Chicago; the mortgages were issued to lower-income residents of the distressed Austin neighborhood. South Shore continues to service the loans.

Bank of America, in an innovative and widely publicized program launched in summer 1990, expanded its affordable housing program to include fixed-rate loans in lower-income communities. The bank even went so far as to identify its target areas by ZIP code and census tracts—a sort of reverse redlining. But what made the program possible was an agreement that Fannie Mae would buy up to $250 million of these loans for sale in the secondary market.

"It's the first geographically targeted lending program in the West, and that does make it unique," Marder told *American Banker*. "We're happy that we helped them do the deal."

Bank of America's Donald J. Mullane told a 1990 CRA conference that "we have a sense that we can do substantially more than $250 million in a three-year time frame." He added, "That has got to be a very profitable service for us. And we're filling a need."

In New York, Fannie Mae is one of the partners in an unusual mortgage securities program that will help two lenders do a great deal of business in moderate-income neighborhoods. The securities, up to $100 million, will be issued by Fannie Mae to back loans originated by Norstar Mortgage Company and Manhattan Savings Bank. The most striking aspect of the arrangement is the buyer of the securities: the New York City Employee Retirement System, the city's largest employee pension fund.

In actuality, the two lenders will buy mortgage insurance from the New York City Rehabilitation Mortgage Insurance Corporation and exchange the loans for Fannie Mae securities. They will then sell the securities to the city pension fund. The pension fund said it hopes the program will make home ownership possible for 1,000 families. Eligible borrowers will be offered loans with as little as 5 percent down. "We hope this program will serve as a model for similar initiatives with pension funds throughout the nation," said Martin D. Levine, a Fannie Mae vice president.

Fannie Mae's role as a limited partner in rental housing developments is helping push construction of more than two dozen projects across the country. Some of these also involve local lenders and nonprofits, as well as local or state governments.

In Lowell, Massachusetts, for example, a 19-year-old, 265-unit complex is being converted into a townhouse and garden-style development, with a certain proportion set aside for rental by low-income families. Fannie Mae, which has committed to a $5.7 million equity investment, is one of two limited partners in the project being developed by the Coalition for a Better Acre Incorporated, a local nonprofit. Financing is coming from two area lenders, Bank of New England and Shawmut Bank, as well as other private and government sources, including HUD and the Commonwealth of Massachusetts. With its investment, Fannie Mae qualifies for low-income housing tax credits.

In addition, Fannie Mae is working with nonprofits such as the National Community Development Association and trade groups such as the Mortgage Bankers Association and the National Association of Home Builders in demonstration projects tied to affordable housing. While Fannie Mae's role in these efforts varies, in general it is committing to buying mortgages originated by participating lenders.

Freddie Mac's Commitment

Not content with a passive role in affordable housing, Freddie Mac has made a series of investments in low-income initiatives and taken a much more public stance than in years past. Recognizing the congressional scrutiny the corporation is under and the political sway that social initiatives have in the current Congress, some cynics may question Freddie Mac's impetus as new-found religion.

But the answer may be in the tenor of the times, which clearly is pushing lenders and loan buyers down the economic ladder. In June 1990, Freddie Mac named a First Boston Corporation official, Carl W. Riedy, Jr., as a vice president to head its affordable-housing initiatives department. The department's mission: to consolidate and boost Freddie Mac's efforts to invest in low-cost housing and to buy home loans extended to lower-income individuals.

"We intend to play a much more active role" in financing affordable housing, Riedy said not long after his arrival. His own philosophy, he said, is that "there is no single solution, no free lunch, and no magical program. To achieve our goals, partnerships are necessary, as resources and risk must be shared."

But Freddie's efforts are tied to economic realities, and the corporation's commitment has been questioned in the wake of a decision spurred by the national contagion of real estate troubles. Freddie suspended its cash purchases of multifamily housing loans late in 1990, a move aimed at slowing a growing wave of delinquencies. A spokesman for the Mortgage Bankers Association of America told American Banker that the industry was "outraged" by the move, but Freddie Mac said the cash purchases—usually used for newly originated loans, while more seasoned loans are securitized—represented just 15 percent of its multifamily transactions in 1990.

A prominent researcher in the CRA field argued early in 1991 that Freddie Mac "is more or less disbanding" a lot of its low-income housing support programs. "They have no appetite to get into this at all. They're so gun-shy now," he said.

But if the near-term future is shaky, Freddie has shown a willingness to get involved with some innovative projects—a fact that institutions should not lose sight of. And publicly, the agency still insists that widening housing availability for low- and moderate-income families "is a critical part of Freddie Mac's mission."

Among the programs Freddie has taken on were:

• Tiered-payment mortgages, which Freddie Mac began securitizing in 1989. Available from a wide range of lenders, these provide borrowerswith the benefits of conventional, fixed-rate mortgages with low initial payments and without negative amortization. Freddie's willingness to securitize such loans is a major inducement for lenders to make them.

• A major mortgage-purchase commitment began October 1, 1990, in Michigan, where Freddie Mac has agreed to buy up to $500 million in mortgages originated by lenders participating in the Freddie Mac Seller/Servicers program in the state. Mortgage insurance is being provided by private mortgage insurers, and up to 10,000 borrowers are expected to be served. Monthly income and debt-to-income ratios have been adjusted to help would-be borrowers qualify.

• Offering mortgage credit certificates to lower-income homebuyers. In a program initiated with the Rhode Island Housing agency, Freddie Mac offers these as tax credits that reduce the amount of federal income taxes withheld from a first-time homebuyers' pay. The additional take-home income helps the buyer meet regular mortgage payments. Lenders treat the credits as income.

Freddie Mac also has invested a lot of effort toward buying multifamily loans on properties that rent below market rates. The deals take a number of forms, according to officials at the corporation. In Jasper, Missouri, for instance, a $2.7 million mortgage was preapproved by Freddie Mac and used to finance a low-income apartment complex for 176 needy families. In Whittier, California, a $3.4 million mortgage sold to Freddie Mac helped finance an 89-unit senior citizens complex that is in turn subsidized by the Department of Housing and Urban Development's Section 8 rental Assistance Program. And in Dallas, the corporation helped turn an apartment complex near a hospital into housing for low-income people with AIDS.

Freddie Mac also has been talking with nonprofits and lenders about developing mortgage-backed securities containing a higher-than-normal mix of loans from disadvantaged areas. Buying such a security would provide an incentive for investing in poorer neighborhoods and could signal an increased commitment to affordable housing—meaning that institutions buying such securities could use them to enhance their CRA records.

Other Secondary Market Players

In part because of the difficulties lenders have faced in selling their low-income loans, a handful of new entities have emerged to provide a secondary market for affordable housing loans. None is remotely the size of Fannie or Freddie, but they are doing their part, and lenders should take note of them.

Two major pension funds in New York City, for instance, have bought large blocks of mortgage loans from the Community Preservation Corporation. President Michael D. Lappin said that while insurance companies seem to prefer the security of dealing with Fannie and Freddie, "We've done very little work with [the secondary mortgage companies]. They're difficult to work with because they don't understand local concerns."

Among the larger of the lesser secondary players is the Local Initiatives Managed Assets Corporation, or LIMAC, an offshoot of the nonprofit Local Initiatives Support Corporation formed in 1987. LIMAC buys and securitizes loans made by community development lenders; it also securitizes commercial real estate and mixed-use projects. Its first issue, for $10.5 million in 10-year bonds, was heavily subscribed by insurance companies. LIMAC activity has helped expand local LISC capabilities in half a dozen cities, LISC officials said.

LIMAC has been set up to purchase bridge and gap loans, and was recently working with Freddie Mac on a $100 million demonstration project in which LIMAC would buy and assemble pools that would be swapped for Freddie Mac securities.

A smaller secondary market has been formed by the Neighborhood Housing Services Association (NHSA), a spin-off of the nonprofit Neighborhood Reinvestment Corporation. NHSA had bought some $37 million in housing loans from local Neighborhood Housing Services chapters by 1990 and sold them to insurance companies and philanthropic groups at below-market costs; it acquired 331 loans totaling more than $5.1 million in fiscal 1989 and has bought more than 3,300 since 1976. These purchases boost the assets of the revolving funds in the Neighborhood Housing Service network.

The secondary market deals also help make projects doable. In Kansas City, for instance, NHSA provided gap financing for a 47-unit rental apartment complex for the elderly; by buying $300,000 in loans, it enabled the $2.6 million project to be completed.

Insurance companies are a good market for far more than the NHSA loans; they offer a major source of permanent financing at attractive interest rates, according to American Security's Karen Kollias. Given the reserves and the way they are regulated, she said, insurers can offer longer-term investments than banks or thrifts, and their lower cost of funds enables them to offer long-term fixed-rate mortgages, something lenders are not always eager to do. Aetna Life & Casualty, for instance, has had a neighborhood reinvestment program in force for more than a decade. It provides permanent mortgages on projects housing low- and moderate-income families, but some conditions apply. A local bank or thrift must make the construction loan, and the project must have a nonprofit as a sponsor or partner of the developer or as the developer itself.

Kollias said such ventures expose banks to some of the basic components of community development—public subsidies and nonprofit sponsors. A bank "also has an incentive to participate since Aetna has already committed its permanent loan, which eliminates the bank's risk in having to hold onto, or 'portfolio,' a loan it might not be able to sell to the secondary market," Kollias noted.

Another potential secondary market are state housing finance agencies, a number of which have long been active in issuing mortgage revenue bonds for low-income housing. SAMCO's Doris Schnider, for instance, said she has been talking with the California Housing Finance Agency about a secondary mortgage program in which the agency "would take us out with tax-exempt financing" once a construction loan had been made.

Housing-related lending is expected to remain the foremost means for financial institutions to perform community reinvestment. An increasingly popular method of delivering those loans involves pools and consortiums that spread risks, pare costs, and leverage the impact of individual bank and thrift loans.

CHAPTER 5

CONSORTIUMS AND GROUP INITIATIVES

THE GRANDFATHERS THRIVE

A few organizations have been pooling lending money or collecting equity stakes for low-income housing and community development for more than a decade—some even before the Community Reinvestment Act arrived in 1977. Just as South Shore Bank has been a model for lenders, these nonprofit consortiums and intermediaries are the beacons that have lit the path for others who have set out in the past few years.

Officials with these consortiums freely concede that CRA is the energizing force behind much of the recent activity, even at their own shops. But they don't see themselves as being in business to satisfy CRA requirements; if participating banks are motivated chiefly by compliance concerns, so be it. The more participants, the more money that flows to the consortiums and the more projects the nonprofits can take on.

Each of the consortiums examined in this section are grandfathers in terms of relative age. But don't look for any infirmities; they are flourishing, at least according to the numbers. Institutional interest and lending are at all-time highs, and their leaders have been important resource people in the movement to create more public-private partnerships for community development. And there will be more. Hundreds of banks and thrifts are expected to sign on to such ventures in the next few years.

The Community Preservation Corporation

Established in 1974, when a fiscal crisis was shaking New York, the Community Preservation Corporation (CPC) has compiled a glowing record through bad times and good. As of mid-1990, it had been responsible for creating more than 26,000 housing units worth more than $750 million, with virtually no defaults. Its chief executive, Michael D. Lappin, said he could recall only one project that defaulted, forcing the corporation to go to a mortgage insurer to collect.

CPC had a strong history of lender involvement from the outset. It was born following a study by the New York Clearing House Association banks looking for ways to arrest the abandonment that was racing through the city's poorer sections. Specifically, the banks wanted to explore a partnership with government to halt the deterioration. They were joined not long afterward by the Savings Banks Association of New York State.

The resulting corporation was built on a strong foundation—commitment from the city of New York and a large group of the city's biggest commercial banks and savings institutions. The initial leadership of David Rockefeller, then head of Chase Manhattan Bank, gave the CPC a lot of credibility from the outset. But it was the idea, and not just the personalities, that clicked. CPC was set up as an independent not-for-profit entity supported by 39 institutions. It would lend money under its own authority with the aid of two credit lines, one for secured construction loans, the other hinging on an agreement by lenders to purchase notes secured by long-term mortgages made by CPC.

As a bridge between the financial community and government, CPC has worked with the latter to overcome the regulatory and program hurdles that impeded investment. It also has given government an understanding of what was needed to spur private investment. In turn, CPC has provided institutions with a font of information about workable public programs and how they could lend to the affordable housing market. Not surprisingly, then, CPC has been examined closely by others around the country interested in setting up consortiums to work with small developers.

That market "tends to be anticompetitive" because of its complexity, Lappin said. Several different government programs are often combined to create affordable housing, including tax-reduction and rent-increase programs needed to provide incentives for development. "We created the market," Lappin said flatly. "We brought in borrowers who had never been to a bank before."

CPC didn't lure borrowers by offering "gimme" rates. It has generally charged borrowers the prime rate plus two and a half points, plus a one-point commitment fee, Lappin said. With the lack of competition in the market, "we didn't have to shave rates." Still, the corporation has had as many as 25 bidders for six-month development projects, he said.

As it has evolved, CPC has brought in additional investors outside the banking community. In 1984, for instance, two major New York City employee pension funds agreed to invest up to 2 percent of their assets in CPC loans, and by mid-1990 CPC had $550 million in pension fund investments, Lappin said—far more than the $195 million committed by banks and thrifts. In a recent report, CPC said it sells almost all its loans to pension funds.

Seven major insurers also agreed in 1986 to forward-commit to buy $100 million of Fannie Mae pass-through securities backed by loans of affordable homes and condominiums financed by CPC and others. "We have more long-term investors than we need now," Lappin said, adding that the availability of public mortgage insurance has been a key to luring these big investors. Indeed, almost all permanent mortgages made through CPC are partially insured with one of two New York State mortgage agencies, and all loans sold to the city pension funds are 100 percent insured.

Banks and thrifts contribute to the credit lines in sums proportional to their asset size. While a credit committee of bank and thrift executives reviews the loans, Lappin paints the contributions as very hands-off investments. "The banks do nothing but lend us the money," he said. When they have tried to serve the low-income housing market themselves, they have stumbled, he said. And while CPC rules offer institutions a chance to opt out of the construction credit every five years, none had done so by 1990.

The mechanics of the funding are worth noting, for they involve much more than institutions dumping money into a kitty. Under a revolving credit agreement with lenders, the CPC is to receive up to $52 million through January 31, 1993, for financing these construction loans. The notes bear interest at the prime lending rate of the agent bank, and no compensating balances are required; in 1988–1989, rates ranged from 8.25 percent to 11.5 percent.

CPC is the principal private lender in the city's 10-year plan to revitalize vacant buildings, and the $200 million in loans contemplated in 1990 created its biggest year ever, far above 1989's $133 million. With its success, the corporation has expanded to six counties outside the city. Asked about the difference between its program in blighted inner-city neighborhoods and more rural areas, Lappin said, "We have no agenda on affordable housing. It means different things in different communities."

It may have no agenda, but CPC has provided plenty of advice for others. "To duplicate CPC's success, local communities must rationalize their low- and moderate-income development processes and programs," the corporation said in its latest annual report. "At the same time, investments made to finance such projects must have access to long-term financing, principally through the secondary mortgage markets."

The Windy City has long had the sails of community development filled by a steady breeze of bank-led consortium lending. The vehicle is the Community Investment Corporation (CIC) in Chicago, established in 1984. Like CPC, CIC originates and services loans financed by collateral trust notes bought by member institutions; the notes are secured by mortgages. As in New York, bank and thrift representatives serve as the CIC's board and on its loan review committee, and the corporation uses city, state, or federal subsidy programs to keep rents affordable.

The CIC, which had 36 Chicago-area banks and thrifts as members in 1990, concentrates on rehabilitation of multifamily properties. In tandem with city loans, in its first six years it generated $112 million in financing, enough for more than 7,000 units.

Signing up for SAMCO

The Savings Associations Mortgage Company in California, better known as SAMCO, predates even the CPC. Launched in 1971 by 11 savings institutions, it had grown to 52 members at year-end 1989 and 87 by December 1990. Asked about the recent membership spurt, President Doris Schnider conceded, "I would say the driving force is CRA." In announcing one new member, she said its arrival "demonstrates the credibility we have in the financial community in providing an efficient means of meeting CRA requirements."

As the lines between banks and thrifts have blurred and the savings industry continues to shrink, SAMCO has agreed to accept commercial bank participation. It admitted its first bank, Columbia National Bank in Santa Monica, in the spring of 1990, and added several more later in the year. One was Mitsui Manufacturers, the Los Angeles bank whose CRA travails have been related in an earlier chapter. "SAMCO offers Mitsui the flexibility to choose projects to fund through California, while enabling us to earn CRA credit for participation in its loan projects," said Jerry W. Johnston, the bank's president and chief executive.

Like CPC, SAMCO's lending just keeps growing. It had made $251 million in loans in its history through October 1990, Schnider said, with $40 million of that in 1989 and $51 million in the first 10 months of 1990. All of that is tied to housing, and at least 51 percent of its projects must be dedicated to low- or moderate-income affordability. The corporation has been making multifamily loans since 1980 with absolutely no delinquencies, she said.

Participating lenders have the right, as SAMCO is doing its underwriting, to direct their loans. "We put the projects out for sale, and they can pick and choose which ones they want to lend to," Schnider says. "Most of them like it that way. The comments we get from lenders indicate that they want to be involved in where they're lending."

Among the participants are the state's largest thrifts, including Home Savings of America, American Savings, First Nationwide Bank, and Great Western. Schnider allows that the California Community Reinvestment Corporation, a recently formed bank consortium that will be discussed in the next section, is competition. But the thrift group is holding its own. "Fortunately for SAMCO, we've been around so long that people come to us," she said. "SAMCO has become a focus for a lot of our members," agreed John Hartnett of the California League of Savings Institutions.

SAMCO "has become an excellent conduit through which substantial contributions to community reinvestment are made [by] member associations," said Great Western in its Community Reinvestment Act Statement. The thrift said it gave $3.8 million to the consortium in 1989 and well over $20 million since 1977. First Nationwide has been involved in SAMCO's management and also had purchased more than $20 million in loan participations.

Neighborhood Housing Services

An umbrella of local public-private partnerships under the aegis of the Neighborhood Reinvestment Corporation, a nonprofit chartered by Congress in 1978, Neighborhood Housing Services is truly a national organization. The network of some 270 NHS partnerships has spread to more than 140 different cities, towns, and counties in 43 states and the District of Columbia. More than half of those living in its collective neighborhoods, with more than 3 million residents, are minorities.

Unlike CPC or SAMCO, NHS is not a consortium essentially financed by lenders. It is a network than relies heavily on public monies from municipal authorities and federal grant programs, and its members are locally funded and operated—self-help organizations that rely as much on community residents and local government as they do on financial institutions. This framework may be a bit more daunting for lenders than a CPC, but the opportunities for their input are significant. Consider the Neighborhood Reinvestment Corporation's board of directors, which includes high-ranking officials from the Federal Reserve Board, Comptroller of the Currency, Federal Deposit Insurance Corporation, and National Credit Union Administration.

Through 1989, NHS members had rung up some impressive numbers, triggering a cumulative $6.6 billion in reinvestment, making more than 22,000 below-market loans totaling more than $200 million, doing almost $2.7 billion in conventional lending and $147 million in commercial reinvestment, and taking credit for 96,000 housing units built or rehabilitated. In 1989 alone, nearly 23,000 homes were rehabilitated through 220 NHS partnerships. NHS also has a secondary market, the Neighborhood Housing Services Association, that was discussed in the previous chapter.

NHS helps steer residents who do meet conventional credit requirements to participating lenders—a considerable source of potential business. Residents who do not qualify may receive a loan from NHS's revolving loan fund, capitalized by contributions from banks and other corporations, local governments and foundations, and the Neighborhood Reinvestment Corporation. Contributions from more than 2,000 institutions and local governments added up to more than $30 million in 1989.

Increasing the flow of capital to its neighborhoods amounts to a multifaceted effort "that means examining the nuts and bolts at various points—marketing the neighborhood, sound underwriting at local institutions, creative use of the revolving loan funds, and working with downstream institutions such as the secondary markets and the security purchasers," said George Knight, executive director of the Neighborhood Reinvestment Corporation. A memo to members from the Federal Home Loan Bank of Atlanta notes that among the eligible activities for its Community Investment Fund program are two affiliated NRC programs, the Apartment Improvement Program and Mutual Housing Associations.

In New York City, where there are a half-dozen NHS partnerships serving all of the city's five boroughs, 13 banks and thrifts were signed up for the Citywide Loan Program, which will provide up to $5 million in financing for loans to mixed-use and multifamily properties with up to 20 units. The program's principal aims: remedying deferred maintenance in poorer neighborhoods and providing special financing opportunities for small business and property owners seeking to upgrade their commercial and retail space. Up to $100,000 can be borrowed for moderate rehabilitation, and up to 80 percent of value may be borrowed for more extensive rehab work; rates will float up to 2 percent over prime during the construction period, and be fixed at 2 percent above prime at the closing date of a 5- to 10-year repayment loan.

Here again is evidence of extensive lending activity in disadvantaged areas being undertaken at market rates. NHS is a nonprofit, but it is not flinging money with submarginal returns toward risky borrowers as part of a charity effort. The rehab program, NHS said in a brochure, aims to bridge "a serious credit gap for loans from conventional lenders who use standard underwriting criteria."

Another New York NHS program is being financed by IBJ Schroder Bank and Trust Company, a wholesale bank with a Japanese parent. Schroder agreed in 1990 to commit $500,000 to NHS for a revolving loan fund for credits at below-market rates; through this, NHS will extend loans to low- and moderate-income residents at rates between 3 percent and 8 percent. NHS said it hoped the program would "provide an avenue for other wholesale banks to increase their participation in the partnership."

In New York as of 1990, NHS had loaned more than $5 million directly, packaged more than $12 million in government loans, and stimulated more than $227 million in reinvestment. Delinquency rates were running only about 5 percent, and the average loan was in the range of $9,000 to $10,000, according to executive director Francine Justa. But banks, with 19 percent, and thrifts, with just 4 percent, were hardly in the limelight among the cast of contributors to NHS of New York City in 1982–89. The public sector gave 32 percent, for instance, and insurance firms 18 percent.

Still, local lenders have come out foursquare for the NHS concept. "We can all pay a little now to NHS and keep people in their improved homes, or we can pay a lot later for all the costs of homelessness and blighted neighborhoods," said James M. Large, Jr., chairman and CEO of Anchor Savings Bank. "The reasoning behind the NHS effort is aimed at a problem that isn't going to go away anytime soon—the crucial need in America's cities for affordable housing," said Richard Braddock, president of Citibank. "We prefer to describe such initiatives as enlightened self-interest."

Bank One in Columbus, Ohio, is another lender pleased with its association with NHS. It provided $284,000 for acquisition and a major portion of the rehabilitation of two abandoned buildings bought by Columbus NHS. The two buildings had been vacant for more than a decade. They are being converted to apartment units, four of them specifically for use by the handicapped. "We look forward to future projects with CNHS," said Ron Newsome, an assistant vice president at the bank.

Local Initiatives Support Corporation

Another nonprofit usually shortened to its initials, LISC, this New York-based corporation is a more complex entity than the others examined here. Two of its major arms, the National Equity Fund and the Local Initiatives Managed Assets Corporation, will be discussed elsewhere in the book under low-income tax credits and secondary market players, respectively. But LISC itself is responsible for assembling funds from corporations—including banks and thrifts—and leveraging them through investments in nonprofit community development corporations and public-private partnerships doing both affordable housing and economic development around the country.

LISC, formed in 1979, bills itself as the largest private nonprofit development intermediary in the nation. In its 1990 report, the corporation said it had helped CDCs finance 21,500 units of affordable housing and 5.5 million square feet of commercial space throughout the nation. Like the CPC, it provides financial and technical assistance that helps ensure the viability of community-based projects by small developers.

In its own words, LISC "operates as a social investment banker." Its repertoire includes loans, grants, equity, and gap financing for high-risk projects. Far and away the greatest portion of its investments are in the form of equity investments, mostly through the NEF and two related funds covered in the next section. Those totaled almost $79 million in 1989, compared to $13 million for loans and guarantees and $6 million for grants.

Sometimes LISC will work in partnerships involving lenders in one of its 23 principal service areas around the country. In Washington, D.C., and Seattle, for example, LISC is working with government, foundations, and a number of local lenders in "HomeSight," a program aimed at making home ownership possible for low-income families.

To further New York City's Housing Production Program, the Dime Savings Bank has loaned LISC $500,000 for CDC projects' predevelopment costs and invested an additional $3 million in the National Equity Fund. "LISC's leveraged dollars mean our financing has a far enhanced impact," said Ellen Nathanson, first vice president and community affairs officer at the Dime.

In Dade County, Florida, a small group of lenders that includes Great Western Bank is creating a revolving loan fund that will work with LISC money to finance redevelopment projects. Over three years, the partners aim to generate $2.1 million in funding.

In Ohio, Bank One Cleveland kicked in support for a $114,000 loan to a 12,000-foot shopping center in a poor area in southeast Cleveland. The project was financed by LISC with an assortment of other partners, including foundations, the city government, and a major oil company.

National Housing Partnership

Dating back to 1970, the NHP is among the oldest public-private housing partnership ideas around. It is the largest apartment owner; according to the corporation's 1990 annual report, it claimed to own, as a general partner, 60,000 units subsidized by the federal government, more than any other owner.

Like the other intermediaries mentioned earlier, the NHP gets much of its support from private corporations, including financial institutions. In 1990, it listed 18 commercial banks and thrifts among the corporate stockholders of NHP Inc., the holding company. It also had a revolving credit line of $30 million with various banks in 1990, with receivables from housing partnership investors pledged as collateral. Interest rates were pegged to prime, certificate of deposit plus 1 percent, or LIBOR plus 1 percent—rates that clearly were not below-market "loss leaders." In using the line, NHP must maintain certain financial ratios, its report noted. The company also has commitments for unsecured lines of credit from lenders, up to $47.4 million.

NHP also enters into joint ventures with financial institutions. It did so in 1989–90 in Washington metropolitan area with Virginia's Signet Bank in a $56 million construction refinancing, and with Maryland National Bank for "favorable" financing and an equity package for another housing project.

Momentum in Maryland

Not quite as hoary as some of the other consortiums discussed here, the Development Credit Fund in Maryland offers one of the more intriguing models that other banks might consider emulating. Set up in 1982, the DCF is a multibank nonprofit established specifically to provide credit to "socially and economically disadvantaged" business people in the state. As such, it shows that multibank consortiums can work with small business development as well as housing.

Participating banks have included Maryland National Bank and Equitable Bank (acquired recently by Maryland National), First National Bank of Maryland, Mercantile Safe-Deposit and Trust Company, Sovran Bank-Maryland, and Union Trust Bank. The banks initially committed $7.5 million a year for three years in a revolving loan pool, according to the Comptroller of the Currency's "Community Development Finance" publication.

The State of Maryland has proven a valuable ally. Its Small Business Development Finance Agency kicked in $2.5 million over the same period to capitalize a revolving loan fund and guarantee the DCF loans, the Comptroller's publication noted. The City of Baltimore also provided an initial grant to help defray the DCF's expenses. Such backstop funding from government may not always be available, but banks and thrifts should leave no stones unturned in the hunt for public partners for community development programs.

In the first years of the program, loans going to working capital or machinery and equipment ranged from $5,000 to $500,000 and were set at a top rate of prime plus 1 percent; they have been 80 percent guaranteed by the state development finance agency. Late in 1988, the DCF got authority from the Small Business Administration to use SBA's guaranteed loan program. That enabled the fund to up its maximum loan to $750,000.

Another Maryland nonprofit, often compared to LISC, deserves mention here. The Enterprise Foundation, formed in 1982, organizes and supports locally based nonprofits involved in housing rehabilitation. Much like LISC, it offers small grants and low-interest loans to needy groups and assists neighborhood groups in finding additional financing. Thanks to professionals on its staff, it provides advice on design and construction techniques that can help small developers save money. It, too, has worked with banks and thrifts to create additional housing, particularly through the low-income housing tax credit program discussed later in this chapter.

REGIONAL INITIATIVES: SPREADING THE RISK

The success of consortiums like the CPC and SAMCO, coupled with mounting CRA pressures, has sparked a number of regional efforts. Most of them have been formed quite recently; some are still being pieced together. Again, there is little in the way of heroic individual initiative required from the banks or thrifts that take part. These pools are relatively painless ways of spreading their own risk and satisfying part of their CRA requirements by making money available for professional staff to administer and disseminate.

The impetus for these efforts has varied. Some has been spawned by trade groups, like the Massachusetts Bankers Association effort that will be examined shortly or a loan pool organized by the Washington (D.C.) Bankers Association. Other programs were set up by institutions that saw the collective benefit of joining hands and leveraging what any of them could do individually. A group of some three dozen pools are largely divorced from bank sponsorship. Known as community development loan funds, most are being run by social activists bent on generating seed money for business development in troubled neighborhoods.

The CCRC

Perhaps the largest and best known of these fledgling pools is the California Community Reinvestment Corporation, or CCRC. Formed late in 1989, it brought together 46 commercial banks that pledged a total of $100 million to finance low-income multifamily housing in the state. The state's four largest banks are represented, as are a host of small institutions.

Properties eligible for CCRC funding must have at least five units. While the executive director, Daniel Lopez, and a handful of staffers do the outreach efforts and the screening of projects, the actual commitment of funds is made only after approval by a loan committee—the same process that takes place with the Community Preservation Corporation. The loan limit is $15 million.

The CCRC concentrates on take-out financing, providing permanent fixed-rate loans, and only 51 percent of the units need be affordable to low-income households. Loans are being made through the consortium to nonprofit and for-profit developers, and the CCRC aims to sell its loans in the secondary market to boost liquidity. In its first fiscal year, which ended in September 1990, the consortium committed some $33 million in loans. One California banker said that permanent financing of multifamily housing was a logical focal point. Historically, he said, it is "an area none of the major banks did well."

As chairman, the CCRC has a highly visible banker, Donald Mullane of Bank of America. Mullane is an executive vice president and head of $18 corporate community development at the bank, which is contributing about million toward the pool. (As loans are approved, commitments are drawn in proportion to the size of each participating bank.) Mullane said that member institutions will have the chance to advocate—and participate in—their own local projects; he told a CRA conference in 1990 that community banks can set up subpools within the main pool. Borrego Springs Bank might serve as the agent for five other tiny banks, he said, noting that some participations could be as small as $1,000.

The ability of Lilliputian banks to make their voices heard will assuage the fears of many that their funds could be targeted for projects far outside their communities, said attorney Mark Aldrich, principal of the Bank Compliance Group in Irvine, California.

Some other concerns have been voiced. "I think [the CCRC] made a mistake when they decided not to get into construction loans, so as not to restructure the marketplace," said the CPC's Lappin. "That means they can't routinize lending." In his view, "They're more responding to advocacy groups, without thinking the process through." He also faults the CCRC for not using a state mortgage insurance program from the outset to make its loans more appealing to long-term investors.

But the CCRC did develop its underwriting criteria to be consistent with Fannie Mae guidelines, said John Trauth, director of the San Francisco Development Fund, the nonprofit firm that helped shape the CCRC. He added that the consortium plans to package its loans and sell them as mortgage-backed securities, with Fannie Mae as a credit enhancer.

While the Federal Reserve Bank of San Francisco was a major behind-the-scenes player in the formation of the CCRC, those familiar with the effort give a heap of credit to the Development Fund. And the firm is spreading the gospel, working with lenders groups to set up pools in Florida, Hawaii, Washington state, and Nevada. Some of these consortia are likely to involve thrifts as well as banks.

The Florida consortium will be made up of lenders in the greater Orlando area seeking to pool $50 million for affordable housing, said Kathy Kenny, deputy director at the San Francisco fund. It was expected to be operational by early 1991. The other pools were not as far along, she said, noting that it generally takes 9 to 10 months to complete the operating structure and turn on the loan spigots.

Kenny gives considerable credit to lenders for making the pools come together. The organizing usually starts with a task force of local chief executives, she said, who put committees together to determine policies and assess credit needs. "Each of the lenders put in tons of hours" to help the CCRC get off the ground, she said.

While affordable housing is the focal point of the pools the Development Fund is advising, the California Bankers Association has been making noises about a similar type of effort to spur economic development. "A lot of banks don't do mortgage financing," said Larry Kurmel, executive director of the California Bankers Association. "They're really commercially oriented institutions. So we're looking at creating a device similar to CCRC that would do targeted economic development." Such a program would be set up and operated by the association, he added.

Complications in Atlanta

Another highly publicized loan consortium was set up by 11 major banks and thrifts in Atlanta. Known as the Atlanta Mortgage Consortium, it was launched in mid-1988, shortly after the Atlanta Constitution startled the city, and the nation, with its extensive series of articles examining an apparent racial bias in mortgage lending. As of late 1990, it had grown to 13 banks and 9 thrifts.

That intense national spotlight had a lasting impact on the ensuing Atlanta initiative, bankers and regulators agree. Rushed into operation, the program offered $20 million in the first year and $24 million in the second to low-income borrowers at terms that proved more than merely concessionary. The ratios used to qualify borrowers were so liberal, some regulators say, that many new homeowners could be in over their heads. In fact, the ratios were scaled back in the second year after troubles mushroomed during the first months of the original program. What the Atlanta experience underscores is the notion that the best intentions don't always make for the right results. It is a good object lesson in not rushing into any program without careful groundwork.

In an effort to qualify more people—and to mollify community activists—the banks raised their "back ratio" from 42 percent to 50 percent. This meant that would-be borrowers were able to get loans that committed 50 percent of their gross incomes to house payments and other debt obligations, well above the 33–36 percent lenders usually stipulate. The liberalized standard "was more of a political thing than anything else," James C. Mynatt, a first vice president at Trust Company Bank, told *Southern Banker*. But with it, many AMC borrowers, already burdened with car payments and installment debt, just couldn't make ends meet.

As of mid-1990, more than 9 percent of the loans made under the AMC program were delinquent. A May 1990 study by Ronald Zimmerman, a vice president at the Federal Reserve Bank of Atlanta, found "many instances of credit deterioration," including repossessions, garnishments, and accounts turned over for collection. "How are you revitalizing a neighborhood if you're sucking all the discretionary income away from the people? We're out of our comfort zone on this lending criteria," Zimmerman told *Southern Banker*.

Moreover, Zimmerman said, by pricing its loans 100 to 200 basis points below prevailing market rates, the AMC had essentially made them unsalable in the secondary market. Too, the lenders had agreed to absorb all origination and closing costs. His conclusion, based on reviewing results from one of the banks, was that the AMC participants "appear to be losing money."

But returning the back ratio to 42 percent in the program's second funding year, while it made regulators more comfortable, angered community activists because it whittled down the number of qualified borrowers. "Now they've backed off and created a huge level of ill will in the low-income and advocacy community," Craig Taylor, a member of the consortium's board, told *Southern Banker*.

Regulators are seldom openly critical of community investment efforts, but Zimmerman didn't sugarcoat his findings. He concluded that "most people, including lenders, appear not to have given much thought to the logic behind" the ratios used to qualify borrowers. He added that a number of AMC borrowers could have obtained loans from conventional programs at market rates, meaning that "in effect, the AMC lenders underpriced their own conventional loan programs for these applicants."

Zimmerman acknowledged the difficulty of making conventional loans to low-income borrowers. At the time when the data for the Atlanta newspaper series was being gathered, "local and state authorities were offering more attractive home mortgage loans with below-market interest rates and more flexible lending terms" than were local banks. He added, with some irony, that "these programs were financed with proceeds from bonds purchased, for the most part, by local financial institutions."

One upshot of all the furor is that AMC lenders are casting about for more public or philanthropic participation to help ease their burden. That hasn't been easy. Bankers say that a limited number of experienced nonprofits in the Atlanta area, combined with a crazy quilt of local jurisdictions, have hurt efforts to put together the kind of public-private housing partnership programs found in cities like New York, Washington, or Chicago.

The Massachusetts Initiative

Several other regional consortiums were still in the formative stages in 1990. Perhaps the most ambitious was in Massachusetts, where the Massachusetts Bankers Association was leading a massive $1 billion statewide program to create more affordable housing, better access to banking services, and economic development funding.

This effort, announced early in 1990, wasn't born in a vacuum. The racial tension touched off by the Charles Stuart murder case was still running high, and community activists had been emboldened by a Federal Home Loan Bank of Boston study showing a pattern similar to Atlanta's— whites were far more likely than blacks to get mortgage loans. At the same time, New England was spiraling deeper into a recession, and real estate losses were snowballing at some of the state's largest banks. While the troubled economy might in the past have kept banks on the sidelines, they knew they had to act. "This is not an issue that will go away," said MBA spokesman Robert Fichter. "I'm happy to say that most bankers are taking it seriously."

Some 40 community groups, from Boston and around the state, had been talking and negotiating in earnest with bankers for seven months prior to the January 1990 announcement. "We learned their economic needs, and they learned about the realities of banking," said Richard F. Pollard, then chairman of the MBA. "These new programs respond directly to the needs they expressed, while recognizing our fiduciary responsibilities to our depositors and stockholders."

Plans call for the banks to generate some $465 million in loans and investments to create the $1 billion in economic activity. This investment will include separate efforts in affordable housing, minority business enterprise, and new branches and ATMs in poorer neighborhoods; the first two will be overseen by corporations, having community members and bankers as directors, that were established specifically for those purposes. This thoroughness, said consultant James Carras, attests to the level of sophistication among bankers and community leaders in the state.

To oversee affordable housing programs, the trade group created the Massachusetts Housing Investment Corporation, a not-for-profit loan pool committed to raising $100 million for purchase, rehabilitation, and new construction of rental, co-op, and single-room occupancy housing. A related entity, the Massachusetts Equity Fund, seeks to generate a similar amount in corporate equity in low-income tax credits, a concept that will be examined in the next section. In addition, 10 banks are participating in the Community Home Buyers Program set up by General Electric Mortgage Insurance and Fannie Mae, which began in Massachusetts in March 1990. Eventually, participating banks plan to make $100 million in loans to first-time home buyers through the program.

The Massachusetts Minority Enterprise Investment Corporation was created as a for-profit lending entity for minority small businesses. It is targeting loans from $2,500 to $250,000, and will be funded through lines of credit from member banks, who have also supplied initial capital.

The overall effort "will be the best example in the nation of a comprehensive approach" to solving the problems of minorities and low-income areas, said the MBA's Pollard. Brave words, certainly and a lot of eyes will be turned to Boston to watch how things develop. If the program meets many of its goals, it will almost certainly be widely emulated, though perhaps not on the same scale.

But the formula has raised some doubts. The degree of participation it gives community groups is certain to politicize the process, say skeptics. The CPC's Michael Lappin noted that his corporation has no public people on its board, just bankers. "We won't give money away and have it used as a political tool," he said. But in Massachusetts, a traditionally liberal state where political emotions run high, the notion of giving activists greater access to the economic levers has a certain inevitability—particularly at a time when society has begun to refocus on easing the burdens of its most disenfranchised.

New Seeds Are Planted

A number of affordable housing pools had more shape on paper than in reality late in 1990. One was being formed in upper New York State, where Fleet/Norstar and several other regional banks created the Community Lending Corporation to pool money for short- and long-term mortgage lending in communities between Buffalo and Albany.

Essentially, the CLC will try to replicate what the CPC is doing in New York City, with takedown lines for construction loans and permanent financing, said James P. Murphy, executive vice president and director of public policy and external relations at Fleet/Norstar. Norstar was the first bank to pledge a commitment and a capital infusion (respectively, $3 million and $35,000) to help the new organization set up headquarters and a staff.

Murphy said he expected that about 15 commercial banks and an equal number of thrifts would sign on for the CLC, with a goal of $90 million in short- and long-term lending money and a credit committee to oversee the loans. "They'll have to look to niches and work through them," Murphy said. "It's very doable, and they should focus on affordable housing, single-family as well as multifamily." The group's success, he added, may hinge on how well local initiatives can be hitched to the consortium's financing. Lending made through the consortium "will count for CRA, but most of the institutions that are involved won't have CRA problems," Murphy said.

Some pooling already is under way in upstate New York. Fifteen lenders in the Albany area have joined to provide $7.5 million in long-term and short-term financing for renovation, construction, and permanent financing of affordable housing units. In Syracuse, six lenders are offering $3.3 million in special financing for the purchase of rehabilitated homes; the city of Syracuse has a goal of rehabilitating or building 450 homes by 1992.

In California, where a tremendous amount of consortium activity is already under way, yet another group was being formed. The California Housing Partnership Corporation, a nonprofit set up by the state legislature, is seeking private corporate investment in low-income housing programs. Like the CPC in New York, the program aims to allow landlords to take part in subsidy programs that would raise rents to market rates.

A developing pool in North Carolina will, at least initially, involve only savings institutions. Created by the North Carolina League of Savings Institutions, the consortium is modeled after California's SAMCO, said Paul Stock, executive vice president and counsel of the league. He said that the SAMCO concept seems to work well for small institutions—most of the trade group's members are small thrifts—adding of SAMCO, "They will work until the underwriting can be properly done."

Stock said that the Community Investment Corporation of North Carolina would be capitalized and owned by the North Carolina League. Interested members would be asked to put up fees based on their asset size, but the numbers would be small, ranging from $1,000 to $2,500. While initial membership would be limited to members, the league has been considering a proposal to include community banks. "We may well decide that a broader base would be useful," he said.

Prior to creating the CIC, North Carolina thrifts had no access to loan pools, "unless they're doing it in their communities, with three of four getting together. But I think you could consider that more a participation than a pool," Stock said.

The leadership role taken by the associations in Massachusetts and North Carolina underscores the increasing activism of state trade groups. Some of that activism comes as a response to the shrinking roster of financial institutions, particularly thrifts, in recent years; with membership dues sliding, the associations must sell more services or find new ways to broaden participation. Community development experts expect that a number of state associations will follow suit in the next few years. As the chief link between lenders and the political arena, trade groups are well positioned to negotiate and carry out community investment initiatives.

Community Development Loan Funds

While outside the confines of consortiums organized by bankers, community development loan funds represent a growing resource for partnership efforts to reach lower-income neighborhoods. Spread around the country, most are very small intermediaries funneling capital to their home communities or states; the total funds being managed in 1990 was $60 million.

The bulk of the CDLFs, which date back to 1969, have a focus on housing, but others were organized to fund small business, and some do both. A few, such as the Low-Income Housing Fund in San Francisco and the McAuley Institute in Silver Spring, Maryland, have a national scope. Some work with as few as a handful or even just one lender, while others, like the Fund for an Open Society in Philadelphia with 547, list hundreds of participating lenders.

The National Association of Community Development Loan Funds, a resource and education center serving the funds, was launched late in 1989 and listed 36 members in the United States and one in Montreal by the following year. Most members are aligned with socially responsible investment causes and tend to support groups with whom banks and thrifts have little contact, such as developing community land trusts, micro-businesses, and housing cooperatives. "Their credit products are development credit products to nonprofits," said the Woodstock Institute's Jean Pogge. Run by volunteers and by paid community development specialists, these loan funds are low-overhead operations, similar in some ways to community development credit unions.

Loans made through these CDLFs can be virtually microscopic by bank standards—as low as $1,000, or even lower. The funds generally loan money for at least a year, and rates can vary from 0 percent to slightly below market rates, said NACDLF executive director Martin Paul Trimble. As with other intermediaries, they offer technical assistance and training for borrowers.

Individuals donate 40 percent of the capital committed to the funds, according to the NACDLF, so the remaining 60 percent is being divided among financial institutions, insurance companies, religious groups, and foundations. The appeal for banks and thrifts may seem a little obscure: there are no loan guarantees, rates are below-market, and volumes are very low. But the CDLFs frequently serve as brokers for loans a bank could not profitably uncover, and they do so with loan-loss rates of less than 1 percent, the association said.

Moreover, some of the CDLFs are working with such mainstream efforts as the Federal Home Loan Banks' Affordable Housing Program, described in the previous chapter. The Low-Income Housing Fund, for instance, got a $1 million commitment from the program for 10 years, which it expects to produce more than 1,300 housing units. The San Francisco FHLB will provide a direct subsidy of $387,415 to First Nationwide Bank, the California-based thrift; it, in turn, will write down the cost of the $1 million from the market rate to 3 percent. First Nationwide will loan the money at 3.7 percent to the LIHF, which will issue loans at 5.3 percent.

Local governments and nonprofits have set up other "micro-loan" funds, separate from those under the NACDLF. One administered by the City of West Hollywood, California, for instance, is a revolving loan fund with nine participating institutions. Here interest rates can be far higher. The West Hollywood pool charges up to four points above the lender's prime rate.

Bank of America makes grants into some of these micro-business funds, a few of them making loans as small as $500, Donald Mullane told a 1990 CRA conference. If the bank were trying to make the loans itself, it would sustain losses of 25 percent and would be considered part of management if it attempted to monitor the credits, he said. He added: "To make small business loans in inner-city areas is the toughest form of lending there is."

Some micro funds are spreading loans in rural areas. Bankers sit on local loan committees in Arizona and Southern California organized by the Micro Industry Credit Rural Organization (MICRO). The group seeks to organize and train entrepreneurs, many of them women, who start micro-enterprises in largely Hispanic areas along the Mexican border. In three years through mid-1990, it had made loans to 239 businesses totaling less than $750,000. Those numbers may be less than alluring to lenders, but defaults are running at just 3 percent.

One of the program's organizers, James Farias, said media and CRA pressures were used to "convince" local lenders to help finance the program. But from its halting start, the MICRO revolving fund had swelled to more than $1 million in 1990, and the project's leaders hoped it would become self-sufficient by 1993.

And Southern Development Bancorporation, the Shorebank spinoff noted in Chapter 3, has created a micro-enterprise revolving loan fund in rural Arkansas called the Good Faith Fund. It makes very small, short-term loans for self-employment, with the average loan ranging between $500 and $2,000.

LOW-INCOME TAX CREDITS TO THE RESCUE

While loan pools, credit lines to consortiums, and investments in public-private partnerships may be the preferred routes for many institutions looking to do their part for low-income housing, an important vehicle—still so new in some areas that the showroom aura lingers—has been rolled out: the low-income housing tax credit. Already, several programs incorporating these credits have launched thousands of housing projects around the nation, and observers think they will be an important means for bank and thrift community investment in the 1990s.

A product of the Tax Reform Act of 1986, the low-income housing tax credit was meant to give corporate America an incentive for making investments in rehabilitating distressed real estate. The program has become the major tax initiative remaining in the housing arena, given the general dismantling of the favorable tax status for real estate tax shelters. It was extended by Congress late in 1989, and attempts have been continuing to make it a permanent fixture. The National Low Income Housing Coalition, an advocacy group, claims credit for designing the concept.

Like other consortiums, these tax credit programs comprise a pool of funds managed by nonprofit managers working with local developers. The principal difference, of course, is that a CPC or a SAMCO involves loans, and therefore debt; the tax credit programs involve equity investments. Instead of getting returns based on market rates, investors reap rewards based on lowering their taxes over a 10-year period. The largest of these tax initiatives, the National Equity Fund, projects annual tax savings of 105 percent of a company's payment and annual returns of 20 percent or more—a worthwhile investment from any yardstick, and miles better than most banks and thrifts did with commercial real estate in the late 1980s. A good deal of that money is gone forever, poured into chargeoffs and costly workout efforts that have only marginal recovery prospects.

Equity investments were specifically cited as a valid community investment activity in a question-and-answer booklet on CRA issued by the FDIC in 1990. The agency stipulated, however, that such investments must serve a public or community purpose and that "general partners should be quasi-public or private, for-profit or nonprofit organizations." The Office of the Comptroller of the Currency said the credits offer "a potentially powerful new tool for developers and investors and can increase significantly the financial feasibility of a variety of housing development and rehabilitation projects seeking bank financing."

Projects created by housing tax credits have a sterling record: None has ever gone into foreclosure, according to Frederick D. Wacker, community affairs officer at the Federal Home Loan Bank of Atlanta. But developers involved with the projects are having difficulty securing permanent mortgages, he said. And the National Housing Partnership complains that the tax credit program "is so narrow and complex that few apartment units can be created or preserved at any given time."

The tax credit mechanism itself is not complex. A bank or thrift (or any interested company) makes an equity investment in a tax credit program as a limited partner. In turn, it receives low-income housing tax credits, which can be taken annually in amounts ranging up to 90 percent of a project's eligible costs. Investor capital is disbursed to nonprofit community groups or nonprofits in joint ventures with for-profit developers.

The credits are dollar-for-dollar tax reductions, which offer the equivalent of a tax-free yield to qualified investors, says Charles E. Riesenberg, managing vice president of the community development corporation at First Bank System in Minneapolis. The difference between what a company pays for the credit and the tax savings represents the gross profit on the investment.

Credits are allocated by the individual states in which the housing is located and calculated over a specified 10-year time frame. Once the buildings are completed, the start of the credit period and the accrual of tax credits cannot be deferred beyond a year; if unclaimed, they are irrevocably lost. And because low-income housing alone creates little or no profit for developers or investors, it is the tax credits that provide the lure.

Many Fortune 500 companies have signed on for the credits, which once again puts institutions in the position of being just part of the pack. But regulators see such investments as a good thing. "It's the type of activity that banks can do, and it's reasonable to ask of them," Ronald Zimmerman of the Atlanta Fed told *American Banker*.

The National Equity Fund

The Chicago-based NEF, born in 1987, bills itself as "a national nonprofit investment manager of affordable housing projects." If that sounds much like LISC, consider its lineage: The NEF is a subsidiary of LISC created specifically to mine the tax credit area. The NEF itself has two flourishing affiliates, the California Equity Fund and the New York Equity Fund.

Financial institutions represented a minority of the three funds' corporate contributors in 1990—23 of 59—but the proportion of depository institutions is higher than it is in LISC. Contributions stood at $141 million in 1990. That money was channeled into seven national and regional corporate tax credit partnerships, producing $370 million in affordable housing; frequently the NEF investments created a sort of gap financing that "moved projects from 'good idea' to reality," said NEF Chairman David Stanley.

Some 95 projects in 23 cities throughout the country have been or are being carried out under the NEF banner. The cities range in size from small (Petaluma and Healdsburg, California,) to medium-sized (Raleigh, North Carolina, and Hartford, Connecticut), to major (Boston, San Francisco, Los Angeles, and New York). More than 5,000 housing units had been built by 1990, with 92 percent of them dedicated to low-income occupants.

For corporate contributors, these investments require little more than a willingness to commit funds—a situation that, as noted earlier, doesn't carry as much weight with examiners as company-sponsored projects. But they do show up on the list of activities regulators say count toward CRA, particularly for wholesale banks. Investors are part of an annual limited partnership, a blind pool with no projects preselected. They are approved by the NEF's board and monitored by the fund's staff, which also provides technical assistance to developers.

Among the NEF's biggest backers is Freddie Mac. In March 1990, the corporation announced it was investing $10 million in the 1989 NEF, making Freddie Mac the largest single investor in the $77 million fund. Earlier, a $6 million Freddie Mac investment in the NEF in 1989 helped launch low-income housing projects in Kansas City and Grand Rapids, Michigan. In all, Freddie Mac pledged to contribute $40 million to low-income tax credit programs in 1990.

The 1989 NEF Fund was set up to create rental housing for the poor and the homeless in 15 cities in an effort that will end late in 1991. The cities: Boston, Cleveland, Hartford, Indianapolis, Kalamazoo, Kansas City, Missouri; Los Angeles, Miami, Minneapolis, Newark, New York, Philadelphia, Raleigh, the San Francisco Bay area, and St. Paul.

NEF officers say they plan to keep the pedal to the metal, involving more investors and raising more equity. Their 1990 goal of $100 million was achieved in November 1990 when renowned investor Warren Buffett announced a $25 million investment in the NEF. That was far above the $77 million raised for the 1989 fund. "We will invest these funds in an ever-greater number of projects in an ever-greater number of cities," NEF chairman Stanley said.

The two state-based funds, while modeled on the NEF, have some differences. The California Equity Fund was created to allow corporations in the state to utilize available state tax credits in tandem with federal credits. The New York Equity Fund itself is jointly sponsored by LISC and by the Enterprise Foundation, the prominent Maryland-based nonprofit founded by developer James Rouse in 1982 to foster community development.

As of mid-1990, the California Equity Fund had raised $40 million, $10 million each from Security Pacific Corporation, Great Western Savings Bank, and Freddie Mac, as well as smaller sums from other institutions. The money is being used to help finance a package of 4,000 low-cost housing units; renovation efforts were under way in the Bay Area, greater Los Angeles, and San Diego, and new construction was going up in San Francisco, Los Angeles, and Sonoma County.

Bankers were enthused about the program. "CEF allows us to invest in low-income housing with the assurance that our funds are well placed and well used," said Steven Strange, senior counsel for City National Bank in Beverly Hills.

In New York, 20 CDCs were using $49 million in equity investments to renovate 1,250 affordable units in the Bronx, Brooklyn, and Manhattan. Homelessness is a particular target: the New York fund has been targeting 10 percent of each project site to accommodate homeless families. At the 75-unit Townsend Avenue Enterprises project in the Bronx, one in 10 units will be set aside for the homeless.

A number of New York's biggest banks and thrifts are contributors. Chemical Bank, for instance, anted up $1 million in 1988, and the Dime Savings Bank gave $2 million in 1989.

Following the Lead

Cities and states around the country are activity organizing equity funds to take advantage of the low-income housing credits, said consultant James Carras of Carras Associates. Chicago and Maryland have active funds, and others are being organized in Atlanta and Massachusetts, to name a few locations. The Massachusetts effort seeks to raise equity capital for multifamily housing projects with at least 50 percent of the units affordable to low- or moderate-income households. Carras maintained that bank investors can expect a return on their equity from 16 percent to 22 percent.

In Atlanta, plans call for 20 major local corporations to invest a total of $5 million each year in a fund to finance multifamily housing on city-owned land; included would be such major banks as C&S/Sovran Corporation, Sun Trust Banks Incorporated, Bank South Corporation, and First Atlanta Corporation. The first project being considered for funding in Atlanta was a single-room occupancy building with more than 300 units. The Massachusetts Equity Fund seeks to raise $100 million in capital in two stages. It would also focus on multifamily housing, with 50 percent or more units affordable to low- and moderate income households.

Another model worth considering is in place in Minneapolis. The Metropolitan Housing Partnership is being headed by two financial firms, First Bank System and Northwestern National Life Insurance, the two general partners. Developers of multifamily housing can tap into the fund;

typical projects are $3 million in size and provide 500–600 units, said First Bank's Riesenberg.

Corporate investments in the Minneapolis pool range from $250,000 to $1 million; they pay this to the partnership over 10 years in equal installments, Riesenberg noted. Corporate donors execute investor promissory notes for the unpaid balance of their commitments. The managing partners here take the role filled by the staff at the various equity funds. They review each project for IRS compliance, monitor project managers' performance, and provide necessary financial statements and tax schedules for investors, Riesenberg said.

The First Bank executive said he expected the 1990 partnership fund to increase to $20 million, almost double the 1989 total, with about the same number of partners—13. An offering for the partnership, issued in the spring, was extended a number of times, he said; meanwhile, the group "tied up" seven development projects, contingent on receiving the needed financing.

Five local banks are in the partnership, he said, but a goodly amount of funding is coming from General Mills and other major corporations in the area. Fortune 500 companies are a "a big market here," he said. But the partnership is investigating some deals with community banks, at a scale where the resources of a giant corporation are not needed. Riesenberg said the partnership is "a natural" for insurance companies, but he said he had been unable to interest either Fannie Mae or Freddie Mac.

The Enterprise Foundation also operates a number of local tax credit initiatives that have attracted financial institutions. Chemical Bank, for instance, has committed $5 million for acquisition, construction, and financing of two projects in a low-income tax credit syndication run by the foundation in conjunction with Fannie Mae. In another project, in Baltimore, Fannie Mae is the sole limited partner in another foundation-run effort that renovated 78 units of low-income rental housing. Fannie Mae invested $848,000 in exchange for tax credits.

In a related, far larger effort, Fannie Mae made an $11.8 million equity commitment to the Enterprise Foundation's Housing Outreach Fund in exchange for tax credits. The funding will be used in building smaller nonprofit-sponsored rental projects. By late 1990, projects had begun in Pensacola, Florida, and Miami.

In Rhode Island, Freddie Mac chipped in $1 million to become a limited partner in the $5 million Rhode Island Equity Pool, LP, a financing pool offering tax credits that is expected to help create homes for up to 400 low-income households. Fannie Mae also contributed $1 million, and four financial institutions collectively gave $3 million: the Bank of New England and three local institutions, Rhode Island Hospital Trust, Citizens Savings Bank, and the Eastland Bank. While returns are not guaranteed, the pool strives to give the limited partners a 15 percent return, said Jeannie Engel, a spokeswoman for the Rhode Island Housing and Mortgage Finance Corporation, the general partner.

Returns on community reinvestment aren't always easy to calculate, and that is especially true for grants and charitable donations, where the payback is in community betterment and good will. Yet these noncredit activities have an important philosophical connection with conventional CRA activities.

CHAPTER 6

GRANTS, GIFTS, AND OTHER GOOD WORKS

EDUCATION, THE ARTS, AND COMMUNITY BETTERMENT

As we have seen, mounting regulatory pressures for stepped-up community investment have had the biggest impact in the areas of housing and economic development. That is proper; regulators and banking observers agree that the CRA law's focus on wider access to credit naturally leads to lending in those areas. But banks and thrifts are doing a good deal more for their communities in other, sometimes more visible, ways. As good corporate citizens, institutions are looking seriously at ways to improve education, cultural vitality, and services to the disadvantaged. Sometimes a relatively minor gift can be leveraged many times through good publicity and good follow-through.

Many of these efforts are longstanding and clearly independent of any links to CRA. Compliance examiners probably won't be making note of most of them, and community groups may be indifferent. But experts say they can effectively supplement CRA-driven activities, spurring additional business for the institution and creating a "socially responsive" label that is likely to take on more importance as the decade goes by.

Helping Education

Community outreach is one form of education, but many banks are doing a good deal more than merely trying to ascertain local credit needs and working to help meet them. They are out in the local schools—"adopting" schools, teaching adult classes in personal finance, and instructing students about economics, banking, and finance. Trade groups have resources to offer

here; the ABA, for example, has a Personal Economics Program that
provides bankers with training tools such as videotapes, slides, and study
guides.

These activities can carry some weight with CRA examiners, even
though the CRA regulations don't specifically mention educational support as a desired activity. Evidence comes from Tennessee, where Sevier
County Bank made a number of presentations about banking and finance
in the local schools. R. B. Summitt II, the bank's executive vice president, said he placed correspondence from the schools about this training
in the bank's CRA file. An FDIC compliance examiner made a special
note of the activity and complimented the bank's consumer education
programs, he said.

"Educating the community about the services out there, how to use the
services, and how to get them is the first step to reaching CRA requirements,"
George Bowen, a vice president at U.S. Bank of Washington in Seattle, told
ABA Bankers Weekly. American Security Bank, one of the nation's premier
community development lenders, lists educational efforts in its CRA statement. It noted that "the information and relationships that develop" from these
efforts "serve to heighten the bank's knowledge of the community and are
helpful in gauging banking requirements of the community."

As noted in the earlier section on housing, some banks and thrifts have
incorporated educational programs on mortgage terms and home finance
into lending efforts in lower-income communities. And a number of major
banks around the country are working with MasterCard and the Small
Business Administration in a series of credit conferences around the
country aimed at women who own or want to own businesses. Participating
institutions include Citizens and Southern National Bank, Seattle-First
National Bank, Wells Fargo Bank, and State Street Bank.

Several major banks in Chicago are contributors to the Woodstock
Institute, which uses their funding to prepare a commercial lending fact
book that is widely disseminated. Northern Trust Company also has supported institute-sponsored credit workshops for low-income residents, said
Woodstock president Jean Pogge. The contributions are "probably CRA to
some extent, but we don't ask for a lot," she said.

Still, a seminar featuring a banker discoursing on mortgage points and
credit criteria can't really be considered part of the school-based educational mainstream. Spurred largely by understandable concerns about the
capabilities of high school and college graduates in the increasingly intense
global economic warfare, banks and thrifts have "adopted" schools or

formed related partnerships with long-term goals of turning out better-edu-
cated adults. Too numerous to begin to list here, these efforts frequently turn
up in bank CRA statements. And some major banks are contributing
millions each year to programs designed to improve teaching or writing
skills.

While these myriad good works may not belong in an institution's
CRA file, they are strong testimony of community investment—seed
money to fertilize the minds of tomorrow's workforce. And there have been
yowls of concern raised about the apparent decline in the abilities of many
of today's graduates; educational support comes under the heading of
enlightened self-interest.

Many institutions around the country have "school banking" programs
in local high schools. Some 40 Massachusetts high schools have
"branches" run by students, some of whom have gone on to careers in
banking, said Georgeann Abbanat, deputy commissioner for the Massachusetts Division of Banks. "It's really an exciting program. It really
benefits everyone," she said, adding that she considers sponsorship a
legitimate CRA-related activity, though not in the same league as meeting
credit needs.

A bevy of institutions have put concerted efforts into education campaigns battling drug use. In several instances, chief executives have stood
front and center, saying they wanted themselves and their banks to be
counted in the war on substance abuse—clearly a public policy issue that
carries considerable weight in the community.

Fleet/Norstar Financial Group has been distributing an antidrug video
to schools and community groups in its Northeastern markets. It estimates
the cost of the video campaign at $450,000, a sum that will come from its
Fleet Charitable Trust. "This could be considered part of our Community
Reinvestment Act compliance, but really, it's going beyond the CRA
curve," James P. Murphy, executive vice president for public policy, told
American Banker.

Supporting the Arts

One might think that support for the performing arts would be tied more to
private banking programs than to general corporate giving. After all, most
of the biggest donors to the arts are the nation's richest people; the boards
of opera, dance, and theater companies and symphonies are filled with
names from local banks' most-wanted customer lists. The connection isn't

lost on bankers, and bank chief executives spend considerable time rubbing elbows with wealthy patrons at gala receptions and dinners.

But community investment is more complicated than giving thousands every year to the Chicago Symphony or underwriting overseas trips by classical musicians. Those donations, worthy as they are, may do little or nothing to broaden public access to the arts. Many institutions have pointed their arts giving downstream, to programs with accessibility to lower-income people—and a bigger potential reservoir of community good will. These efforts can support the performing arts or fine arts and serve as investments in new forms of expression or in preservation of the classics.

This kind of support is showing up in Community Reinvestment Act statements. Great Western Financial Corporation, for instance, says its charitable contributions program "keeps us in close touch with the needs of our communities and allows frequent contact with other community leaders who are involved in these activities." Citicorp said its arts support is aimed "particularly [at] those that contribute to the economic development of cities, neighborhoods, and schools."

Not all underwriting has involved professional performers. Provident National Bank in Philadelphia helped establish "Creative Kids," that city's first arts festival for children. It was a joint effort between the bank and 24 arts groups, and community outreach was part and parcel of the bank's efforts. Branch managers met with local civic leaders to encourage support for the event, and Provident also produced and displayed festival posters and brochures. Dominion Bankshares Corporation in Roanoke, Virginia, has sponsored performances by a puppet troupe of mentally handicapped puppeteers.

Even the biggest bank givers are seeking out ways to fund community arts groups. Chase Manhattan is a good example. Under former chairman David Rockefeller, the bank was the foremost corporate arts sponsor in banking. It still does a great deal to support the biggest names in music and dance, but Chase also has a Small Grants Program for the Arts aimed at not-for-profits with a lot less visibility. The bank has made grants ranging from $1,000 to $5,000 to these groups.

Faltering earnings certainly endanger the kind of giving financial institutions have been doing in recent years. Yet the arts will continue to get their share of bank funding; the potential for good works, recognition, and positive spin on customers is just too great. "For every dollar spent on the arts, an additional three or more dollars is generated in hotel, restaurant, retail operations, transportation, and parking revenues within most local economies," proclaimed the Business Committee for the Arts. "The arts increase employment tax revenues, commercial and residential real estate projects, tourism, and attract new industry and business."

One banker puts it more simply. "We support the arts because to do so is good business," said Warner N. Dalhouse, Dominion Bancorp's chairman and chief executive. "A strong cultural base makes for a strong community and a strong economy."

Community Betterment

Improving education and donating to the arts are integral to improving life in the community, but some financial institutions have decided to broaden their giving still further. Generally speaking, these grants—most of the funding is supplied by grants or gifts—can be lumped under the heading of community betterment. This is community investment at its most elemental.

For certain banks, the door is open to virtually any group involved in creating housing. Chemical Bank, for instance, awarded $395,000 in general support grants to 65 New York-area nonprofits in late 1990 as part of its Housing Opportunities Program. The bank has given out $1.8 million under the program in five years. Money goes to groups that actually develop low- and moderate-income housing and those that offer technical assistance to such groups.

Great Western Financial Corporation launched an unrestricted grant program in 1987 to support the work of nonprofit organizations involved in projects designed to add to or revitalize low-income housing stock. Called the Leslie N. Shaw, Sr., Memorial Awards, in recognition of the work of a former Great Western community development director, these have gone to up to three nonprofits a year. In both 1988 and 1989, three groups received a total of $200,000 from the thrift company to further their work.

In Philadelphia, Provident National Bank has designed a grant program to help free community development groups from having to continually solicit funds for operating expenses. The bank's idea: Providing the groups with multiyear funding would make them less dependent on lobbying and enable them to pursue their own goals. Provident offered to commit $45,000 over three years to any agency whose main focus is rehabilitating residential or commercial real estate. The caveat was that the grants would be for core operating expenses, not for specific programs. Provident billed the grant program as "the newest component of Provident National Bank's CRA initiative" and mailed out application forms to 75 agencies in the greater Philadelphia area and 35 other larger charities.

A different twist on the same theme involved Valley National Bank in Phoenix a few years ago. Valley invited 15 rural communities in Arizona to take part in a contest focusing on specific short-term community betterment projects. The three best were to receive awards of $10,000, $7,000, and $5,000, respectively. Fourteen towns agreed to take part and were sent collateral materials that included posters, a volunteers' kit, and $250 for incidental expenses. The campaign cost the bank $38,250, but officials reckoned that publicity alone more than compensated; some 50 newspaper articles alone were devoted to the contest.

Foundations

Many banks have set up foundations to facilitate gift-giving to worthy organizations. Foundations have obvious tax advantages, and institutions frequently use the earnings from the endowment to fund the awards they issue. Major banks have foundations involved in a wide spectrum of charitable giving, most of it going to the work of nonprofits involved in social causes. Frequently this foundation money is used to finance the nonprofits' operating expenses, while the actual cost of its programs is handled by the bank itself. Foundations at Bank of America, Wells Fargo, and the defunct Crocker National Bank, for instance, have been involved over the years in supporting the San Francisco Development Fund, the nonprofit seeking to generate more affordable housing. But it is their parent banks that actually have financed the programs established by the Fund.

Foundation grants can also be a good means for wholesale banks to help their communities. The Bankers Trust Company Foundation created a $500,000 grant program in August 1990, for instance, to help increase the capability of community organizations to manage newly renovated housing for homeless families and to deliver social services to these resettled families.

The foundation at First Colonial Bankshares in Chicago was established in 1989 and is being funded out of profits at the holding company. "We want to focus our dollars on places and situations where our contribution is having a meaningful impact, where $1,000 will make a difference," said First Colonial president Robert Sherman. Sherman contended that regulators are probably more inclined to look favorably on banks that engage in such continuing community support than those who don't. "I think it's easier on us because we are rooted in the communities we serve," he said, adding that such giving is "what CRA is all about, what outreach efforts are all about."

Clearly, larger banks and bank holding companies have a better opportunity to put their names in front of the public through wide-ranging grant programs. But institutions need not be the size of Citicorp or BankAmerica Corporation. Fourth Financial Corporation, with less than $4 billion in assets in 1990, has spread its largesse around Kansas, supporting everything from community theater to zoos to donating property for public parts to giving money to a city for a new sign. "Wherever the community, you can bet Bank IV is the catalyst for projects and programs that benefit its citizens," the bank's 1989 annual report proclaimed.

With the recent surge in environmental concern, banks can be expected to do their part to help spread conservation or protection messages—community betterment aimed at everyone. Wells Fargo Bank contributed $400,000 to a $3.4 million advertising campaign last year spearheaded by the Metropolitan Water District of Southern California. The promotion urged residents to "save water for a future we can all bank on." Wells planned to distribute more than a million water conservation kits, written in English and Spanish, through its 167 branches in southern California.

Environmental clean-up or protection campaigns have mushroomed in a number of areas around the country. But in tying themselves to these campaigns, financial institutions are generally trying to market their own products—buy a CD and help save the bay, for example—rather than making outright grants to the group or cause behind the clean-up.

HELPING THE NEEDY

Scrooge wasn't a banker, and banks and other financial institutions have historically been well-recognized contributors to food and clothing drives, particularly in the holiday season. But the 1990s will bring pressure to do more, and not just seasonally. Some of that will undoubtedly involve work by bank volunteers, but look for institutions to be more involved in assisting programs that serve the homeless and the malnourished. To turn away from the underbelly of society will be to court charges of indifference or heartlessness—charges that may get back to examiners probing a bank's reputation in the community.

Many of the most visible efforts to help the homeless will be in major cities, where the situation is the gravest and the need for funding most apparent. In New York, for instance, some of the city's biggest banks, including Chase Manhattan and Manufacturers Hanover, are actively engaged in programs to help the homeless. In Los Angeles, John Singleton, chief operating officer of Security Pacific Corporation, was recruited to head the fund-raising effort for a new building for the Union Rescue Mission. The mission operates programs designed to get homeless people back in the work force.

Institutions in a couple of smaller communities have raised the fund drive for the needy to a high level—one that promises to pay off in the coinage of community good will down the road.

Commonwealth Federal Savings Bank in Valley Forge, Pennsylvania—site of some very harsh weather one colonial winter—organized a "Hope for the Homeless" drive to collect winter clothing. Beginning in 1988, the drive accepted new and used clothing at the thrift's 31 branches. Its "Fight the Pain of Hunger" campaign collected more than 2,500 cans of food from customers and employees for distribution to local area shelters in 1989-90.

Across the country, in Ventura, California, the Bank of A. Levy touched off a do-good (or perhaps, do-better) battle when it helped a local radio station raise funds for the needy during the Christmas season. Listeners were told about a needy family or individual and urged to contribute to the fund at one of the bank's 22 branches. Bank of A. Levy made the first contribution, and then a rival bank rose to the bait, saying it could raise more funds at its three branches than the Bank of A. Levy could at all of its branches. Overall, the program at the two banks attracted more than $6,000. Nearby Foothill Thrift and Loan in Agoura Hills, California, holds an annual Thanksgiving food drive in which it invites the public to bring canned food donations to any branch. What's more, the thrift matches the contributions, pound for pound.

Some institutions will be able to hitch their efforts for the needy to local or statewide campaigns. Huntington National Bank in Columbus, Ohio, has pledged just over $50,000 to the Caring Program for Children, a statewide initiative designed to provide health benefits to children between the ages of six and nine whose family income is below the poverty level and have no health insurance. Huntington's gift will provide two years of care for 110 children.

Institutions should be thinking, too, about rolling up their sleeves when disaster strikes—a time when aid for temporary care or rebuilding is urgent and high-profile. A number of California banks rushed out reduced-rate lending programs in the aftermath of serious brush fires that destroyed more than 600 homes in California in 1990. Still, most of these efforts seemed spurred as much by trying to match the competition as by any original desire to reach out to the fire victims.

One institution involved in that effort is worth highlighting, however. Home Savings of America, Los Angeles, has created something of a disaster team, established in the aftermath of the 1987 earthquake in Whittier, California. The team was in action in 1989 at both the San Francisco earthquake and in the coastal Southeast, devastated by Hurricane Hugo. The thrift concentrates on its own customers in the affected areas, contacting them and alerting them to an information number in Pasadena, where they can talk to a disaster specialist.

Helping the Elderly and the Handicapped

The affluent elderly have become a prime target for banks around the country. Older customers are loyal to institutions, tend to sock away a good deal of their money in traditional depository accounts, and control 68 percent of the average bank's time deposits, according to the American Bankers Association. Well-heeled retirees don't need assistance. But those elderly who are not well off can use a hand, and some institutions are including them when drawing up a list of community investment recipients.

That may not involve major sums. Centennial Bank in St. Ann, Missouri, is providing office and training space, computer time, and related forms of assistance to a local program called the Older Volunteer Service Bank. The program urges volunteers to give their time to help elderly people who need special care. "We felt there was a need for this type of program because 20 percent of our market is over the age of 55," said Centennial president Jerry Byrd.

A few institutions have elected to organize and fund projects to refurbish housing owned by senior citizens. First Interstate Bank set up a program in Fresno, California, that it called the Fabulous Fresno Paint-a-

Thon. The bank provided promotion, phone services, and a lot of volunteer labor in addition to funding. Fifty homes belonging to seniors financially unable to pay for the work were painted in a single day.

Some institutions are working aid for the elderly into lending programs. The Dime Savings Bank in New York participates in the Senior Citizens Home Improvement Program, which provides loans up to $15,000 for the elderly at just 3 percent interest. Still others are taking banking services to the elderly by setting up branches in retirement homes. Some banks are going at this market in a big way. First Fidelity Bank plans to have a dozen offices in retirement homes before long. Several are already open, with deposits ranging from $1 million to $11 million, according to a bank spokeswoman.

New Haven Savings Bank in Connecticut has taken the special service idea to its logical conclusion—offering to bring financial and other services to elderly customers at home. Under "other services," the thrift includes in-home health supervision, companion placement, household financial management, housekeeping, and transportation. While the program is being run by the thrift's trust department, it does use the services of Elderlife, an organization of professional geriatric care specialists.

While such red-carpet treatment won't be feasible for many institutions, any added attention to the elderly market may involve stepped-up community outreach. Older people often feel connected to their area in ways younger persons don't, and they really care about what the institution is doing to make others' lives better, said bank marketing consultant Michael P. Sullivan. Good works that appeal to their sense of community betterment could generate new deposits as well as good entries for an institution's CRA files.

Help for the handicapped has come in a wide variety of forms—from program contributions to loans for building facilities to sponsorship of special events, to name a few. A number of institutions also have set up facilities specially designed for use by the disabled. Provident Bank of Maryland, for example, recently launched a program to provide banking services for the hearing impaired through the use of a special terminal—operated by the customer—that sends messages via a special phone number. Customer representatives staff a message center during banking hours and respond to messages received at night or on weekends on the next business day. A similar program is in effect at Norstar Bank of Upstate New

York, which has an 800 number for the hearing impaired and a specialist assigned full time to the line.

A number of banks around the country have set up Braille teller machines for the blind, but Fleet National Bank in Rhode Island has been offering a range of special services to the blind since the early 1980s. A bank representative sets up the accounts, which include special style checks, a check writer—a device that holds the checks and guides the user in filling them out properly—and Braille statements.

Sometimes helping the handicapped involves getting out a message. Norstar Bank of Upstate New York was the primary sponsor of Freedom Row 89, an eight-day, 150-mile trip by four disabled athletes of the U.S. Disabled Rowing Team. The bank's involvement reflected that "the time has come to focus on the capabilities of the disabled," said chief executive Robert F. MacFarland.

Grants and loans, of course, will be the principal ingredients of many institutions' help for the handicapped. And why not? Such assistance can easily be incorporated into an ongoing strategy for community investment. The Bank of Boston's computer subsidiary, Randolph Computer, recently donated $25,000 to the Computer Dealers Lessors Association's Charitable Foundation. The funds were to be used to buy computer equipment for the disabled. And the Dime Savings Bank of New York made an $825,000 permanent acquisition loan for These Our Treasures, a Bronx school for children with developmental handicaps.

THROWING OUT A LIFELINE

As much as financial institutions have been doing for the disadvantaged, the issue of lifeline banking has had a lot of bankers' blood simmering. More than any other compliance issue, the debate over lifeline—literally, accounts that provide a lifeline to the banking system for the disadvantaged—reminds bankers that in many outsiders' eyes, banks and thrifts are closely linked to public utilities and have an obligation to provide certain services for society at large.

Banks don't care for that association. With shareholders to satisfy and a host of other nonbank providers lined up to snatch away their business, bankers have been uneasily treading a path between voluntarily providing basic banking services such as low-cost checking and savings accounts and fending off more onerous proposals. But the drift of events is pulling them toward offering more. The FFIEC said that in weighing nonlending activities for a CRA assessment, it would consider an institution's record of offering noncredit services—a clear allusion to basic banking. Most major banks' Community Reinvestment Act statements include a recounting of their basic banking programs.

"It's helpful to advertise the availability of the services that you are offering that benefit low- and moderate-income persons, including government check-cashing and the offering of low-cost checking accounts," consultant Rick Eckman told a Consumer Bankers Association compliance conference. If the neighborhood is predominantly Hispanic, he added, that promotion should be in Spanish. Some banks have acknowledged the needs of Hispanics by setting up specialized services. National City Bank in Norwalk, Ohio, provides bilingual signage and a special check-cashing-only teller to accommodate workers employed by local agricultural firms.

The Consumer Bankers Association maintains that the basic banking account set up by Manufacturers Hanover Corporation helped the company in 1989 during its application to buy the New York City branches of Goldome, the savings bank. The Federal Reserve's analysis of that application considered the basic account as part of its assessment of the bank's community reinvestment record.

Basic banking programs aren't exotic or unusual. In a 1989 survey, the Consumer Bankers Association—which has made the basic banking issue one of its principal causes—found that only 7 percent of the 81 major metropolitan banks it surveyed placed any eligibility requirements on basic banking accounts. (The CBA noted that no clear definition of basic banking accounts exists. It said they are generally typified as no-frills checking accounts which feature a low monthly service charge, no or low balance and/or opening deposit requirements, and a limited number of checks per month at no additional charge.)

Nine out of 10 banks surveyed said they promote the accounts in lobby brochures, while a much smaller percentage, about 3 in 10, said they use paid advertising or community outreach to promote them. Public attitudes would seem to reinforce those efforts. A Gallup Poll commissioned by the American Association of Retired Persons found that 73 percent of consumers believe that financial institutions should offer basic banking services, and 76 percent think they should cash government checks, up to a set amount, for persons registered to cash checks there.

American Banker's Consumer Survey in 1989, however, provided bankers troubled by the clamor for mandatory basic banking with some relief. It found that two of three consumers oppose mandating that banks provide basic banking services for the poor, and a similar percentage believe banks should not be forced to lend in areas in which they would choose not to do so.

An ABA survey released in 1990 found that 59 percent of the commercial banks surveyed offered low-cost banking accounts in 1989, up from 53 percent the previous year. The ABA, which has also circled its wagons on the lifeline issue, maintains that most banks offer these services but are not doing a good job of broadcasting that fact.

Some banks that have promoted basic banking as part of community outreach efforts have discovered, however, that it isn't always a top priority with some lower-income consumers. Officers of Indiana National Bank in Indianapolis found that community leaders were far more interested in property-improvement loans.

Bank of America has extended its no-frills banking to the lending side with a program called "Basic-Bank of America special income credit." Targeted at people who do not meet standard credit criteria, the program has given loans to persons in low-paying jobs, students, and retirees, according to executive vice president Donald Mullane. The bank is limiting loans through the account to households earning no more than 80 percent of the median for the area. Mullane said the bank's low-income checking account and special income credit were developed following conversations with community groups. Bank officials sought advice on underwriting standards; when the groups thought some were too stringent, the bank altered them. None of these products involved safety and soundness issues, Mullane said.

The Washington Pressure Cooker

Much of the heat that lifeline continues to generate comes from Washington. Particularly controversial have been ongoing efforts to compel banks to cash government checks for noncustomers. A bill incorporating provisions to mandate such activity, pushed by longtime champion Senator Howard Metzenbaum, D-Ohio, was beaten back in summer 1990 after furious lobbying by bank trade groups in no mood to negotiate.

Bankers insist they are not moved by elitist notions of keeping out a rabble of welfare recipients trying to cash government checks, though they acknowledge such a scenario could hurt customer service. Lobbies would be crowded with throngs of government check recipients at the beginning of each month, when the checks are usually mailed, the argument goes; institutions would then have to arrange to have more cash on hand and to hire extra part-time tellers and schedule more armored car deliveries.

More than anything, though, bankers see government check-cashing requirements as an onerous imposition of government control. "We are opposed to any approach that suggests the government is mandating the services banks have to offer," Gary Kohn, Senate lobbyist for the Independent Bankers Association of America (IBAA), told *American Banker.*

A good number of banks already do offer such services. A study by the Public Interest Research Group found that 31 percent of 500 institutions in four selected states—California, New York, New Jersey, and Oregon—offered government check cashing to nondepositors. A voluntary check-cashing program for welfare recipients sponsored by the Massachusetts Bankers Association had garnered some 200 bank participants with more than 1,800 branches by fall 1990. Bankers in Connecticut have no choice: A state law requires them to cash such checks for free.

The IBAA argues that opening up all banks to noncustomer check cashing would hike fraud within the banking system, as well as impose a heavy new burden on small banks already straining under the regulatory load. The ABA warned in a mailgram sent to members banks in mid-1990 June that "powerful consumer organizations and interest groups such as AARP are vocal in support of [basic banking] proposals. It is essential that we meet their show of strength with one of our own."

Peggy Miller, the legislative representative for the Consumer Federation of America, argues that despite banking trade groups' intransigence on the issue, lifeline banking is not a big deal for individual banks. "I've had 30 or 40 bank presidents tell me it's nothing," she said. Legislation on the issue has been watered down to the point that banks "have run out of substantive complaints."

Miller said she is "very leery" of efforts to tie the provision of lifeline or check-cashing services to CRA, although she noted that some negotiations between banks and activist groups have made those services part of an eventual agreement. She added that the CFA fought efforts to make evidence of such services cause for bumping up an institution's rating by one full grade. "We're not happy with the shift [toward linking lifeline with CRA]," she said. The law is very clear that community reinvestment means providing credit, she argued.

Yet regulators approving merger applications in recent years, like the Manufacturers Hanover deal mentioned earlier, have clearly incorporated basic banking into the community reinvestment formula.

Others have noticed the widespread, if tenuous, linkage between lifeline and community reinvestment. CRA has proven that banks can be pressured on social ends, Robert Litan, a senior fellow at the Brookings Institution, told *U.S. Banker.* "So we've already moved down that road. Banks don't want us to go any further. That's one reason banks are fighting the [lifeline] issue to death." The CBA's late Craig Ulrich maintained that regulators "did some lawmaking of their own" when they made a connection between CRA and basic banking issues.

While banking trade groups have carried the fight, thrifts have been largely silent. James Grohl, a spokesman for the U.S. League of Savings Institutions, said he could not recall the group getting involved in lobbying on basic banking, nor had it ever really taken on the issue in an active way. But in general, thrifts support the bankers' fight. "We're not that keen on having to cash checks," he said. "Branches don't keep a lot of cash on hand," which could lead to logistical problems if check cashing were widespread, he added.

A leading thrift lobbyist in New Jersey argues that basic banking—and particularly government check cashing—proposals being considered as part of potential legislation in that state shouldn't apply to thrifts. "They don't do payroll programs for the government, like First Fidelity or Midlantic," said Frank A. Willis, referring to the state's biggest banks. "They don't have compensating balances for that. So my argument is that thrifts should be absolved from those requirements."

Still, the CFA's Peggy Miller finds thrifts more open on the lifeline issue than banks. "I don't find them as negative, in part because of the way they were set up," she said, referring to the origins of many savings institutions as vehicles for small savers.

One piece of good news for bankers was a suggestion in June 1990 by Postmaster General Anthony Frank—formerly chief executive of First Nationwide Bank—that the Postal Service might consider establishing check-cashing services in its local offices. But he cautioned that the service would have to generate substantial fees and not hurt customer service, and that the matter would be studied at length before any decision could be made.

Representative Doug Barnard of Georgia, a former banker, introduced a bill in summer 1990 that would authorize the Postal Service to do government check-cashing. Bankers applauded the move. "We support it. It's a good alternative to the Metzenbaum amendment," Steve Verdier, House lobbyist for the IBAA, told *American Banker*. "We would be interested in [the Barnard bill] regardless of what Metzenbaum does," added Joe Belew of the Consumer Bankers Association. "It would be a good thing for banks if it passes."

Even if the Post Office does eventually step in and handle government check cashing, financial institutions cannot afford to become complacent. Political pressures will continue—if not on check cashing, on basic banking accounts with minimal fees. Lifeline banking and CRA "are on parallel tracks," says New York attorney Warren Traiger. "What goes into the political push on CRA will go into lifeline banking and government check cashing."

"I don't know why banks aren't pursuing this area more aggressively," said Lyndon Comstock of New York's Community Capital Bank. "If they don't, the only alternative is to have lifeline imposed on them. I don't think the legislators will sit by and let that [situation] go by indefinitely."

Extending services to poorer Americans has only recently become a significant criterion by which any financial institution is being been judged. Given the current tenor on the congressional banking committees and the access of consumer activists to the corridors of power in Washington, however, experts believe these services will keep mounting in importance; any perceived indifference to the community at large will leave a stain that will be tough for an institution to erase. As we will see in the next chapter, banks and thrifts pushing community causes are the ones who will score best with regulators and consumers alike.

CHAPTER 7

THE SHAPE OF THINGS TO COME

WHAT THE NEW EXAMS REVEAL

Even as 1991 got under way, bank and thrift executives were hard-pressed to glean much intelligence about what examiners were looking for in the new ratings system. Evaluations were coming out in more of a trickle than a stream, and a lot of the evidence was merely anecdotal. The agencies themselves were playing things very close to the vest; some were refusing to release results without Freedom of Information Act requests.

One high-ranking regulator said it was difficult to pinpoint any areas of weakness among examined institutions because there was no process at his agency for studying the early batch of exams with an eye toward spotting trends. Other observers said it was premature to talk about patterns. Fed Governor LaWare said in September 1990 that it would take six months or more to get an accurate picture of how well the industry was faring.

But a few things were clear. In general, the same pattern under the old system is true under the new: The vast majority of institutions are being rated in the middle, with a few considered outstanding and a few poor. Actually, more thrifts had reportedly been rated as being in "substantial noncompliance" than banks.

Experts monitoring the process say it clearly is harder than ever to get an outstanding rating. "What is happening is that some banks are making major progress in what they're doing and how they're viewing CRA," said Virginia consultant Robert Raven. "As the examiners go out, they get more experience of what to look for"—and the hurdles get a little higher. He added that the examination process is taking longer than it used to.

"The curve undoubtedly has shifted away from outstanding. It's definitely moved to the right; the exams are tougher now than a year ago," said Charles Grice of the Community Reinvestment Institute.

Regulators have insisted there is no standard grading curve, but early results released by the Fed found about 10 percent of those examined had been deemed outstanding, 80 percent satisfactory, and the rest—with one early exception—rated as "needs to improve." "Nothing in the law says that a certain percentage must be unsatisfactory," Fed Governor LaWare told a CBA conference on CRA. "There is no mandated bell curve here."

Grice, who had examined many of the early evaluations, said the Fed's pattern was generally at historic norms, and the FDIC curve was flatter, meaning more high scorers in proportion to the satisfactory group. The OCC appeared to be the toughest grader among the banking agencies, he said; the OTS is "even a notch further over" on the low side, particularly in the Western region. "They've been brutal." Almost all the Western institutions had been evaluated by early 1991, he said, a pace far quicker than in other regional offices. A high-ranking OTS official agreed that some regions are proceeding faster than others.

The Western OTS office had given a few "noncompliance" and dozens of "needs to improve" ratings, Grice said. It is hard to tell if compliance in the region was poor, or it the low scores were the result of institutions not having been examined in as much as 10 years, he added. And there is general agreement that thrifts are playing catch-up. "A lot have spent a majority of their time in the past year trying to get solvent," said Raven. "Some are very involved in CRA; there are others that virtually have no program. On the whole, they are not as far as along as banks."

The Good and the Bad

Institutions that have received outstanding ratings in the new ratings format didn't put their systems in place overnight: They have long track records in helping their lower-income service areas. Those rated satisfactory, not surprisingly, did some things well and others less well. There were no strong indications at this writing what assessment areas are weighted more strongly than others. Good documentation, attention by directors, and willingness to create products for lower-income consumers appeared to be enough to compensate for any other deficiencies and bring an institution a satisfactory rating. A summary look at a selected group of evaluations sheds some useful light on the examination process.

The Good
First Interstate Bank of California and Bank of America, two of California's biggest banks, got outstanding ratings from the Federal Reserve Bank of

San Francisco and the OCC, respectively. At both institutions, examiners praised the thoroughness of programs for delivering on CRA.

Examiners complimented First Interstate's efforts to communicate CRA aims throughout the organization, its statewide task force, and the attention to CRA paid by the managing committee, senior vice president John Popovich told *American Banker*. Bank of America scored highly with examiners by showing management commitment, a leadership role in loan pools for lower-income credits, and a wide range of products and services made to lower-income people, executive vice president Donald Mullane told the newspaper.

Boatmen's National Bank in St. Louis, which received an outstanding from the OCC, earned praise from examiners in virtually all the assessment factors. Among other things, the examiners singled out the bank's detailed records—including a daily library—of bank contacts; active director involvement; a good CRA training program; a variety of effective marketing efforts; and participation in a number of government grant or loan guarantee programs.

First Nationwide Bank, the major thrift in San Francisco, received an outstanding from the OTS. The evaluation itself gave the thrift a grade in each of the 12 assessment factors; with seven deemed outstanding and five satisfactory, the rating swung to the former. Among the areas that were deemed first-rate were ascertainment of credit needs, distribution of credit extensions, the record of opening and closing offices, and participation in local projects.

In weighing the thrift's local investment record, the OTS said First Nationwide "has a well-documented, exceptional record of participating in local community development and redevelopment projects, and has established itself as a leader in this area."

The Bad
The most publicized "substantial noncompliance" rating in 1990 was given to Farmers and Merchants Bank of Long Beach, California. The fact that Farmers happens to be rated as one of the nation's soundest banks gives ammunition to the argument that strong CRA compliance can be a drain on resources. Indeed, president Kenneth G. Walker argued after the rating was released that soundness is one of the strongest attributes the bank could offer its customers.

Farmers and Merchants hasn't ignored CRA issues. It was a founding member of the CCRC, the low-income housing pool in California, and met with city officials in Long Beach to discuss affordable housing there. But a regulator hinted that the bank's weak commitment and inadequate process dragged it down.

A small Florida institution, Banyan Bank of Boca Raton, got a "needs to improve" from the Federal Reserve Bank of Atlanta. A fairly weak-performing small bank, with assets of $34 million in June 1990, Banyan was taken to task for having no CRA plan and no involvement by directors in CRA.

Examiners said its rating was mitigated by the fact that management had recently changed, and added: "The bank has not actively sought lending opportunities in community development programs. However, the bank is small and relatively new, which has precluded its participation in many programs." (More detail on the criteria used in formulating the ratings will be offered in the next chapter.)

The Examination Approach

By all accounts, the primary areas examined up front are the extent (or existence of) a CRA plan, knowledge of and relation to the institution's local community, and CRA involvement by senior management and directors.

"There's far more emphasis on process from beginning to end," said Virginia consultant Raven. "How do you determine community needs? What kind of outreach do you have? [The examiners] go out into the field and talk to community groups to find out. How do you analyze the data? How are you organized?" A secondary emphasis is on communications within the bank concerning CRA issues. And examiners are looking for evidence of communication from the top. "It all goes back to what happens at the board meeting," said one consultant.

HMDA files are reportedly the top priority for loan data review. James Daniel of Oklahoma's Friendly Bank said the main thrust of the exam at his bank was the HMDA data; the examiners were looking for measurable results, with the HMDA data compared against generalized numbers for the affected census tracts.

"Thorough" is a word often heard about the new examinations. "The exams are quite detailed. And the examiners don't have the latitude they've had in the past," said David P. Parish, vice president and director of housing and community investment at the Federal Home Loan Bank of Boston. "It's more of a checklist they have to run through."

At the FDIC, special review section chief Ken Quincy said, "You have the normal inconsistencies you have in a new program." A lot of review work has been going on, he added. "The comfort level of the examiners has to go up," said one FDIC examination official; since the information is going to the lay public, examiners have to learn to put their findings in layman's terms.

Still, the joint examiner training helped greatly, said several regulators involved with the program, as did the month of lead time between the end of training and the first exams. The regulators brought out differences among the various regions, put them on the table, and tried to resolve them.

The FDIC is doing safety and soundness and compliance concurrently, and Quincy said it is important that the examiners talk to each other: Problems would erupt if the safety and soundness examiners start classifying loans that the compliance examiner has commended for CRA purposes. "We want the safety and soundness examiners to understand we need more flexible standards, but we don't want compromised standards," Quincy said.

Detailing the examination procedure at Bank of America, Donald Mullane told a CRA conference that examiners made 50 branch visits at random in geographically disbursed areas. They went to sensitive areas and interviewed all of the branch managers, asking about the extent of CRA involvement and the bank's goals. The examiners also pored through the meeting minutes for the board of directors, the social policy committee, and the managing committee, Mullane said.

"They are thorough sticklers for detail. They are going to force you to detail in your minutes or on your call memorandums exactly what you did," he said. "And they want detailed board minutes. And if you're a small community bank, I can't emphasize enough how involved your directors have to be."

Documentation was cited as one of the keys to the top-notch results at Bank of America and First Interstate. First Interstate cited records backing its efforts. "If you say you put on workshops for first-time home buyers, you better have a flyer and a memorandum detailing who attended," senior vice president John Popovich told *American Banker*.

Appeals

The agencies have been unyielding in their opposition to any sort of formal appeals process that could change a rating once it had been determined. Said Ken Quincy: "Where would it end? What about the community groups? They'd want to appeal a bank's good rating, too. I don't think any of us think it's necessary. There's a built-in appeal process through review and examination. The exit interview gives sufficient opportunity for a bank to respond."

As has been the practice, examiners and management have a good deal of opportunity to discuss findings during an exam, giving the bank a chance to ensure that all the proper information is factored into the exam. "From the time the examiner leaves the bank until the final evaluation is filed, a bank has the opportunity to clarify substantive concerns," Dennis Deischler, a high-ranking official at the OCC, told CBA researchers Dawson and Forbes. "However, clarification of misunderstandings or misinterpretations does not mean financial institutions can change substantiated conclusions."

Reactions

Bankers who have gone through the public ratings evaluations have decidedly mixed reactions. But the consensus seems to be that the exams are indeed more rigorous than ever—and word of that rigor has triggered anxiety among those still awaiting their exams. "Some of the problems [raised] have been in anticipation of exams, and not yet in response to exams," said California consultant Mark Aldrich. "That's slowly working its way through the system."

"I have to tell you, there was nothing untoward in this CRA examination, any more than there was in any of the former ones, except that they were extraordinarily thorough," said Bank of America's Mullane.

Others speak of big changes. The latest exam was "dramatically different from the old one," said James Daniel of Oklahoma's Friendly Bank after the two banks in his investor group each got satisfactory ratings. "Never assume you're all right," he advised a CRA conference. "We thought we were excellent, but we had some deficiencies." But he said the public portion was "very circumspect," and that unless a bank has a serious problem, this should not emerge as an issue.

"We've had very encouraging feedback" from examiners, said Fleet/Norstar James Murphy as the exam there was taking place. But he added, with a touch of resignation, "I'm sure we'll get rapped here and there by a community group or regulator. That's part of the territory."

Some bankers are understandably irritated. "They want us to give the bank away," fumed Kenneth Walker of Farmers and Merchants to *American Banker*. He insisted that the examiners were preoccupied with "technicalities."

While interest among community development advocates has been understandably high, frustration over the slow release of ratings was also high. "Nothing they [regulators] have done has been interesting to community development practitioners," said the Woodstock Institute's Jean Pogge in late November 1990. Advocacy groups would like to compare "outstanding" ratings from the various regions to see what differences exist, she said.

"From my perusal of the evaluations I've seen, they are generally much more ambiguous than people might have hoped," said Deborah Goldberg of the Center for Community Change. "They don't tend to give lots of detail, and the numbers are not always consistent. Actually, they generally don't give numbers at all." Particularly for large institutions, the evaluations make no mention of what locations the assessments are based on, she added, nor is there discussion of different kinds of markets or the extent or consistency of the CRA market. "There's a heavy emphasis on process," she said.

One researcher offered the theory that "the best is yet to come"—that regulators purposely selected the "easy" institutions first and are saving the toughest ones for later, when examiners have more experience under their belts. That approach ties in to safety and soundness, he said, adding, "The regulators don't want to offer a lot of public failures. They wanted to make the point that this [ratings process] was a nonissue" for activists.

THE REGULATORS' BALANCING ACT

Judging by the small number of comments received about the final FFIEC guidelines published in July 1990—about a dozen—one might think the regulators would have relaxed a bit as the new examination process got under way. Hardly. The four federal agencies are very much aware of the eyes turned to community reinvestment and past complaints about lax enforcement. But they are also mindful of the red ink bleeding from even some of the country's best and brightest banks.

CRA creates "a heavy burden on us as regulators," Fed Governor John LaWare said. The agencies must take extreme pains to emphasize the lack of any relationship between a CRA rating and an institution's safety and soundness, he said. LaWare conceded that "we've spent an enormous amount of time and money training examiners," but the result is "not a perfect process."

Efforts to improve CRA evaluations have triggered internal changes at some of the agencies. The FDIC, which had just 22 core compliance examiners in 1990, planned to have separate compliance and safety and soundness examinations in late 1991. The exams have been performed concurrently, with the average time for a compliance exam in 1989 running to 50 hours, said Ken Quincy, chief of the special review section at FDIC.

The Office of Thrift Supervision, which had been conducting separate compliance exams using specialized examiners, spent much of 1990 developing a corps of specialists for each district office. That system was put in place, though "the program needs some refining," said one official there.

More than examiner staffing is being scrutinized. The FDIC is aiming to hire outreach officers, who are not examiners, in each of its eight regional offices in 1991. Director of community affairs Janice M. Smith said these officers will act as liaisons with examiners in a process similar to that in place at the Fed.

All the agencies are trying to develop a better feel for what wholesale and specialty banks should be doing in the CRA area. The FDIC, for instance, planned in 1991 to tackle that dilemma, having spent the latter part of 1990 monitoring and reviewing the results, Smith said; the results would be compared on a regional basis.

"Some think CRA has changed, but it has not. The reporting of it is the change," said one prominent regulator. "For the most part, the examiners have been trained, but they're still trying to refine their thinking." He added, "It's a learning process for all of us. One thing we talked about with the other agencies is having a debriefing in the first half of [1991] to talk about what have we learned."

State regulators are trying to keep up with their federal counterparts. In Massachusetts, officials want state and federal exams "to come from the same place," said Georgeann F. Abbanat, deputy commissioner for community reinvestment and outreach at the Massachusetts Division of Banking. While it's possible for the two agencies to disagree, "usually it's very close. We're looking at the same assessment factors and the same facts," she said. She added that the Massachusetts department will be sending out CRA questionnaires, with information based on assessment factors, to try to get banks to think about CRA issues every year.

Release

Perhaps nothing associated with the new evaluation process was making regulators hotter under the collar than the issue of releasing the public CRA

ratings. With community groups itching to get their hands on these evaluations, the agencies were insisting they would not be stampeded into creating
any central clearinghouse or central registry of the ratings.

They specifically rejected the idea of putting out an annual compilation
of ratings and evaluations for each institution examined during the previous
12 months. "The agencies believe this should not be an interagency undertaking, and that they will sufficiently fulfill the intent of Congress by
making the evaluations and ratings available to the public through the
examined institutions," the FFIEC said in July 1990.

Each federal agency elected to deal with disclosure on an individual
agency basis. Initially, people interested in finding out who had been
examined could do so by filing Freedom of Information Act (FOIA)
requests with the appropriate agency, the regulators decided.

The stickiness of the release issue showed up in sharp and ironic relief
when the Federal Reserve met resistance from its fellow agencies when it tried
to collect recent evaluations to do some comparisons. The response from a
couple of the agencies: File an FOIA request. "If the agencies are relying on
Freedom of Information [requests], they're creating their own problems," said
a vendor in Maryland. "This is supposed to be public information."

The inability to obtain the ratings in an easy and timely way frustrated
consumer and community groups, who accused the agencies of subverting
the will of Congress. "Congress wants the ratings public, but the agencies
seem to be saying, 'They didn't mean us.' They're putting the onus on the
banks," said the Woodstock Institute's Jean Pogge.

Some observers said regulators were wary of seeming too chummy
with the activists. Others said they were deeply worried about the health of
the banking industry and wanted to keep the lid on any potential CRA
uproar. "The regulators are as nervous as the industry about public ratings
disclosure," said Deborah Goldberg, of the Center for Community Change.
The center developed a standard FOIA request that was being sent periodically to the agencies in late 1990 to collect evaluations.

Continuing pressure to ease the release of the ratings finally took its
toll. The FFIEC voted early in December 1990 to urge each agency to
publish at least quarterly an updated list of institutions it had examined.
Gradually, the four agencies moved in that direction. The OCC was the first
to act, said Goldberg, appointing a person in the communications office to
release the list of those institutions that had been evaluated. An OTS official
said lists would be available quarterly from the regional offices.

The FDIC has set up series of monthly updates indicating when ratings
for various institutions will become public; copies of the evaluations them-

selves will be available through the corporate communications office for fees that would be associated with an FOIA request, said Ken Quincy. But the agency was having some trouble implementing the system. In mid-January, the FDIC was still trying to assemble evaluations from regional offices around the country for the July 1–December 31, 1990 period. "Frankly, the systems weren't ready for this," said Quincy. Glitches in an automated system meant that the FDIC had to gather the evaluations manually from the various regions, some of which were ready to report on their results, while others weren't.

Community groups can be expected to keep pressing for more disclosure. While she deemed the efforts to improve dissemination "a small step forward," the Center for Community Change's Goldberg added, "I think it's stupid not to give out the rating" when the agency releases the list of who has been evaluated. "I think they should include the rating and the information that you can get the evaluation directly from the institution." She also objected to the fact that some of the agencies still planned to charge a fee for release of the evaluation itself.

One community affairs official said the regulators prefer that the evaluations be released by the institutions. "One of the purposes of the [ratings] process is to try to foster dialogue at the local level," he said. "That's why we try to take ourselves out of the process and make the rating publicly available through the institutions."

If regulators felt compelled to remove some of the hurdles for obtaining a CRA rating, they were no less concerned about how they could be used. Fed Governor LaWare, speaking to a consumer group, said that "all of the procedures for public release are not worth putting in place unless the disclosures are used constructively." He emphasized that the agencies don't want acrimony or harping over individual ratings. "I would hate to see the process bogged down in discussions with regulators as to whether a bank's public evaluation and CRA rating was precisely correct," he said.

Handling the HMDA Data

Collecting and sorting the reams of data created by the new HMDA requirements will be a tremendous challenge for the regulators in 1991. Many of the loan/application register reports will still be on paper; one vendor in the geocoding field said regulators "are scared to death that semis [trucks] filled with paper will be backing up to their doors." The Fed's

LaWare contended that a projected 1.7 million pages of data being created by the HMDA registers would create a towering stack of paper 30 feet higher than the Washington Monument.

Electronic delivery would dissipate that paper nightmare, but the agencies had not established a common electronic format by the end of 1990, so vendors were offering to select the correct format for institutions, depending on the regulator.

Regulators will be using mapping programs to supplement hard-copy reports showing perceived performance and where HMDA compliance might be a problem. With these programs, the agencies can compare a specific institution's records with overall loan levels for a city, or target low-income neighborhoods. Ronald Zimmerman at the Federal Reserve Bank of Atlanta said in 1990 that the aggregates were still producing skewed results, but that the register created by the new system would be helpful; by allowing a breakout by race or sex, borrowers could be directly compared.

Observers familiar with HMDA said the new system will create yet another balancing act for regulators as they try to satisfy institutions and community groups. The regulators' decision to release the raw HMDA files—"sanitized" by removing names and other confidential material—has been troubling to many banks. But the FFIEC stood firm, saying it "believes that the release of the raw-data files is consistent with the statutory directive to maximize public disclosure of the HMDA data. Such disclosure will not add to the regulatory burden on the reporting institutions."

The agencies did take the lenders' side, however, by refusing to compute the elapsed time between an application and the date of final action. Community groups had sought those computations, arguing that unusual delays may signal discrimination, but the regulators said that too many factors might come into play to make these numbers valid.

While the FFIEC intends to mail the disclosure statements produced by its HMDA analyses in October 1991, it was widely believed that the complexity of the job will push that release in 1992. Release alone, however, won't give the agencies cause for relief. "If this information comes out and receives a lot of play in the news media and political arena, it's going to put enormous pressure on the regulatory agencies to find more discrimination, or at least be able to assure us that they have thoroughly examined the banks," consultant JoAnn Barefoot told an ABA workshop late in 1990.

What Regulators Are Saying

Enforcing the will of Congress to crack down on CRA compliance has compelled regulators to don a tougher public face. But their message to the industry has not been all thunder; it has been softened by warm words and assurances that effective compliance is within the reach of a majority of institutions. "Most banks have complied, consciously or unconsciously, with the aims of CRA since before the act was in existence," said the Fed's LaWare.

Still, banks haven't had to look hard for the tough talk. "CRA has got to be woven into the fabric of the banking system in the country," LaWare asserted. Institutions may need to be more creative and concentrate on cash flow rather than collateral when judging lower-income borrowers, he said.

"CRA is not charity," Sandra Braunstein, a community affairs program manager at the Fed, told *Freddie Mac Reports*. "We do not promote the use of programs that lose money. Programs that don't make money do not stay around like a community development effort that makes money."

"There are no magic formulas or cookie-cutter approaches to community development financing. It takes being proactive, innovative, and entrepreneurial," said the Atlanta Fed in a paper issued to members. Moreover, regulators want evidence of follow-through. Thrifts taking part in the Home Loan Banks' Affordable Housing Program, for instance, are being expected to include among their monitoring efforts "audits of applications and supporting documentation, loan-record analysis, specialized reporting and data gathering, and site inspections."

Institutions need to know their lending area and be aggressive about seeking out opportunities, said David Parish at the Federal Home Loan Bank of Boston. That is true in rural areas as well. "The problems are somewhat different, but the techniques are pretty much the same," he said.

Mixed with the sterner messages have been assurances that regulators intend to be scrupulously fair, and that they recognize that institutions can only take on so much risk. The agencies are obligated to make certain that "examiners are well trained and are instructed that there is no single way to get a good CRA rating; that they recognize the long-term nature of some programs; and that they recognize there are alternative indicators of soundness," Griffith Garwood, director of the division of Consumer and Community Affairs at the Fed, told *Freddie Mac Reports*.

"We have taken the view that the banks are not required to take excessive risk," said Ronald Zimmerman at the Atlanta Fed. "We would like for them to start with smaller, more manageable [housing] projects, maybe 50 units, to get their feet wet," he told *Business Atlanta*.

Regulators also insist that community reinvestment will work best if consumer groups and local governments are involved, rather than dumping the load onto financial institutions alone. "Community groups can help play a constructive role by recognizing that economically unsound community lending programs are counterproductive in the long run," LaWare said. He urged community groups "to recognize the need to initiate constructive dialogue and discussion on community needs with banks on an ongoing basis."

And there have been some suggestions of a carrot for the industry for effective community reinvestment. Two economists at the Federal Reserve Bank of San Francisco suggested in a 1990 paper that banks could be rewarded for good CRA performance by getting expanded powers, or that loan guarantee programs should be expanded to encourage more even geographic distribution of credit. However, Congress has been in no mood to increase bank powers lately.

Noncredit Activities

The assortment of noncredit activities described in Chapter 6 have made institutions better corporate citizens and more likely to win business from community groups and local governments. But as components of a strong CRA program, they may be little more than decoration on a well-baked cake.

"There are things that just don't satisfy the requirements. They're supplementary," said the FDIC's Janice Smith when asked about activities like support for the arts, education, and the needy. "We're looking at the lending side first. That's not to say there aren't other things they could be doing. Some of these things are good ways to learn networking."

Regulators say examiners weigh these charitable and civic gifts in the process of their work, and make a judgment in view of the institution's entire CRA effort. One federal community affairs official said she is likely to give banks credit for their support of education because it is such a vital part of community betterment. Clyde Paul Smith, president of the First Women's Bank of Rockville, Maryland, divides CRA activity into two tiers, credit-related activities and civic-minded ones. He said regulators weight each tier accordingly, giving the civic work the least credit.

If anything, the agencies are showing signs that they are open to new approaches to community investment. The Federal Reserve gave approval to First Financial Corporation of Wellington, Kansas, a tiny holding company, to establish a subsidiary that would buy a tract of land for agriculture-related activities, including testing of alternative crops, equipment, chemicals, and farming methods.

"The board's order is significant because it permits a rural bank to engage in an activity targeted to local needs, even though the activity has little relationship to traditional CRA credit and housing concerns," noted the FFIEC. "It signals a willingness by the board to entertain innovative approaches to meeting the needs of diverse communities."

OPPORTUNITY KNOCKS

Along with the calls for proactivity, documentation, and outreach runs a constant thread among regulators' and trade groups' approach to CRA: The notion that community reinvestment presents an opportunity for banks to gain favor and new business. "Above all, CRA should be viewed as more than an obligation. It can also be a business opportunity," said former ABA President Kelly Holthus. "The association said that CRA can be looked at as a social obligation, but it can equally be looked on as a marketing opportunity," said Robert Fichter of the Massachusetts Bankers Association.

The *opp* word is even being used when talking about disclosure of less-than-fabulous ratings. "I believe the disclosure of a rating is an opportunity, not something we should be tremendously afraid of," said the Fed's John LaWare. LaWare has been urging banks to publish their CRA ratings, along with their responses in local newspapers. Even those rated "needs to improve" should do so, he said, releasing the ratings along with "any positive ideas they have about how the bank might proceed to address [its] CRA responsibilities going forward . . . In other words, banks can turn the CRA evaluation into a positive opportunity to open, or continue, dialogue with the community." Over time, he believes public CRA ratings will be a boon to the banking system.

"The banker who goes beyond business as usual, earning a high CRA rating in the process, may find abundant new marketing opportunities opening up," noted the ABA in its *CRA Executive Summary for Community Bank CEOs*.

"Some attitudinal and institutional restructuring may be in order, but since when has that been an obstacle between a good businessman and a good business opportunity?" wrote the CBA's late general counsel, Craig Ulrich.

Bankers Respond

Prominent bank and thrift executives around the country have come to publicly endorse community reinvestment as a potentially profitable venture. "We intend to make money at it. If you run it as a profitable business, you can get your officers on board," Malcolm S. McDonald, vice chairman of Signet Banking Corporation in Virginia, told a CRA conference. "There is an opportunity for us to put money into the community, with the hope of it being repaid," Wells Fargo vice president Mel Carriere told *American Banker*. "The [credits] don't end up as bad loans or chargeoffs."

A number of chief executives have publicly uttered the phrase that CRA *is the right thing to do,* but more than obligation is involved. "I think there is more the banking industry can do that is developmental . . . finding better ways," said James Murphy, executive vice president of Fleet/Norstar, the Northeast superregional. "Given the way the economy is heading, and the demand, I think there are great opportunities for banks to make the best of an untoward situation."

Community development corporations—many a direct result of CRA—can be real engines for economic revitalization and job growth. "It's a long-term economic benefit for our community," Dennis A. Carroll, president of the First National Bank of Hartford, Wisconsin, said of a small-business incubator formed through its CDC. He told *Independent Banker*; "The new businesses will be hiring people, and that's the name of the game. They are going to do some banking, and they're going to do some buying in the community. Obviously we'll reap some of this."

For minority banks, especially, community development lending is a natural niche. Community reinvestment played a big role in the recovery of the Boston Bank of Commerce, a small black-owned bank that has been cited as the community reinvestment leader in Boston. President Ronald A. Homer sees continued opportunity: "Since a good part of our deposits and loans are based in the community, it was part of our strategy to develop a strong, loyal, and profitable customer base," he told ABA *Banking Journal*.

Theodore Roosevelt National Bank in Washington goes after churches and nonprofits and finds that they can offer a significant deposit base. President Harold Fischer said that for every deal he has done with them, he has gotten more in deposits than he put out in loans. And community outreach in itself can be good marketing, say several CRA consultants. Small businesses have other needs besides capital, such as cash management and retirement planning and products.

Profitability and Loss

Well-organized, carefully targeted CRA programs have proven to be profitable and produce low loan losses. American Security and South Shore Bank, certainly, have done well in community development lending—witness the 1.6 percent return on assets that American Security was touting for its community development lending arm in 1990. South Shore earned 0.85 percent on assets in 1989, and it was over 1 percent the year before; City Lands Corporation, a development arm of its parent Shorebank Corporation, had a 28 percent return on equity in 1989.

Attorney Warren Traiger said of CRA lending, "If you're smart, you can make money at it. Not as much as in your best areas, but you can definitely make money at it." Community reinvestment activity "reflects sound banking practices, with credit experience in line with that of Boatmen's overall loan portfolio," Boatmen's National Bank said in its CRA statement.

"CRA is not bad business. [With] CRA, properly underwritten, loans to lower-income people are good ones," said Bank of America's Donald Mullane. He maintained that all the bank's CRA-related products stand alone, and all make money. "We don't have a program that we offer to lower-income people or to developers, or whoever, that is not profitable," he told a CRA conference in San Francisco.

"There is no significant difference between loan delinquency rates in South Central Los Angeles and our experience statewide," said Great Western Bank chief executive James F. Montgomery. "The argument that low-income home buyers aren't good lending risks just doesn't hold water if you know your underwriting."

Continental Bank Corporation expects its new array of CRA-related investments to do just fine. Executive Garry S. Scheuring told *American Banker* the bank expects a 15 percent return on its business units pursuing community reinvestment. In Florida, the Black Business Investment Corporations, the statewide network for minority capital explored in Chapter 2, reported an 11 percent return in 1990 and 0.4 percent loan-loss ratio—numbers that a lot of major banks would have been delighted to report.

Equity investments in housing intermediaries and low-income housing tax credit programs can generate annual returns in the high teens or higher—one reason, perhaps, why a lot of nonbanking corporations are represented in lists of investors in those enterprises.

Return in the capital markets is usually associated with risk, but that isn't necessarily true for community development lending. Consider the defaults or loan losses for these profitable efforts:

• For the first five years of the Chicago Neighborhood Lending Programs begun in 1984, First Chicago, Harris Bankcorp, and Northern Trust showed a combined default rate of 0.1 percent, according to the Center for Community Change.
• At South Shore, net losses in 1989 were 0.12 percent of outstandings, compared to 0.87 percent for its peer group—the sixth consecutive year in which losses were below the peer group average.
• Community Preservation Corporation, the New York City program that earns market rates for its participating lenders, has had virtually no defaults since it began lending in 1975.
• A low-income housing project in Phoenix that had a brush with default was the only problem loan cited by Low-Income Housing Fund of San Francisco among more than 90 development projects around the country, 80 to 90 percent of which provide housing for very poor or homeless people.

WHICH WAY CRA

The CRA brushfire banks and thrifts fear most in the near term, the one sparked by poor CRA ratings, was a fire in search of tinder in the first days of 1991.Most observers agreed it was too early to conclude that ratings disclosure would create a commotion or be more of a nonevent. But seen through the filter of those fearing a hail of bad publicity, it was more of the latter.

"I don't think there will be an enormous anything," at least not initially, said Peggy Miller at the Consumer Federation of America. "It will help some, if there are fairly sophisticated efforts" on the part of community groups to work with those ratings that are made public, she said. "It's one more piece; it helps."

"There may be a great profusion of do-goodism. Or it could be a colossal nonevent," said Clifford Rosenthal, executive director of the National Federation of Community Development Credit Unions. Allen Fishbein of the Center for Community Change, however, sees an impact: He thinks the release of ratings will make churches and local governments far more selective about where they put their funds.

"I have some friends on the regulatory side saying they would like to see things happen" to turn up the spotlight on CRA, said one researcher early in 1991. "They're saying they still think it's going to happen." Boston consultant James Carras said the fact that an overwhelming majority are getting satisfactory ratings is going to raise a lot of concern from advocates. "There will be a response," but he said he couldn't predict its shape.

Regulators continue to tread cautiously. One high-ranking regulator said the public-ratings exercise "has everyone on edge. It's not comfortable for us as regulators. We will be hanging people's dirty linen in public." Robert T. Parry, president of the Federal Reserve Bank of San Francisco, told a CRA forum that disclosure "will also subject the regulators to greater scrutiny. And you'd better believe we have an incentive not to allow grade inflation in our ratings."

Alarms about potential bad publicity continue to be sounded by consultants. "Every CEO—even in small towns—should assume that one of these mornings, he will open his paper and see his CRA rating compared with his competition," said JoAnn Barefoot, a former deputy comptroller and head of J. S. Barefoot & Associates in Columbus, Ohio. "If you have a good record, stand by it," she added. "CRA should not be used for blackmail."

One thrift trade group official said he feared the CRA ratings release would turn into another big negative for thrifts, another "thrift story."

No matter what the ratings, "I would hope that both community groups and banks would be more inclined to use the CRA evaluations as a jumping-off point for constructive discussions about what needs to be done in the community and how the banks might play a role," said Fed Governor LaWare.

Those few banks that do get outstanding ratings may be understandably inclined to crow about them. First Interstate Bank of California was asking the Fed late in 1990 how far it could go in using its grade for promotional purposes, and Bank of America put out a press release and took out an advertisement in the *Los Angeles Times* calling attention to its rating.

The Political Agenda

The forest of question marks surrounding the public ratings process will eventually be cleared, but the longer-term direction of community reinvestment, experts say, will hinge on the national public policy agenda. Community advocates, backed by Congress, are in ascendancy now, but that rise is a fairly recent event.

"I think it's a matter of where the political pendulum is swinging," said New York attorney Warren Traiger. "I think it will turn very much on the political makeup, on who's in charge of the subcommittees on [Capitol] Hill," said one prominent regulator.

"I think [CRA activity] will be tied to who has relationships with banks," said Charles Grice of the Community Reinvestment Institute. That would mean more of a role for cities and pension funds and less of a role for activist groups like ACORN.

Grice said he had expected more fireworks than he had seen by early 1991, but the anxiety level was still high. "Lenders are more afraid than they should be. There's a much broader audience watching banks now, and lenders are enormously paranoid," he said. Said another researcher: "I think there is paranoia, but not as much as I'd like to see for things to really pick up."

Many activists "haven't connected the dots yet," said Grice; he still sees a widespread lack of awareness about how to use CRA as a means of bringing money to their neighborhoods. Another tool to do that could be in the wind, however. Virginia consultant Robert Raven said there is a growing feeling that in 1991 the federal agencies are going to come out with another pronouncement extending the same type of data collection being used with HMDA to all lending, including credit cards.

Meanwhile, new pressure groups are starting to make their weight felt. The NAACP will be agitating for additional hiring through CRA protests in a new strategy, outlined late in 1990 in an interview with *American Banker*. While CRA does not deal with employment, the civil rights group plans to ask banks to commit to hiring more blacks as a requirement for dropping protests. "The CRA legislation requires that community groups have a voice, and the NAACP, being one of the largest community organizations in the country, would naturally have a responsibility in this," Edythe Hall, the organization's administrator for minority business and employment, told the newspaper.

But minority hiring is not a CRA function, regulators insist. "If a bank or holding company chooses to make an [affirmative action] agreement purely on its own, that's its business," Fred Bagwell, vice president of the Federal Reserve Bank of Richmond, told *American Banker.*

Another discrimination issue, however, is looming in the form of the expanded HMDA reports. Regulators, consultants, and community advocates agree the data is likely to show continuing lending bias—and, given the publicity accorded the earlier mortgage-pattern stories from Atlanta, Detroit, and Boston, a titanic controversy could be brewing.

Some voices are unequivocal about the danger. As CRA has evolved, "ascertainment [of community credit needs] was the big issue of yesterday and geocoding is the big issue of today, and discrimination may be the biggest issue of the future," JoAnn Barefoot told an ABA workshop in late 1990. She added; "The HMDA data are a time bomb sitting under your bank."

One Fed official said the continuing link between CRA and discrimination "has literally overwhelmed the CRA issues of credit extension. We need to make an intellectual distinction between CRA and discrimination. It would help the debate to separate this out."

Community Groups Look Ahead

Community reinvestment advocates, while buoyed by some of their recent victories in Congress, are far from jubilant. "Community groups haven't gotten all the things we've asked for [from Congress]. But we got more than the banks did," said the NFCDCU's Clifford Rosenthal.

Activists still feel somewhat betrayed by regulators, the target of much of their steam in years past. There have been complaints that their conversations about banks are passed on to bankers, but community groups are not clued in about conversations between banks and regulators.

Doubts have been heard about the near-term future of the CRA movement, including disclosures. "The downside [of public disclosure] is that if 90 percent of the banks get 1–2 [ratings] again, then we're in a worse position to argue," said Jane Ubelhoer, a Washington lobbyist for ACORN. "Now, if they say the community's credit needs are being met, we have a harder case to make."

Some fear that regulators will quash some community development programs because of marginal profitability. "Federal regulators must understand that we're talking about different levels of profitable return. Or

The Shape of Things to Come 205

else many of these programs could be canceled," Dr. Calvin Bradford told the National Training and Information Center (NIC).

The HMDA reporting changes, while a potential gold mine for activists, has triggered some concerns. National Peoples Action in Chicago has been urging its members to write to the Fed to protest the fact that loan data on HMDA statements will no longer be available immediately from lenders, as it was previously. They foresee a long delay in 1991 when all the register data is being processed. "The information that communities finally get could be out of date, possibly costly, and could only be obtained from some slow-acting office in Washington," the group said.

Some advocates are continuing to target Uncle Sam at least as aggressively as they are banks. Gale Cincotta of NTIC warned that unless the government restores some subsidies it has cut, there won't be enough low-rate mortgages in years to come. "These neighborhood lending programs worked because the lenders and the communities were committed to them," she said. "Now it's up to the federal government to hold up its end of the partnership."

One development being watched as 1991 dawned was the formation of a national CRA coalition that would include churches, unions, Indian and women's organizations, and various advocacy groups. Spearheaded by the Enterprise Foundation, the group would be funded by private foundations and would concentrate on research and education, said ACORN's Ubelhoer. "It would not be going to banks and filing challenges," she said. The idea for the coalition has been attributed to Representative Joseph Kennedy, the force behind the move to publicize CRA ratings.

The coalition's organizers hoped to go to foundations in February 1991 for planning funds. Anne Hoskins of the Center for Policy Alternatives said the group had set up bylaws and has attracted "mainstream" nonprofits such as Enterprise and LISC—entities with considerable corporate support that should give the group added legitimacy with the financial community.

Proactivity Rising

Community development supporters do sense that institutions are increasingly proactive, and that attitudes have clearly changed from several years ago. "Today, the bankers really want to do something. It's a matter of educating them on what to do," said Brenda LaBlanc of Citizens for CommunityImprovementinDesMoines.

"More banks are coming to us rather than us going to them," said the NFCDCU's Rosenthal. "I don't spend a lot of my time pounding on the doors of unresponsive institutions. They talk to their peers, and the circle is not that big." ACORN's Ubelhoer said bankers have become friendlier and more willing to meet with ACORN staffers. Some in St. Louis have actually gone to ACORN's offices in search of CRA-related loans, she said. Bankers "are calling us now, and asking us about our projects," Virginia Peters, executive director of the Wesley Housing Development Corporation in Alexandria, Virginia, told the CBA's Dawson and Forbes.

The Woodstock Institute's Jean Pogge cited Northern Trust Company, with whom Woodstock set up a home buyers program even though Northern ordinarily limits its retail lending to its trust customers. Even something as small as a free used computer can be a gold mine to a CDCU or strapped community group, she added.

Some bankers are responding to the proactivity message, though they may phrase it a little differently. "We made an initial decision that everything we did would be preemptive. We weren't going to have community groups walking up and down in front of the building carrying signs," said Bank of America's Mullane. Instead, the bank chose to "offer products before they insisted that we offer them."

Banks in Vermont are definitely becoming more proactive and spending more time developing programs, said John Ewing at Bank of Vermont. Safety and soundness remain a concern, "but we believe that with a little creativity, you can do community lending that is really quite effective."

Enlightened self-interest is at work, observers say. "I think there is genuine concern for the problems of affordable housing in their markets," said Kathleen Kenny at the San Francisco Development Fund. "Institutions see that it's part of the economic vitality of the area."

"Banks should view the new CRA focus of regulators and the public as a permanent business condition," says State and Federal Associates, a Virginia consultant. "The need to reach out to all segments of the community, with viable products and services as well as with expressions of interest and community spirit, will continue."

hile more and more banks are reaching out to respond to concerns in will

Bankers Divided

While more and more banks are reaching out to respond to concerns in lower-income communities, entrenched resistance remains and will keep the industry's response in check. One attorney in the field believes most banks will still do the minimum because "they still see CRA as charity cases." Consultant Laurie Glenn in Chicago said she still hears this "charity" label, adding that she sees a sort of generation gap at work. Bankers who have come to prominence in the past five years understand that CRA can be good business, but older bankers don't see that, she said. Moreover, older and smaller banks are less tuned in to CRA.

This resistance bothers community development bankers like James Fletcher at Chicago's South Shore Bank. Other banks "don't act. I think that we get very short-sighted in business in this country," he said. "They say that in the short term, [they] can make more money over there than over here. They don't see there's a long-term benefit in getting involved in this payoff down the road."

Other bankers recognize that small-business development, a CRA area, is key to the development of local economies. Dennis Rash, head of NCNB's CDC, said it is unrealistic to expect that major corporate relocations will "jumpstart" local economies. Instead, "the development of small businesses is the single most likely means of nurturing economic development," he said.

But small business and CRA don't often go together in banker's minds. "Banks work well once they know the customer, but most banks don't want to know what the low-mod community wants or needs," said one consultant. Bankers are more likely to voice frustration that CRA agitation seems to focus on quick solutions and gobs of money on their part. Bankers, a patient and cautious lot, aren't willing to empty the vaults.

They do understand the rationale for pressure tactics. Community groups "understand the name of the game. The name of the game is to leverage their strength," said Security Pacific's Irving Margol. "Rightly so. I would do the same thing."

An executive at a major thrift that has worked extensively with nonprofits said she warns them that institutions aren't lending to them because they are eager to do so; if the loans go bad, that may send institutions running to regulators with an "I told you so" message that could hurt future lending.

Other frustrations include information, a keystone of the lending process; banks say they are getting too little or it is too fragmented to be useful. "Many of the bankers I've met are thirsty for a role to play in community reinvestment, but are frustrated by the myriad of competing interests at the community level," consultant James Carras told *Ba...ker & Tradesman*. "There are so many programs, and so few resources."

Better information about programs and experiences would improve community lending, bankers agree. A lot of informal networking has been going on among community development lenders, but there is widespread acknowledgement that this should be more institutionalized, said American Security's Karen Kollias.

What Does the Recession Hold?

The deepening recession in early 1991 did not bode well for increased community reinvestment. Massive chargeoffs, particularly at the nation's largest banks, were shutting off much new lending; too much time was being spent cleaning up the old loans, a great many of which had been made to real estate developers and bore no relation to CRA. Banks charged off $30 billion in 1990, and 25 percent of the banking industry was posting such losses that it had effectively stopped lending, said *Business Week.* And a Fed survey found that half of responding banks said they have cut their lending to small business, one slice of the CRA pie.

"We have no appetite for risk right now," said Clyde Paul Smith of First Women's Bank of Rockville, Maryland, in what was a widespread refrain. An attorney with a number of bank clients said that prudence will remain a crucial issue unless federal or state governments agree to increase sub-sidies—an unlikely event in most areas.

The sluggish economy in Arizona hurt one community reinvestment effort: the launching of a multibank CDC. The CDC organizers were hunting for in-kind contributions and services and support from state government. Without that, said officials involved with the effort, the project could not move ahead.

Arizona is hardly alone, but regulators say safety and soundness concerns will not make CRA disappear. Janet Gordon, a community development official with the OCC, agreed that "difficult markets" exist in certain areas of the country. But these "should not preclude banks from continuing to work with their local government and nonprofit organizations in finding ways to make these kind of deals work," she told a 1990 forum on bank CDCs.

Fed Governor LaWare conceded that regulators are scrutinizing real estate loans, but added, "We believe that there need be no conflict between CRA and safety and soundness." That sentiment was echoed in Mas-sachusetts, home to some of the nation's most troubled real estate waters. "This is the worst cycle for business in some time," said Robert Fichter of the Massachusetts Bankers Association, which has been organizing a massive community reinvestment program. But he added, "I haven't heard of a single bank—as much as safety and soundness are on a one-lane road—no one has said, 'I'm sorry, I have to drop out of all this.'"

The economy could hurt some of the biggest CRA players, said Robert Raven of State and Federal Associates. "We think banks that have made public [commitment] goals are going to have a problem," he said. "We may have banks not meeting their goals, or to try to do so, they will have to lower their standards."

But institutions that do reach out in hard times can expect to win praise. Francine Justa, executive director of the Neighborhood Housing Services in New York, cited the participation of 13 banks and thrifts in a neighborhood rehabilitation loan program. "At a time of severe fiscal restraint at all levels of government, the support of the private sector is essential to maintaining the city's housing stock," she said.

New Avenues Emerging

No matter how long the recession lasts, existing community reinvestment initiatives will survive it. Expect more commercial banks to join consortiums and pools, including some that were once restricted to thrifts. That is happening in California, where a number of banks joined SAMCO in 1990.

And observers predict that a growing number of commercial banks will join the Federal Home Loan Bank system—roundly disparaged by banks when it was a regulator—to qualify for the Affordable Housing Program and other inexpensively funded ways to satisfy CRA obligations. Under FIRREA, commercial banks with at least 10 percent of their assets in residential mortgages can join.

Task forces developed to CRA issues have sprouted and will continue to pop up. A number of banks have joined with insurance companies to form the Low- and Moderate-Income Housing Finance Task Force, a national group working to overcome impediments to financing lower-income housing. An even broader effort has been launched under the banner of "A Social Compact with America's Neighborhoods." Leaders of the financial, insurance, and other industries have organized to give advice and to serve on committees and boards of community groups and loan providers targeted toward low- and moderate-income communities.

Other programs are considerably more local. The Pennsylvania

Bankers Association organized a Community Reinvestment Task Force in 1990 to help members meet their CRA responsibilities. And the Massachusetts community reinvestment initiative, detailed earlier in the book, aims to bring together local leaders and bankers in a highly structured, goal-oriented program.

Other efforts may be more local still, involving groups of bankers in specific cities. The president of a small bank in west Los Angeles, for instance, has been trying to organize a CRA effort on a citywide basis. "I think people are beginning to see need for that," said consultant Mark Aldrich.

And there is an ongoing call for new players. Banks have been eager to share community reinvestment duties with other providers, and community development intermediaries have been courting—often successfully—insurance companies, pension funds, and small mortgage companies not subject to HMDA. Those efforts should continue to bring in more resources.

Collaborative efforts should continue to increase because so many bankers acknowledge their effectiveness. As Irving Margol of Security Pacific noted at a CRA conference, "Left on our own, [community reinvestment] is too big for us. But if we become the catalyst to bring the organizations together, everybody benefits."

The public-private partnership idea has proven itself time and again, and experts predict more to emerge as both institutions and governments hunt for resources. Consultant James Carras said there were 20 low-income housing consortiums early in 1991, up from just a handful a year earlier. The Enterprise Foundation got a $2 million federal grant in 1990 to help two dozen cities establish such partnerships to improve affordable housing programs.

Future legislation is an unknown, but various ideas for improving delivery of financing in inner-city neighborhoods have been offered. Clifford Rosenthal at the National Federation of Community Development Credit Unions has proposed something called the Neighborhood Banking Corporation, which "would serve as the financial and technical infrastructure for a network of nonprofit, community-based financial institutions which specialize in serving low- and moderate-income people." He conceded late in 1990 that the idea has been largely dormant, but could be reexamined in 1991.

State and city pressures could also create new structures for community reinvestment. As noted earlier, more than 30 states have enacted legislation with CRA linkages, and more states are considering them. Some consultants see the linked deposit issue, for states and for cities, as a coming battleground, with banks' CRA ratings being a crucial factor in determining who gets those deposits.

The powerful National League of Cities has been considering the linked deposit issue, said Charles Grice of the Community Reinvestment Institute. Moreover, he said, state treasurers are talking about negotiating CD rates with banks based on their ratings.

This potential new battery of CRA players, umpires, and coaches will change the nature of the game. There will be lobbying, publicity, and new pressures—the things that create problems for reactive banks. But for proactive institutions that have demonstrated an abiding concern for community issues, these can be turned into something constructive— into opportunity.

CHAPTER 8

CRA COMPLIANCE

A QUICK PRIMER ON CRA

Community Reinvestment Act performance may still seem like something of a roll of the dice for institutions concerned that their regulator—and the individual examiners sent by that regulator—may be looking for programs or actions that could be viewed differently by another agency examining another bank or savings institution across town. "There is a lot of concern about the role of individual examiners in the process," said a New York attorney with a number of savings bank clients.

But the federal agencies have left no doubt about their intent to standardize the examination process as much as is physically possible. Extensive consultation, joint training of examiners, and joint announcements about CRA measurement (beginning with the 1989 joint statement) have pulled the agencies together on CRA as never before. The results are there in pronouncements and guidelines, in voluminous detail.

The Ground Rules

CRA applies to all federally insured commercial banks, savings banks, and savings and loans, whether their charter is state or federal, but it does not apply to credit unions. CRA monitoring is still divided among the agencies as it has been since the beginning: national banks are examined by the Office of the Comptroller of the Currency; state-chartered Federal Reserve member banks and bank holding companies by the Federal Reserve Board; other state-chartered banks and savings banks by the Federal Deposit Insurance Corporation; and savings and loans and other savings associations by the Office of Thrift Supervision (formerly the Federal Home Loan Bank Board).

Each examining agency is charged with assessing an individual institution's record of meeting community credit needs and must "take such record into account" when evaluating certain applications for approval. These include applications for deposit insurance or a new charter; to open a branch or other deposit-taking facility; to relocate a home office or branch; to merge, consolidate, or acquire the assets or liabilities of another institution; or to form a bank or thrift holding company.

Beyond that, "every covered financial institution has a continuing and affirmative obligation to help meet the credit needs of its delineated community, including the credit needs of low- and moderate-income neighborhoods," subject to safety and soundness, the agencies said in a joint statement. "The law does not say, however, that institutions should meet this obligation by making loans at certain specific levels or amounts. To the contrary, it is clear that credit needs differ from one community to the next, and that the role of individual financial institutions will appropriately differ, even within one market."

To gauge this obligation, the agencies examine an institution's records on CRA compliance as part of broader compliance examinations performed, on average, every 18 to 24 months. So even a bank or thrift that has never applied for a merger or to open another office will be routinely screened to make sure it is performing community reinvestment.

The FIRREA law of 1989 substantially altered CRA enforcement by making two major changes in the law; changing the existing five-tiered rating system to a four-tiered one, and requiring that the results of CRA examinations completed after July 1, 1990, be made publicly available. Under the old system, institutions were rated numerically from 1 (outstanding) to 5 (essential noncompliance.) The new four-tiered system does not use letters but phrases. From best to worst, these are outstanding, satisfactory, needs improvement, and substantial noncompliance.

The publicly disclosed evaluations will include the examining agency's findings and conclusions for each of 12 assessment factors that will be discussed shortly, as well as the specific rating assigned from among the four grades. The evaluation will be sent to the institution with the written CRA examination report. This report will remain confidential, but the CRA evaluation must be made publicly available within 30 business days after being received by the institution. Each agency will have the same format for its evaluations, but can have its own document and own response mechanism. The evaluations do allow for some information remaining confidential, such as references that identify any customers, employees, or officers, including those who supplied confidential information in the course of an examination.

As amended by the agencies in 1990, CRA evaluations must be placed in an institution's file at its head office and at least one designated office in each local community. Moreover, language must be added to the public notice advising the community about the availability of the evaluation, and a copy of the evaluation must be provided on request. However, the institution "is authorized to charge a fee not to exceed the cost of reproduction and mailing, if applicable."

A standardized format is being used in preparing the public CRA evaluations. This has been divided into four sections: a cover page and general information about CRA, including background on the law, the nature of the evaluation, and a description of the factors the agency considers in assigning a rating; a summary of the four ratings and the institution's specific rating; a narrative discussion of performance under the relevant assessment factors; and additional information such as the Metropolitan Statistical Area where the institution is located, branch locations, and where HMDA data can be found.

As a rule, the examiner tells the institution about his or her preliminary findings at the close of the CRA examination. He or she then prepares a proposed evaluation for public release. This is reviewed at the next level of authority within the agency, and after review, the final CRA evaluation is sent to the institution.

Standards and Assessment Factors

At minimum, institutions must meet two broad sets of requirements under CRA. The first involves a series of technical standards, the second a group of a dozen "assessment factors," divided into five performance categories.

Under the technical standards, an institution must:

• Delineate the local community or communities it serves on a map, using methods that do not unreasonably exclude low- or moderate-income areas.

• Write a Community Reinvestment Act statement that includes the delineation map, a list of the types of credit the institution offers, and a copy of the CRA notice. This statement must be reviewed and approved by the institution's

board of directors at least once a year and be available to the public at the main office and at least one office in each delineated community.
• Post a CRA notice in every office lobby explaining the purpose of CRA and how the public can comment on the institution's performance.
• Maintain a CRA public comment file. This must contain the institution's CRA statements and any comments from the public about its CRA performance for the past two years. The file must also contain the most recent public CRA performance evaluation of the institution conducted on and after July 1, 1990.

The assessment factors create the framework used by the agencies to determine an institution's public rating. "In order to get a favorable CRA performance evaluation, the institution must demonstrate that it has a satisfactory or better performance record under these factors, taken as a whole," the agencies noted.

The following is a list of the assessment factors, grouped within their performance categories:

1. Ascertainment of Community Credit Needs:
   a. *Assessment Factor A:* Activities conducted by the institution to ascertain the credit needs of its community, including the extent of the institution's effort to communicate with members of its community regarding the credit services it provides.
   b. *Assessment Factor C:* The extent of participation by the institution's board of directors in formulating the institution's policies and reviewing its performance with respect to the purposes of the Community Reinvestment Act.
2. Marketing and Types of Credit Offered and Extended:
   a. *Assessment Factor B:* The extent of the institution's marketing and special credit-related programs to make members of the community aware of the credit services offered by the institution.
   b. *Assessment Factor I:* The institution's origination of residential mortgage loans, housing rehabilitation loans, home improvement loans, small business or small farm loans, and rural development loans within its community, or the purchase of such loans originated in its community.
   c. *Assessment Factor J:* The institution's participation in governmentally insured, guaranteed, or subsidized loan programs for housing, small businesses, or small farms.

3. Geographic Distribution and Record of Opening and Closing Offices:
   a. *Assessment Factor E:* The geographic distribution of the institution's credit extensions, credit applications, and credit denials.
   b. *Assessment Factor G:* The institution's record of opening and closing offices and providing services at offices.
4. Discrimination and Other Illegal Credit Practices:
   a. *Assessment Factor D:* Any practices intended to discourage applications for types of credit set forth in the institution's CRA statement(s).
   b. *Assessment Factor F:* Evidence of prohibited discriminatory or other illegal credit practices.
5. Community Development:
   a. *Assessment Factor H:* The institution's participation, including investments, in local community development and redevelopment projects or programs.
   b. *Assessment Factor K:* The institution's ability to help meet various community credit needs based on its financial condition and size, legal impediments, local economic conditions, and other factors.
   c. *Assessment Factor L:* Any other factors that, in the regulatory authority's judgment, reasonably bear on the extent to which an institution is helping to meet the credit needs of its entire community.

What the Ratings Mean

In promulgating guidelines about the CRA evaluation system, the agencies have provided great detail on what constitutes the various ratings—from outstanding down to substantial noncompliance—for each of the dozen assessment factors. Those descriptions are too lengthy to be included here; a good summary was provided in the June 27, 1990, interagency guidelines booklet directed at chief executive officers and chief compliance officers.

A number of "grids" that break down performance by area and assessment factor have been developed. The agencies include one in the booklet mentioned above; others have been disseminated by trade groups such as the American Bankers Association and Consumer Bankers Association. These grids are useful aids for institutions trying to understand just what constitutes a certain level of performance in a given area.

The agencies also have developed generalized "CRA profiles" that apply to institutions in each of the four rating categories. A good synopsis of these was issued by the Federal Reserve Bank of San Francisco, and is as follows:

Outstanding

Delineated community meets the purpose of CRA and does not exclude low- and moderate-income neighborhoods.

CRA is an integral component of the planning process.

CRA is explicitly reflected in policies, procedures, and training programs.

Documentation is comprehensive.

Monitoring procedures demonstrate volume and distribution of credit and enables assessment of performance.

Affirmative outreach efforts exist to determine credit needs and address them through innovative product development.

There is a high level of involvement by board of directors and senior management.

Special credit services are marketed aggressively, resulting in loans that significantly benefit the community.

The institution is in compliance with antidiscrimination laws.

The institution acts as a leader in economic revitalization and engages in activities to meet community credit needs.

Satisfactory

Delineated community reasonably meets the purpose of CRA and does not exclude low- and moderate-income neighborhoods.

CRA is not an integral part of the planning process, although objectives have been integrated into policies, procedures, and programs.

Employee training is adequate but may need to be expanded. The institution maintains adequate documentation and monitoring of CRA activities.

Credit services are marketed that address identified community credit needs, resulting in loans that benefit the delineated community.

The institution determines credit needs and addresses those needs through appropriate loan product development.

The institution occasionally involves board of directors and senior management in CRA-related activities.

The institution maintains a satisfactory level of involvement with the community.

The institution participates in economic revitalization and/or demonstrates a willingness to explore other CRA activities.

The institution is in compliance with antidiscrimination laws.

Needs to Improve
Community delineation is unreasonable and may exclude some low- and moderate-income neighborhoods.

Training program is not comprehensive.

Documentation and monitoring of activities is inadequate.

There is limited outreach to the community, and passive determination of credit needs is addressed by standard loan products.

The institution involves the board of directors and senior management very rarely in CRA activities.

The institution maintains limited involvement with the community.

Credit services are marketed on a very limited basis.

Advertisements do not reflect identified credit needs.

Credit types may not reflect identified credit needs.

There is a disproportionate lending pattern, negatively impacting low- and moderate-income neighborhoods.

There is limited involvement in economic revitalization, but management may express willingness to participate in other activities.

The institution is not in compliance with antidiscrimination laws.

Substantial Noncompliance
There is an unreasonable delineation of community that excludes low- and moderate-income neighborhoods.

CRA is rarely considered in planning, policies, procedures, and training programs.

There is no viable program for meeting community needs.

There is no program for monitoring CRA activities.

The institution maintains little documentation demonstrating its level of performance.

Management is not aware of credit needs and may not have developed appropriate loan products to meet credit needs.

There is no involvement by the board of directors and senior management in CRA activities.

The institution has no meaningful interaction with the community.

The institution does not advertise credit services.

Types of credit available may not be reflective of the CRA statement.

There are restrictive lending practices leading to disproportionate lending patters.

The institution is not active in promoting community economic development and shows little interest in pursuing other related activities.

The institution is in substantial noncompliance with antidiscrimination laws.

TIPS FROM THE EXPERTS

Scratch a CRA compliance officer or community lender and you may get an earful of advice on CRA compliance and programs. While there's still a lot of variance of opinion on the do's and don'ts of CRA, there is also widespread agreement on what the best-scoring, most admired banks seem to be doing.

Here, then, are some lessons from the field from a range of different sources: bank compliance people, lenders, and chief executives; regulators; community group organizers and executives of nonprofits involved in development finance; and consultants. They offer not only useful ideas, but considerable food for thought.

Attitude/Approach

Take CRA seriously, and realize it won't be going away. "We spend most of our time trying to get banks to look at the marketplace and look at the process to understand and work in that marketplace, and to be creative," said consultant Robert F. Raven, chairman of State and Federal Associates in Alexandria, Virginia.

"We think most banks have not taken a hard look at themselves," Raven added. "The stakes [a while ago] were not that high. I don't think a lot have truly tried to understand what they need to do."

"Bankers must be involved if neighborhoods are to be revitalized,"

Daniel Callahan, chairman of American Security Bank in Washington, told a pair of Consumer Bankers Association researchers. "We can provide business leadership, and we can profit while being good citizens. It's too bad we have to have CRA to get us to do it, but it's here and it's the law."

Treat CRA as more than merely a compliance issue. Signet Bank, American Security, and Maryland National Bank are among those that have elected to look at community reinvestment not as a compliance matter, but as a line business item, says Julia Seward, community reinvestment officer at Signet. She added that lending is not the whole picture, and that banks need to factor in all of their employees and harness their full resources in order to get an outstanding rating.

"CRA is not a special lending program or occasional good deeds. Instead, CRA is a process that should operate every day in every bank," wrote Banc One CRA administrator Julia F. Johnson in *ABA Banking Journal.*

"If you look at CRA only as a compliance issue, the chances of getting an outstanding rating are very slim. It's got to be tied to a marketing scheme," said State and Federal Associates' Raven.

Be open-minded, and don't assume a community development loan in a troubled area is by definition a bad investment. And don't dismiss CRA activists as blackmailers. "It can't hurt to ask yourself, 'Are we doing everything we can to get credit to all parts of the community?'" First Chicago's Richard Hartnack told *American Banker.*

Lending at below-market rates or waiving standard real estate terms in an effort to make a loan "can make community development lending a self-fulfilling prophecy of failure for certain lenders, who think that these losses are the cause of their reluctance to make the loan in the first place," wrote American Security's Karen Kollias in *Secondary Mortgage Markets.*

The CRA protests that hit First Union Corporation in 1989 may have stemmed in part from an earlier published remark by chairman Edward Crutchfield that community activists were practicing a form of blackmail. Said a former executive at the bank: "I think they were laying in the weeds for him."

Think about CRA as providing new marketing opportunities. "Many people are looking at this as though it's a regulation, and they've got to stop," Douglas A. Hilditch, vice president and compliance officer at First Annapolis Savings Bank, Annapolis, Maryland, told *Southern Banker.* "They've got to look at it as a tool for marketing and a business opportunity. And once they look at it in that light, then they'll be able to come up with ideas."

Allen L. Lastinger, Jr., vice chairman at Barnett, said CRA helps to fully identify market needs. "As we refine our procedures to meet market opportunities, [CRA] becomes a positive thing," he told a Consumer Bankers Association conference in late 1990.

Realize that working with low-income borrowers is hard work. Borrowers "may be the best-intentioned people, but they don't have the resources and the technical expertise to bring the projects off the drawing board and put them up on the land," G. Michael Callahan, a senior vice president at Citizens and Southern National Bank, Atlanta, told *Southern Banker*.

"We kind of joke about it, that we spend half our time underwriting credit and probably the other half serving as an adviser or just a sounding board to the borrower, just trying to make something happen. We've just got to bring them along in many cases. It's a unique challenge."

Institutions may catch some flak for trying to do good. "The banks said, 'We want to do loan pools.' We had some reservations, but then we said 'Okay, let's do them. Let's talk about what the needs are,'" said Tom Fox of the Normal Heights Community Association in San Diego. "But the banks said they don't want input. Suddenly they want to fashion their own concepts."

Fred Wacker of the Federal Home Loan Bank of Atlanta says too many lenders look at community development lending as crisis financing rather than asset financing. Even if a loan seems to go beyond prudence, he says, that shouldn't mean nixing it—"there are a lot of credit enhancements out there that could make it work" if the institution is willing to work to find them.

Commitment

Commitment starts at the top, with the CEO and the board of directors. The chief executive must endorse CRA publicly and privately, said Federal Reserve Governor John LaWare.

"There is no question that the only way CRA is going to succeed is from the top down. If top management is not involved, it is not going to be successful," said Security Pacific executive vice president Irving Margol. He noted that the bank's office of the chief executive gets updates every six weeks from the company's CRA officer.

"Regardless of how committed you may be, if those top people in the company don't share that same level of commitment . . . ultimately, you're not going to succeed," said John Kolesar, formerly head of Ameritrust Development Bank.

Be thorough: Make sure all employees know about CRA, and follow through to ensure the technical requirements are being met. Examiners will get a poor signal early on if these technical requirements get lax attention. These requirements include promulgation of where the CRA statement can be found, a listing of products and services, and a definition of the bank's service area.

Line managers must be integrally involved and committed to the CRA process, says Barnett's Allen Lastinger. While this level of involvement can be "touchy," wrote Julius Loeser, senior counsel at First Interstate Bancorp, in *Banking Law Review,* it is crucial to a good CRA program.

"It's very important that communications be constant and close," Charles Thigpen of Ameritrust DEvelopment Bank told a 1990 Consumer Bankers Association conference. "You can't do anything but roll up your sleeves, get your fingernails dirty, and find out what's needed."

"Many thrifts do not retrain their [compliance] people. They don't check to see if they are still in compliance. They do a pretty good job up front, but do not really have any consistency," the OTS' Jerauld Kluckman told Joseph Dawson and Paul Forbes, who wrote *Understanding CRA* for the CBA.

Don't assume there are any shortcuts. "Some banks have seized upon a CDC in a simplistic notion that in doing so they have thrown their bone to the regulators and earned their CRA points, and can go back to regular banking," consultant John Sower told a forum on bank CDCs. "What they're learning is that life ain't quite like that now."

"There is no safe harbor," asserted Allen Fishbein of the Center for Community Change. He called the new CRA process a "complex task that goes beyond the usual circle of friends."

Proactivity/Outreach

It is widely perceived that most banks are only reluctantly applying their energies to CRA, and activists may be quick to form judgments unless top managers act proactively. "Too often senior management is not spending time talking to [community] people outside [a small group] and are using the bank's CRA personnel to run interference," said Fishbein. "I think that's a lost opportunity, and it can lead to community resentment."

Some sort of outreach to local community leaders is vital, he said, adding, "It's not enough [for an institution] to say, 'We haven't heard from them.'" He added that community leaders will "see right through" a CRA officer who doesn't have the backing of and access to topmost management.

Start at home. Experts urge banks to tap their own people for contacts in low- and moderate-income communities. Churches are often a good place to start in minority neighborhoods, as are community newspapers and local governments.

It may be easier and as effective for a bank to invite community activists in as to send people out. First National Bank in Dayton has been hosting an annual community reinvestment breakfast meeting for a dozen years. As many as 100 people have gathered to tell bank officers what the community needs.

Use calling officers and other lending personnel as an integral part of any outreach efforts. Chemical Bank and Bank of Boston are among the major banks mentioned as having particularly good outreach programs. Chemical has had a "Streetbanker" program for many years, using specially trained lenders as its "eyes and ears in the community."

"Banks with officer calling programs can include CRA questions in customer calls. They can also call at least once a year on people who can talk about community needs," wrote consultant JoAnn Barefoot in *ABA Banking Journal.* James Daniel, president of Friendly Bank in Oklahoma City, said he redesigned the officer call report following the bank's examination so that every call will have CRA data built in.

Consider asking community groups and nonprofits for credit referrals. LaSalle National Corporation in Chicago does so, and will work closely with borrowers to satisfy their needs. Kristin Faust, vice president and head of the bank's community development department, told *American Banker* that LaSalle lenders may even go with borrowers to the City of Chicago to get a bigger loan.

Activists say that banks are too often missing an opportunity to finance nonprofits, many of which have outstanding records as borrowers. Bank of Vermont president John Ewing urges bankers to seek help from nonprofits in drumming up community development. "A bank can't really go out and think up projects," he said.

Clyde Paul Smith, president of First Women's Bank of Rockville, Maryland, said his bank is getting credit for referrals even though it is not making mortgage loans. The bank is not a permanent lender, so it has identified two mortgage lenders and has been referring potential borrowers making under 80 percent of median income to them.

Do formal market research. Not only will this give lenders a better profile of a local community than informal soundings, but surveys offer evidence of CRA compliance efforts, said attorney Warren Traiger. These studies can be directed at lower-income communities only, or at the entire population, with higher-income results screened out, he wrote in *American Banker.* Questionnaires should be in other languages if the neighborhood has a high number of non–English-speaking residents.

Distinguishing yourself from the pack pays off with community groups and regulators. "An individualized plan is key [to success], "said Linda Garvelink, formerly the compliance specialist at the Independent Bankers Association of America. While a lot of banks might want to get by with "boilerplate" approaches, they need to show innovation, she said.

Board Involvement

Directors can no longer protest their innocence when it comes to CRA compliance. Among the most-often mentioned features of the new CRA guidelines is the regulatory emphasis on directors, who are supposed to be well informed on and actively involved in formulating and tracking CRA policy.

"The board must know what's going on," said the Fed's LaWare. In fact, he says it isn't asking too much that a board committee specifically dedicated to CRA meets as often as three to four times a year. Comptroller Robert Clarke says board attention is vital when devising a strategic plan for CRA, giving it continuous oversight, and making sure regular performance reports are created.

Directors are expected to know something about community needs. Directors at huge holding companies, such as money center banks, can't be held to the same standards of those at community banks who live and work in the service area. Still, regulators are expecting to see ample evidence of careful attention to formulating and endorsing CRA policy decisions.

Board members should talk regularly to community leaders and follow up with suggestions to the bank's compliance officer, wrote consultant Kenneth H. Thomas in *American Banker.* Local directors "can stay in touch by reading community newsletters and by regularly attending meetings of community groups," said the Federal Reserve in a memo to institutions.

"At small banks, [directors] live and work in the community, and the regulators expect them to shoulder more of the burden," said California attorney and consultant Mark Aldrich.

Set up a board committee at the holding company level and individual community affairs persons at each unit bank. That has been done at institutions like Barnett and Security Pacific.

California CRA consultant Darla Farr urges banks to set up a CRA compliance committee at both the board and officer level, involving a wide range of areas: loan supervision and policy, compliance, marketing, public relations, contribution, branch operations, and senior management.

Structure

Establish an internal structure for carrying out CRA, rather than relying on a quick fix from a consultant. "You want to institutionalize your base. Having a consultant is good, but you need to do [CRA] from the top down. Then you can bring in consultants," said Chicago consultant Laurie Glenn.

While small community institutions may be tempted to buy an "off-the-shelf" product to handle CRA, "you can't have that because each market is different," said Virginia consultant Robert Raven.

Appoint a CRA officer who has the respect of management and give him or her responsibility to act for the institution. Time and again, regulators and bankers say that having a committed CRA officer in place can be central to making the institution's CRA program run smoothly and demonstrate to examiners the bank's commitment. Comptroller Clarke suggests that banks assign "official responsibility for CRA performance to a high-level CRA officer—nothing promotes success in any endeavor as effectively as tying it to an individual's professional survival and advancement."

Pick a CRA officer with diplomatic skills and, preferably, a track record of working with community groups. Deborah Randolph, a community affairs leader at the First Interstate Bank of Texas, said that CRA officer doesn't have to be a career occupation, but a transitory post to establish the needed connections that will make community affairs self-sustaining. But she does see a critical need for diplomacy and an ability to mediate with community groups.

Consultant Laurie Glenn argues that a CRA officer need not even be a banker, but someone with a political or sociological background. "This is politics. You have to determine who are legitimate community players. You can't get caught up in the turf wars," she says.

Realize that traditional management systems may need modification to boost CRA compliance. Special lending divisions can cut costs as experts are created who know the needed paperwork and the network of developers that make community development lending work; they can reassign costs and generate needed volume, said First Bank's Charles Riesenberg. Creating loan brokers within the bank or designating individuals as loan specialists are other models for improving community development lending.

Too often, the CRA officer and the compliance officer are different people working in different departments, said Virginia consultant Raven. And existing divisions between CRA compliance and mortgage lending, as tracked by HMDA, are barriers to effective performance, he said. "Banks view these as entirely different items, which is a mistake."

Bank One changed its compensation structure for mortgage lenders from straight commission to a mix of commission and salary. It recognized that the old system "created an unintentional bias against lending in neighborhoods where the cost of housing was lower or moderately priced," CRA administrator Julia Johnson wrote in *ABA Banking Journal.*

The need for a centralized tracking system of lending activity grows increasingly critical with bank size. The larger the institution, the more important it is to have such a formal system for compiling records of all it is doing. Security Pacific, which has gained attention for its CRA programs, requires branch managers to complete and maintain an assessment of every community served by the bank. He or she also must develop market and demographic data, including information on population trends, employment, income, and home ownership.

Create a system of benchmarks to track CRA performance. Phillips Gay, vice president for regulatory compliance at First Union Corporation, told a CBA conference that by doing so, if a bank doesn't reach those goals, it can come back with a plan to meet them. First Union has a grading score on each of 64 assessment factors and is a big believer in measurable results, Gay said. He added that CRA compliance "is not so much a technical exercise as it is a management process."

Realize that major holding companies can't simply put a standard CRA structure in place and not customize it for local markets. Community groups don't like the "one size fits all" phenomenon, said Allen Fishbein. "That's the wrong way to start," Fishbein told a Consumer Bankers Association conference. "Large corporations do tend to standardize, but it will set the wrong tone and upset community groups."

But by the same token, banks are hearing that regulators will tend to view a holding company by the CRA performance of its worst unit bank.

So at least some degree of standardization is needed, if only to upgrade the weakest links.

Promulgation/Publicity

Take better marketing advantage of community development deals or local assistance programs that fall under CRA guidelines. Bankers agree that more needs to be done. "There's a good story to be told. We need to be more advocates out there," Signet CRA officer Julia Seward told a CBA conference. "Banks are often their own worst enemies" when it comes to getting recognition, said attorney Warren Traiger.

But only claim credit for what you've done, others say. "If you have any rhetoric in your [CRA] statement, you'd better be able to back it up," said James Daniel of Oklahoma's Friendly Bank. And don't try to lord an outstanding rating over the rest of the market unless you are sure you can sustain it, said consultant Michael T. Sullivan.

Advertise in ethnic publications and community newspapers. Consultants say these ads should make readers aware of basic banking and credit products. Banks should earmark a certain portion of the ad budgets to advertising in these media to offer proof that a bank is encouraging low-income loans, wrote First Interstate's Julius Loeser, senior counsel at First Interstate Bancorp, in *Banking Law Review*. Friendly Bank's Daniel said his bank is making a more concerted job of getting advertising, even in areas where it has no real penetration.

Banks could underwrite minority newspapers, suggested consultant Sullivan. They should also consider the possibility of hiring an advertising agency with an ethnic or minority concentration that will give them entree to that market. On the West Coast, particularly, that could prove crucial in reaching the Hispanic market, he said.

Consider issuing a CRA statement that rivals the annual report in detail and glossiness. Some institutions have begun doing so. "If in fact you do that, you may well have a marketing tool and/or a competitive advantage you can use vis-a-vis other institutions in your market place who don't," said the CBA's late general counsel, Craig Ulrich.

An expanded CRA statement can help show how an institution is providing and communicating an overall CRA program, said consultant Rick Eckman. Moreover, examiners may find themselves relying heavily on the detail a bank provides through such a document. And community groups have come to expect a certain level of sophistication in a CRA statement. Lack that, and banks can become suspect, as did Mitsui Manufacturers in Los Angeles.

"All you have to do is look at their CRA statement" to sense their shortcomings, said Gilda Haas, a spokeswoman for Communities for Accountable Reinvestment, a community group. "You can tell the banks in California that have dealt with community groups. They have beautiful-looking documents with charts; their statements are typeset. [Mitsui] had a map of California with dots in it, they had typos, it was just typed on paper."

Communicate any plans to close branches and be prepared to justify any such decisions. This means addressing neighborhood concerns from public relations standpoint, plus analyzing the marketplace and documenting efforts to continue providing services.

Community development credit unions may be eager to step in and provide services in the area where a branch is being closed—but not without some financial or facility donation on the part of the affected institution.

Products/Loans

Flexibility, particularly in underwriting and equity requirements, can make a big difference in lending to poorer areas. Bankers should be on the lookout for government and other public money that can change a poor loan into a solid one.

Banks should look at ways to offer multifamily real estate-owned property for purchase by nonprofits, suggests Gail K. Hillebrand, a staff attorney with Consumers Union. Subsidy money and low vacancy rates in affordable housing may mean a property can support a loan even though it could not make it at market rates.

Hillebrand also suggests that CRA programs offer second mortgages or home equity loans with underwriting and characteristics to make them acceptable to lower-income people.

Be aware that withdrawing a product meant for the low-income market because it is unprofitable is not going to be well received. An institution simply may have to define profitability differently, says Signet's Julia Seward. Barnett's Allen Lastinger said that rather than withdraw a lower-income product, Barnett will modify it. He said the bank has altered the underwriting criteria on some lending products, for instance, and changed pricing and balance numbers on economy checking.

Consider applying a community development lending model, such as one being made available by the ABA. It takes lenders through five steps:

credit analysis, identifying financial gaps, matching gaps to corresponding financial solutions, matching to community assistance techniques, and then matching to community assistance programs. See Exhibit 8-1.

Documentation

Decide on a system for pinpointing loans made in specific areas, giving regulators the "geographic distribution analysis" they are seeking. "A minimal amount of analysis must be done," Fed Governor LaWare said, adding that banks may want to keep low- and moderate-income loans in a special portfolio to track them.

While more and more vendors are selling software for tracking and mapping loan data, regulators insist that a bank can meet its obligations by sticking pins in a map—as long as enough detail is provided.

Mitsui Manufacturers, whose rocky CRA experience was described in Chapter 2, suffered in part from poor documentation. President Jerry W. Johnston told *American Banker* that while Mitsui did make business loans in poorer neighborhoods in Los Angeles, it "hasn't done a good job of keeping records" on those loans.

Geocoding, as the attachment of demographic data to loan records has become known, has become a critical part of CRA compliance. But programs that simply geocode a bank's loans miss a "a lot of good bets," says First Union's Phillips Gay. First Union has created "city action plans" that record the percentages of penetration in various areas.

Computerized loan mapping can make life easier for banks and examiners. Maps can show examiners, bank officers, and community activists how well an institution is doing, at a glance. "When the examiners come in, we can show them as much detail as they like," says Lew-Jean King, consumer support services analyst with Manufacturers and Traders Trust Company in Buffalo, which has been using a software mapping program.

"Mapping provides two specific advantages," said Peter Hoag, manager of agency information services for the California Office of Thrift Supervision in San Francisco. "One is more effective presentations to senior managers and board members. The maps make a case very clearly. The other is, it improves the efficiency of the examiners."

Only a few years ago, mapping used to require mainframes, meaning that it was the province of only the biggest banks. Now it can be handled

EXHIBIT 8–1
Community Investment Model

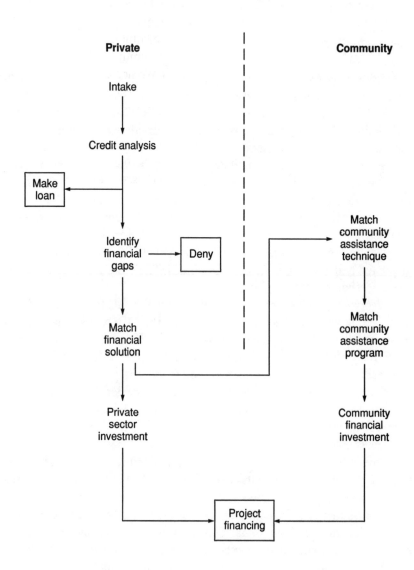

with desktop computers, bringing it down to the level of virtually any community bank.

Make an intensive effort to record contacts and meetings with community groups. LaWare suggests that all interviews and contacts with community groups be recorded, and that banks should write up every interview and put those memos in their files. Institutions should even make note of roles played by officers at CRA or community development conferences, suggests Clyde Paul Smith of First Women's Bank of Rockville, Maryland.

"The center core [of compliance efforts] must be a way and a method of storing data—not only on loans and deposits, but on community groups, and how you tie all of this data together," said Virginia consultant Robert Raven. "If you don't have a good internal system, the entire system is likely to fall apart. You can't build a good outreach program without one."

Understand that HMDA data collection is a key area. Overtones of potential discrimination abound, making the area a hot issue for examiners and the media. Community groups, as well as examiners, may look at HMDA data before anything else. In a protest aimed at Hyde Park Bank of Chicago, for instance, a community group cited the bank's HMDA lending record in its opening salvo.

"However you do it, you need to find out where you are making mortgage loans," said Mark Aldrich at the Bankers Consulting Group in Irvine, California. "I think a lot of our clients are not collectively plotting those distributions. In order to get an outstanding rating, they will have to be prepared to hand that [data] over." Massachusetts deputy comissioner Georgeann Abbanat views HMDA data as a key barometer of a bank's CRA record: "Each bank should look at this registry and evaluate themselves."

Needs assessments and other market research can be helpful in showing compliance efforts. Banks can share needs assessment costs, as several banks in western Massachusetts did recently. They hired a consultant to do a comprehensive plan for the area, and shared the expenses.

Managing the Examination Process

The institution needs to be an advocate for its position and try to control the process as much as possible, experts say. Signet's Julia Seward suggests talking to the CRA examiners before the exam begins in order to pick up advice or useful information.

That advocacy role can be buttressed by paying attention to what rivals are doing. Seward said that the OCC appears to give wide discretion to regional offices. "Try to understand what your regional office seems to want. You'll be judged in part against others in your area," she says.

Bring together all the necessary information and have it on hand for the examiners. "Condense and summarize [CRA-related]information at least once a year into a CRA Report," suggests California CRA consultant Darla Farr in a newsletter from the Federal Reserve Bank of San Francisco. "This communicates to your CRA examiners and saves time and exasperation during a CRA compliance examination. It also creates a useful information tool and trail for management."

Take a systematic approach to managing the examination. The Consumer Bankers Association offers a seven-step guide that institutions might consider.

1. Begin with the last examination report.
2. Be sure that corrective action has taken care of all "objective" or technical criticisms.
3. Be sure that action has been taken on serious "subjective" criticisms.
4. Document corrective actions, as well as prospective policies and ongoing activities.
5. Encourage a positive attitude on the part of staff toward the examination process.
6. Ensure that the staff understands the process and the examiner's stake in it.
7. Prepare a public communications plan for dealing with the disclosure of the CRA rating and performance appraisal.

Damage Control Efforts

Develop plans for dealing with the possibility of a less-than-stellar rating. Consultant Michael T. Sullivan suggests that the plan include a written statement of the issue involved; potential outcomes; identification of the key players, inside and outside the institution and including community activists, news media people, and opinion leaders; and development of an implementation plan.

California consultant Aldrich states, "Banks with poor or marginal ratings must be ready to explain why those are bad and what they are doing now. There will be a damage-containment need."

Go on the offensive to counter criticism. Sullivan suggests that a bank explain its position and outline future plans for the community. If the bank itself announces its rating, it has better control of the ensuing press coverage.

Farmers and Merchants Bank of Long Beach, California, appeared to take something of a public beating late in 1990 when a newspaper report announced that it had received a "substantial noncompliance" rating. In the ensuing press coverage, the bank was forced to defend itself and admitted that the Federal Reserve had told it that an application for a new branch would be turned down.

Consider including a "mea culpa" section in the CRA statement. Attorney Warren Traiger said this confession of shortcomings can help examination performance and provide a clear signal that a bank or thrift is serious about compliance, even if it did not score well with examiners.

Using Resources

Make sure someone at the institution has an understanding of the various local, state, and federal programs that can plug into community develop-ment. As noted earlier, these can provide critical gap financing for marginal projects.

Some of these programs are well known; others are not. "State housing finance agencies have great resources that I don't think enough financial institutions know about," said Frederick Wacker of the Federal Home Loan Bank of Atlanta.

Investigate the use of intermediaries experienced in community rein-vestment, as well as pension funds and foundations. The intermediaries often use revolving credit lines or equity investments from financial institu-tions that clearly count toward CRA compliance; foundations and pension funds can provide direct equity contributions.

"These sources of equity effectively reduce the amount of debt financ-ing required and subsequently, the project cash flow needed to support debt repayments," the OCC noted in its "Community Development Finance" booklet. "They strengthen the capacity of the borrower, reduce loan-to-value ratios, and generally, reduce risks associated with community development lending."

Keep up with advice and commentary from miscellaneous sources—

trade groups, trade journals, newsletters, and newspapers. With CRA continuing to evolve and become more public, more articles and forums on the subject are showing up. Reading community newspapers can keep institutions abreast of what neighborhood leaders want and could help shape credit products.

CHAPTER 9

GETTING HELP

ASSOCIATIONS AND OTHER RESOURCES

Banks and thrifts have been bombarded with material from their regulators in recent years, much of it related to community reinvestment. Institutions know who their primary regulator is and how to reach its representatives; there is no point here in offering any such list of district and national offices. But banks and thrifts should avail themselves of many of the supplemental materials that the federal regulators have issued. One particularly useful resource is a 34-page booklet put out by the Comptroller's office, *Community Development Finance: Tools and Techniques for National Banks*. Cited numerous times in earlier chapters, this booklet is crammed with ideas and advice.

It is also worthwhile mentioning some of the services the district offices are providing in relation to CRA. These include seminars, workshops, newsletters, white papers, and, in the case of several Federal Reserve Banks, a series of city profiles. Institutions can use these profiles to learn about neighborhoods, government contacts, community group leaders, consortiums, and other programs that could be used to generate more community reinvestment.

The Federal Reserve Banks of Philadelphia pioneered the idea and has produced "lender's profiles" for Harrisburg, Pennsylvania; Wilmington and southern Delaware, and Trenton and Camden, New Jersey. Community affairs officer Frederick Manning said the chief purpose of the guides is to communicate the attitudes of the "underside of the market" toward lenders, and to provide a "road map" for bankers. "A number of cities have had their banking structure change as a result of new players. These [profiles] offer a convenient document to land on the ground running," he said.

Profiles were completed by late 1990 for Oakland, San Jose, Pomona, and Sacramento, all in California, and for Salt Lake City, said Jane Shock, a community investment adviser for the San Francisco Bank. Additional profiles were underway for Seattle, Phoenix, and San Diego.

Another valuable resource was being made available through Ronald Zimmerman, vice president at the Atlanta Fed. He prepared *A Public/Private Partnership Model for Home Mortgage Lending,* an instruction book and accompanying spreadsheet designed to help bankers, community groups, and public officials trying to form lending partnerships to make mortgage loans in low- and moderate-income areas. Using the spreadsheet and pertinent financial data, the model computes the amount of income the applicant has available to pay the loan, and/or the subsidy amount that would be needed to make the loan work.

Regulators are far from the sole source of useful information on CRA, apart from consultants and vendors. The major banking trade groups have been disseminating loads of regulatory updates, giving advice, and holding conferences and workshops focused on CRA. A raft of nonprofit resource groups and intermediaries offer training as well as technical assistance and expertise. And community group organizers, while perhaps an anathema in recent years to most bank CEOs, provide a ready sounding board for institutions keen on learning what community-based groups think and what services they want.

Trade Groups

The major banking trade groups have recognized the importance of CRA compliance and the potential for increased community development lending and are pumping out relevant information. Brief sketches of those information programs appear below. State banking and thrift trade groups also are keeping members apprised of CRA developments; these associations are too numerous to mention here.

American Bankers Association
1120 Connecticut Ave., N.W.
Washington, D.C. 20036
(202) 663-5000

The ABA, banking's largest trade group, has tackled CRA on a number of fronts. Its biggest effort in 1990 was the publication of *Community Relations Action Guide,* a looseleaf book aimed at helping bank managements understand community relations issues and how to formulate programs to deal with them.

The ABA also is putting out a number of CRA products, including training videos, a compliance manual, and a guide to improving community development lending. It also held a conference in 1990 that examined ways to make money through such lending, rather than simply complying with CRA.

A subcommittee on community development lending issues has been meeting to formulate ways of helping bankers develop products and specialists in this arena. In addition, the ABA has set up a database on CRA-related programs and will send materials to interested members or answer questions based on information on the database.

Bank Administration Institute
2250 Golf Road
Rolling Meadows, IL 60008-4097
(708) 228-6200

Through the Bank Administration Institute Foundation, education on areas like CRA is disseminated at seminars and conferences, such as at a conference held November 1990 in Chicago entitled "Responding to Public Disclosure." The foundation also provides in-house seminars for member institutions for groups of 15 or more, or for consortiums of institutions or holding companies.

Consumer Bankers Association
1000 Wilson Boulevard, 30th Floor
Arlington, VA 22209-3908
(703) 276-1750

Like the ABA, the Consumer Bankers Association has been busily putting out information and advice about CRA issues. President Joe Belew has called CRA one of the most important and "thorniest" issues confronting the industry.

The CBA published a guide in 1990 to help members better understand the new demands under the Community Reinvestment Act. Called *Understanding CRA: Views of Regulators, Activists, and Bankers*, the booklet features those views, a text of the FFIEC's joint statement on CRA, and pertinent reprints from the Federal Register. The trade group also has held CRA conferences and issued advisories to members about developments in Congress affecting CRA compliance.

The Independent Bankers Association
One Thomas Circle N.W., Suite 950
Washington, D.C. 20005-5802
(202) 659-8111

The trade group specializing in community banks, the IBAA has addressed community reinvestment in its magazine and at its annual convention. The association also puts out a weekly newsletter, pegged to developments in Washington, that reports on regulatory changes and pending legislation affecting issues like CRA. The IBAA has made a special effort to make members aware of community development corporations.

National Council of Savings Institutions
1101 15th St. NW, Suite 400
Washington, D.C. 20005
(202) 857-3100

The principal trade group for savings banks, the National Council has published regulatory analyses and run workshops on community reinvestment, as well as bringing in speakers to its mortgage conferences. The group also is offering a CRA kit, complete with workbooks, designed for institutions that don't have the resources to devote a full-time person to CRA. It also publishes articles on CRA in its magazine, *Bottomline.*

U.S. League of Savings Institutions
1709 New York Ave., N.W., 8th Floor
Washington, D.C. 20006
(202) 637-8900

Under its Housing Opportunities Foundation, located at the above address, the U.S. League is seeking to provide a clearinghouse and educational service for member thrifts. It has developed public relations materials to help institutions publicize their role in housing finance and is collating information on CRA-related programs to share among members.

The Chicago-based U.S. League has a broader mandate to provide information and contacts for members involved in the gamut of operations affecting savings banks, including community reinvestment. Like the banking trade groups, it holds seminars, workshops, and conventions, and lobbies Congress on issues relevant to member concerns.

Nonprofits, Activists, and Research Groups

Bank and thrift executives anxious to learn more about ways to improve their CRA records or seeking contacts with community groups or public funding sources can turn to quite a few entities around the country. Among those in this listing are so-called intermediaries that provide technical expertise to borrowers as well as a conduit for financial institution investments. While these are the most prominent names in the field, this is not an exhaustive listing, and new names are likely to be emerging in the early 1990s.

Many banks and thrifts are familiar with activist organizations by name, if not by any direct involvement. While local activists are often very loosely allied, these national resource and support organizations serve as mentors, trainers, and lobbying forces linking activists around the country. Still viewed by many bankers as "the enemy," they are gaining increased attention and respect from regulators and some of the country's largest institutions.

Association of Communities Organized for Reform Now
522 8th St., S.E.
Washington, D.C. 20003
(202) 547-9292

Probably the country's largest network organization of community groups, ACORN has chapters in almost two dozen states. It has proven a potent organizer of protests against financial institutions and lobbying force for social responsibility issues.

Center for Community Change
1000 Wisconsin Ave., N.W.
Washington, D.C. 20007
(202) 342-0567

A nonprofit organization providing technical assistance on a host of issues to community groups located in low-income neighborhoods around the nation. Its Neighborhood Revitalization Project "provides technical and legal assistance on how to assess credit needs and develop reinvestment strategies," the group says. It also publishes a newsletter, *The CRA Reporter,* covering issues related to community reinvestment. General counsel Allen Fishbein is a frequent speaker at trade group and regulators' forums.

Center for Policy Alternatives
2000 Florida Ave., N.W., Room 402
Washington, D.C. 20009
(202) 387-6030

A nonprofit educational and research group concentrating on community reinvestment at the state level, trying to ascertain standards in terms of how banks can meet local needs. CPA also works with grass-roots advocates. It attempts to determine the viability of establishing state laws on linked-deposit and other CRA-related programs.

The Churches Conference on Shelter and Housing
1711 14th St., N.W.
Washington, D.C. 20009
(202) 232-6748

A nonprofit dedicated to helping churches find ways to create transitional and affordable housing. It supplies technical assistance to church congregations and has published a handbook, *Building on Faith,* that outlines some of the projects churches around the nation have undertaken. Several Washington-area banks are supporting the group and sending lenders to its forums.

Community Preservation Corporation
5 West 37th St.
New York, NY 10018
(212) 869-5300

A financial intermediary formed to promote affordable housing in New York City, CPC has expanded beyond the city limits and is providing expertise to other communities in other states. It uses a credit line from banks and thrifts to finance construction and permanent mortgages, many of which are sold in the secondary market. CPC also provides technical assistance to developers and other borrowers.

Community Reinvestment Institute
10 Lombard St., Suite 200
San Francisco, CA 94111
(415) 956-1992

Founded in 1988, the CRI was created to bring together financial institutions with community-based low-income housing and business groups in an effort to bolster implementation of CRA goals. It is structured as an information research and dissemination center, "and provides opportunities for lenders, borrowers, and financial services regulators to meet and share ideas," according to a brochure. The institute holds seminars and workshops, provides geocoding materials, and generates books on local credit demands.

Development Training Institute
4806 Seton Drive
Baltimore, MD 21215
(301) 764-0780

The institute does training for lenders, regulators, and associations, concentrating not on compliance but on promoting community development lending and underwriting criteria. It has trained community affairs officers at the Federal Reserve and has on occasion done consulting for individual institutions.

The Enterprise Foundation
500 American City Building
Columbia, MD 21044
(301) 964-1230

Founded in 1982 by famed developer James Rouse, this nonprofit research and advocacy group has been concentrating its efforts on affordable housing. Its mission "is to see that all low-income Americans have, within a generation, the opportunity for fit and affordable housing and economic self-sufficiency," the foundation said in a brochure. Enterprise has worked with more than 100 nonprofits groups in 40 cities, and works to create public-private partnerships that include financial institutions.

Local Initiatives Support Corporation
733 Third Ave.
New York, NY 10017
(212) 455-9800

LISC is the nation's largest nonprofit community development intermediary. It assembles money from financial institutions and other corporations and foundations, and leverages that money in direct investments in community development corporations and public/private partnerships in its 23 concentration areas around the nation. It also provides technical assistance to community-based development concerns.

National Association of Affordable Housing Lenders
43 Commercial Wharf, Suite 9
Boston, MA 02110
(617) 742-0532

Still in formation in 1990, this nonprofit was targeted for a launch in the spring or summer of 1991 in Washington. Interim activities are being handled through Carras Associates in Boston. It will specialize in helping lenders interested in affordable housing in lower-income areas. Membership is open not just to depository institutions, but to mortgage bankers, insurance companies, and the secondary market agencies.

National Association of Community Development Loan Funds
P.O. Box 40085
Philadelphia, PA 19106-5085
(215) 923-4754

An association of some 35 national and regional nonprofit loan funds managing some $60 million in capital in 1990. NACDLF members act as financial intermediaries, provide technical assistance to member funds, and provide a clearinghouse for lenders, borrowers, and others pursuing community development. The funds focus on nonprofit rental housing, micro-enterprise and other community business, and home ownership.

National Congress for Community Economic Development
1612 K St., N.W., Suite 510
Washington, D.C. 20006
(202) 659-8411

A nonprofit advocacy group supporting a dozen statewide community-based development organizations and providing peer support and clout to members. The group conducts research and publishes reports on community development issues.

National Council for Urban Economic Development
1730 K. St., N.W.
Washington, D.C. 20006
(202) 223-4735

A nonprofit information and lobbying group that seeks to increase private reinvestment in America's cities. The council includes among its members private companies, city officials, developers, and individuals. It publishes newsletters and a quarterly magazine and brought out a booklet, *Bank CDCs: Instruments for Community Reinvestment,* in late 1990.

National Federation of Community Development Credit Unions
59 John St., 8th Floor
New York, NY 10038
(212) 513-7191

NFCDCU is a financial intermediary and support organization for community development credit unions. It directs investments into these local credit unions, coordinates programs among them, and serves as a national clearinghouse and information center for financial institutions and others interested in helping CDCUs.

National Housing Institute
439 Main St.
Orange, NJ 07050
(201) 678-3110

A nonprofit publication and research center, as well as a lobbying group, dedicated to promoting affordable housing. Its publications include a magazine, *Shelter-force.*

National Housing Partnership
1225 Eye St., N.W.
Washington, D.C. 20005
(202) 326-8000

Through its operating units, NHP provides real estate investments and management, primarily focused on lower-income multifamily rental properties. Working with credit lines from banks and thrifts and through real estate joint ventures, NHP—authorized by Congress in 1968—has built, renovated, sold, and operated apartments in poorer neighborhoods.

National Low Income Housing Coalition
1012 14th St., N.W., #1500
Washington, D.C. 20005
(202) 662-1530

The coalition "is a membership organization dedicated to advocacy, organizing, and education for decent housing for all low-income people," the group said in a brochure. Leaders are drawn from housing advocates and organizers, tenants, and housing professionals. A sister organization at the same address, the Low Income Housing Information Service, publishes research and policy reports and periodic updates about developments in the field.

National Minority Supplier Development Council Incorporated
1412 Broadway, 11th Floor
New York, NY 10018
(212) 944-2430

The Business Consortium Fund run by the council is a nonprofit minority business development program providing working capital funds to certified minority businesses. It has formed relationships with dozens of banks, which become "certified bank lenders" eligible for participation in the fund's loan programs. The NMSDC itself, working through 47 regional councils, helps match corporate support with more than 15,000 certified minority businesses.

National Rural Development and Finance Corporation
1818 N Street N.W., Suite 410
Washington, D.C. 20036
1-800-233-3518

A nonprofit corporation involved in finance and technical assistance in support of rural enterprise development. It is operating a program funded by grants from the Farmers Home Administration and involving $9 million in financing for new development in 11 states.

National Training and Information Center
810 N. Milwaukee Avenue
Chicago, IL 60622-4103
(312) 243-3035

NTIC is a nonprofit resource center providing community groups "with the tools they need to effect important changes in their communities," the center said in a brochure. Formed in 1972, it lobbied for both the Community Reinvestment and Home Mortgage Disclosure acts. It offers training, technical assistance, and consulting for community groups. It has conducted studies on community reinvestment in cities like Chicago, where it is particularly active.

A sister organization at the same address, National People's Action, is an umbrella group made up of neighborhood, church, farm, labor, senior citizen, and other citizens' groups lobbying for community development.

Neighborhood Housing Services of America
1325 G St., N.W., Suite 800
Washington, D.C. 20005
(202) 376-2400

Neighborhood Housing Services chapters serve hundreds of neighborhoods in 43 states around the country. As an intermediary, the NHS raises funds, provides technical assistance, and makes revolving loan purchases for NHS chapters, Mutual Housing Organizations, and Apartment Improvement Programs. NHS receives funds from financial institutions and secondary market sales of its loans.

San Francisco Development Fund
1107 Oak St.
San Francisco, CA 94117
(415) 863-7800

A nonprofit housing advocate, the Fund was founded in 1963 and has provided financial and technical assistance to a wide range of affordable housing ventures. It has been a leading organizer of low-income housing consortiums in California and other parts of the country.

Urban Land Institute
625 Indiana Ave., N.W.
Washington, D.C. 20004
(202) 624-7000

A nonprofit research and education organization aimed at "responsible leadership in the use of land in order to enhance our total environment." The institute offers educational services and texts such as the *Residential Development Handbook,* which offers strategies for financial, regulatory, and other concerns related to residential development.

The Woodstock Institute
53 W. Jackson Boulevard, Suite 304
Chicago, IL 60604
(312) 427-8070

A nonprofit working with and on behalf of residents in troubled urban and rural economies and focusing on neighborhood investment. The Institute specializes in reinvestment policy, technical assistance, and consulting to community organizations, banks, public officials, and regulators.

VENDORS, VENDORS EVERYWHERE

Whenever financial institutions are struggling to understand a market or a regulation, the sounds of a stampede can be heard. A stampede of consultants, that is, rushing to fill the knowledge breach and ease the burden on hard-pressed managements.

The CRA field is hearing plenty of hoofbeats. In the past couple of years, consultants and vendors have sprung up or branched off from larger outfits to specialize in helping institutions cope with the varied demands of community reinvestment and its documentation. Bankers, trade group officials, and regulators all have remarked on the almost-sudden emergence of an entire industry devoted to CRA. "When I saw [CRA] as a two-line item in the statutes, I thought that was appropriate," said Larry Kurmel, executive director of the California Bankers Association. "Now a whole industry has been built up around it, and I think we're getting a little carried away."

Some of the Big Six accounting firms that have gone heavily into consulting in recent years are talking about CRA, but most consultants and equipment vendors are smaller fry who have gone after CRA compliance as a well-defined niche. Not a few are former regulators or bank executives familiar with the terrain, but still, some bankers are wondering just who is really qualified.

"A lot of banks have to be concerned about the possibility of lots of people hanging their shingles out" and seeking CRA-related business, says Gerry H. Parisella at Canadian Imperial Bank of Commerce in New York. "They need to throw their weight behind people with experience." The leader of a nonprofit research group said there seem to be few standards for people calling themselves CRA consultants, with the result that there are "some bad care-providers out there."

Community activists are also skeptical. "I think some consultants know very little about CRA," said Allen Fishbein of the Center for Community Change. "There is no substitute for outreach by senior management." For their part, some vendors are a bit puzzled that they are not doing more banking business. "We see CRA as a way that we can interact candidly with banks," said David W. Bisbee, regional manager for Receivable Financing Corporation in New York, a firm that will guarantee portions of substandard loans. But as 1991 began, most banks seemed to be hunkered down because of earnings troubles and the weakened economy, he said. Noted one prominent CRA consultant, "One of the last things banks want to do is look at another price tag for a consultant."

As it does in most areas in banking, computerization promises real rewards for institutions that can harness it for CRA compliance, marketing, and documentation. Take mapping, an essential component of the geographic analysis that regulators are demanding. While this can be done with paper and pins, increasingly it is being done on desktop computers through software programs dedicated to the purpose. Mapping will take on even more significance as the new HMDA reporting requirements take hold.

Many of the CRA-related software programs being offered aren't as sexy as mapping; they are concerned with automating recordkeeping, tracking regulations, and otherwise simplifying the compliance process. Still, they aren't for everyone. Some members of the National Council of Savings Institutions have looked into software programs, but "software analysis is not quite so helpful because it is expensive for local institutions," a spokeswoman said.

The following list is intended to help financial institutions locate consultants and vendors selling applicable products or services. It is a representative and not a comprehensive sampling, and inclusion on this list by no means constitutes an endorsement of the company or its products.

Allstate Financial Corporation
2700 S. Quincy St., Suite 540
Arlington, VA 22206
(702) 931-2274

The company, which operates under the names of Receivable Financing Corporation and Business Funding Corporation in regional offices around the country, concentrates on receivables. It will guarantee certain loans to borrowers in poorer neighborhoods, charging 5 percent to 10 percent of the loan as a fee, and monitors the borrowers' collateral—chiefly accounts receivable or insured medical claims—for a service fee of roughly 1.5 percent of the value of the receivables.

The Alternatives Group
3939 Belt Line Road, Suite 355
Dallas, TX 75244
(214) 243-8844

The company offers two principal compliance products tied to geographic analysis: Centrax and Citytrax. These enable banks to do geocoding by census tract in larger cities and by city in smaller communities. Both use demographic data from R. L. Polk, extracting elements pertinent to the delineated community; this data can be input from a computer source automatically into a PC and arrayed geographically, then manipulated in a wide range of ways. The company has pledged that if any of its financial institutions clients gets a less-than-satisfactory CRA grade, it will refund their money.

Bankers Compliance Group
18200 Von Karman Drive, Suite 730
Irvine, CA 92715
(714) 553-0909

A consultant that offers regulatory advice to small California banks, it monitors compliance updates and changes, keeps clients informed, and holds seminars and briefings about important issues like CRA.

J.S. Barefoot & Associates
582 E. Rich St.
Columbus, OH 43215
(614) 221-9009

Headed by former deputy comptroller JoAnn Barefoot, the company specializes in advising financial institutions about compliance issues. Barefoot herself has written and spoken widely about CRA compliance. Manuals and software put out by the company are being made available through the ABA.

Carras Associates
43 Commercial Wharf #9
Boston, MA 02110-9790
(617) 742-0532

The firm, which also has offices in Fort Lauderdale, Florida, is a consultant specializing in community reinvestment and development finance. It develops training programs for institutions and helps banks and regulators with market analyses and community reinvestment planning, as well as doing needs assessments.

Development Finance Corporation
1101 30th St., N.W.
Washington, D.C. 20007
(202) 342-2973

A consulting firm specializing in helping banks organize community development corporations. The company's role includes planning the CDC, preparing an investment proposal, negotiating with regulators, organizing and marketing the CDC, and negotiating the initial investments. It also has prepared a manual and a video on setting up CDCs.

Financial Institutions Marketing Association
111 East Wacker Drive
Chicago, IL 60601
(312) 938-2570

Working with American Data Resources, FIMA offers financial institutions the "CRA National Performance Assessment and Documentation Program" to help institutions identify, implement, and monitor CRA-related marketing opportunities. Participants can send magnetic tape records on deposit and loan customers for computer analysis of marketing penetration by census tract. The analysis can be done on a one-time or quarterly basis.

L. R. Glenn Communications Inc.
1728 N. Sedgwick
Chicago, IL 60614
(312) 951-6577

Headed by Laurie R. Glenn, a former political consultant and First Chicago Corporation officer, the firm advises banks and community groups on CRA issues. It develops strategic plans, serves as a facilitator and liaison, and does publicity work. Glenn also has handled protests directed at banks by community groups.

Harte-Hanks Data Technologies
25 Linnell Circle
Billerica, MA 01821-3961
(508) 663-9955

Working with demographic information from National Planning Data, Harte-Hanks gives financial institutions a package of CRA compliance reports showing where customers live and what the institution's lending patterns have been. It offers these reports by census tract and minor civil division, and documents loan applications, with approvals and denials, by census tract. The company has been providing computerized geocoding to industries since 1968.

Jordan & Associates
P.O. Box 39038
St. Louis, MO 63139
(314) 353-8414

The company offers a PC-based software package called RecordMaster Plus that improves control of compliance records and aims to reduce the time spent searching for records needed for examiner, customer, or other requirements—some of which could well be CRA-related. It also provides implementation assistance, compliance handbooks, and other consulting services.

Professional Knowledge Systems Inc.
20 South Central
Clayton, MO 63105
(314) 721-1510

The company sells an automated version of a CRA compliance manual drafted by the Federal Reserve Bank of St. Louis. The Expert Express CRA Advisor, as the software product is known, is an expert system that gives a user quick access to information on federal and nonprofit assistance programs for housing, economic development lending, and small business.

RJE Communications Inc.
765 N. Mary Ave.
Sunnyvale, CA 94086
(408) 245-7532

The company's Credit Trak Loan application systems can generate the loan/application register mandated by the Home Mortgage Disclosure Act in electronic form or on plain paper. Information needed to document compliance is captured by RJE Credit Prompters, the front-end preprocessor for Credit Trak.

Regulatory Compliance Associates Inc.
550 Dempsey Place, Suite 100
Geneva, IL 60134
(708) 232-7342

Company professionals provide on-site consulting, auditing, and training services, and publish newsletters and software products for use by financial institutions, trade associations, and regulatory agencies. These services help bank managements assess the institution's regulatory compliance and develop action plans to address deficiencies.

Sheshunoff Information Services Inc.
505 Barton Springs Road
Austin, TX 78704
1-800-456-2340

Sheshunoff offers institutions a Community Reinvestment Act/Home Mortgage Disclosure Act Regulatory Compliance manual, a looseleaf binder kit that takes institutions through the steps required to meet CRA obligations. The company also provides market share and competitive analysis reports that help CRA compliance programs, as well as research facilities to help institutions define their communities and the affected credit needs.

State and Federal Associates
1101 King St.
Alexandria, VA 22314
(703) 739-0200

A multidiscipline consulting firm that offers clients a customized approach to CRA compliance. Its services include evaluation, data collection, PC-based tracking systems, internal communications analysis, branch service and branch closing audits, and staff training and development. The company also assesses how highly an institution is perceived in the community, helps define local markets, and evaluates external communications.

Strategic Mapping Inc.
4030 Moorpark Ave.
San Jose, CA 95117
(408) 985-7400

The company's Atlas software enables institutions to map loan penetration in low- to moderate-income neighborhoods in their service areas, showing the number and type of loans in each census tracts. The maps can also be used for such tasks as location analysis, marketing, and branch development strategy.

Michael T. Sullivan & Associates
2911 Wamath Drive
Charlotte, NC 28210
(704) 554-7863

Headed by former banker and bank marketing guru Michael T. Sullivan, the firm specializes in marketing and public relations assistance for banks. He has written and spoken widely on ways for banks to assess and meet community needs and to deal with media inquiries. Sullivan was a coauthor of the ABA's *Community Relations Action Guide,* released in 1990.

James Vitarello Development Associates
2809 Ontario St., N.W.
Washington, D.C. 20009
(202) 332-4455

A consultant specializing in community development, especially the formation and operation of bank community development corporations. Vitarello himself, a former program manager for CDCs at the Comptroller's office, has been providing training at seminars and workshops.

Warren, Gorham & Lamont
210 South Street
Boston, MA 02111
1-800-950-1209

A business publisher specializing in resource books in fields such as law and banking, WG & L recently brought out the fourth edition of *Federal Banking Laws*. The book covers a host of compliance areas, including CRA, and includes forms and checklists to facilitate monitoring.

INDEX

B

Back ratio levels, 155–56
Bagwell, Fred, 204
Baker, L.M. "Bud," Jr., 91
Baltimore Financial Federal, 69
Banco de Ponce, 16
Banco Ohio National Bank, 31, 78
Banco Popular, 16
Bank Administration Institute, 237
Bankers Compliance Group, 248
Bankers Trust Company, 11, 63
Bankers Trust Company Foundation, 174
Bankers Trust Corporation, 80, 82
Bankers Trust New York Corporation, 63
Bank for Socially Responsible Lending, 115
Bank of A. Levy, 176
Bank of America, 32, 136, 161, 174, 186–87, 189, 202
  Basic-Bank of America special income credit program, 181
Bank of Boston, 31, 61, 67, 70, 125, 179, 223
Bank of New England, 137, 168
Bank of New York, 89
Bank of Ravenswood, 93
Bank of Vermont, 34, 90, 92, 122, 125, 128, 136
Bank One Cleveland, 149–51
Banks of Iowa Incorporated, 17
Bank South Corporation, 166
Banyan Bank of Boca Raton, 188
Barefoot, JoAnn, 9, 20, 195,202, 204, 223
Barmore, Gregory, 133
Barnard, Doug, 183
Barnett Banks, 71
Bartkowski, Robert, 38
Basic banking programs
  and community reinvestment, 183
  controversy over, 79–84
  defined, 180
  public opinion regarding, 180
Battered women shelters, 127
Baybank, 19
Belew, Joe, 4, 184, 237

Bell Federal Savings and Loan Association, 19
Below-market rates, 112, 113, 122
Bilingual services, 33, 180
Bisbee, David W., 247
Bischof, Tom, 26
Black business investment corporations (BBICs), 200
  nature of, 71–72
  nonbank participants, 72
Black Business Investment Fund, 71
Blake, Jennifer, 131
Blind, services for, 179
Boatmen's Bancshares, 121
Boatmen's Community Reinvestment Program, 122
Boatmen's National Bank, 21, 22, 33, 60, 187, 200
Boggs, Larry, 17
Borngaars, David A., 20
Bonds
  state and local, 80–81
  state finance agency, 67–68
  underwriting, 25
Borrego Springs Bank, 154
Boston Bank of Commerce, 199
Boston Home Loan Bank, 126
Boston Housing Partnership, 56
Boutique banks, 83–84
Bowen, George, 170
Braddock, Richard, 149
Bradford, Calvin, 36, 205
Branch closings, 228
  alternatives, 22
  CRA protests, 21–22
  factors in, 24
Braustein, Sandra, 44, 195
Brooklyn Neighborhood Improvement Program, 124
Brummell, Charles, Jr., 80
Bryant, Jeep, 74
Buckeye-Woodland CDC, 48
Buffett, Warren, 165
Burkhardt, Terry, 51
Burlington Community Land Trust, 122
Burlington Ecumenical Action Ministry, 92
Business Consortium Fund, 75